I LOST IT
AT THE MOVIES

I LOST IT AT THE MOVIES

PAULINE KAEL

An Atlantic Monthly Press Book
LITTLE, BROWN AND COMPANY · BOSTON · TORONTO

LIBRARY OF CONGRESS CATALOG CARD NO. 65-10908

SECOND PRINTING

"Throwing the Race" is reprinted by permission of *Moviegoer*.
"The Sick-Soul-of-Europe Parties: *La Notte, La Dolce Vita,
Marienbad*" is reprinted from *The Massachusetts Review*, ©
1963, The Massachusetts Review, Inc. *"The Earrings of Madame
de . . . ," "The Golden Coach," "Smiles of a Summer Night"*
are reprinted by permission of *Kulchur*. "Morality Plays Right
and Left," "Is There a Cure for Film Criticism?," "Fantasies of
the Art House Audience," and "Salt of the Earth" are reprinted
by permission of *Sight and Sound*. "Commitment and the Strait-
jacket," "Circles and Squares," "Hud," "The Innocents," "One,
Two, Three," "Billy Budd," "Hemingway's *Adventures of a
Young Man*," and "Films of the Quarter," note on *L'Avventura*,
are reprinted from *Film Quarterly*, by permission of the Regents
of the University of California.

ATLANTIC-LITTLE, BROWN BOOKS
ARE PUBLISHED BY
LITTLE, BROWN AND COMPANY
IN ASSOCIATION WITH
THE ATLANTIC MONTHLY PRESS

*Published simultaneously in Canada
by Little, Brown & Company (Canada) Limited*

PRINTED IN THE UNITED STATES OF AMERICA

Acknowledgments

I wish to express my gratitude to the John Simon Guggenheim Foundation and its president, Mr. Gordon N. Ray.

I wish to thank Peter Davison and William Abrahams of the Atlantic Monthly Press, and Gary Arnold and Alan Hislop for editorial advice and assistance. And I wish to express my admiration and respect for Dwight Macdonald, who despite my hectoring him in print has, personally, returned good for evil.

Acknowledgment is made to the *Atlantic Monthly, Film Quarterly, Partisan Review, Sight and Sound,* the *Massachusetts Review, Kulchur, Art Film Publications,* the *Second Coming, Film Culture,* and *Moviegoer* for permission to use material which they originally published.

Contents

Introduction

꘎꘎꘎꘎꘎꘎꘎

Zeitgeist and Poltergeist;
Or, Are Movies Going to Pieces?

Reflections from the side of the pool
at the Beverly Hills Hotel

"Bring your bathing suit," said the movie producer, who was phoning me to confirm our date for lunch at his hotel, and before I could think of a way to explain that I didn't have one with me, he added, "And remember, you're meeting people for cocktails in my suite at six, so just bring your change of clothes." Now I was completely out of my depth: I just said I would join him at 2:30 and hung up. Somehow I didn't want to come right out and say that I didn't have a change of clothes in the evening sense that he meant. Los Angeles dislocates my values, makes me ashamed of not being all the things I'm not and don't ordinarily care to be. Each time I get on the jet to return to San Francisco it's like turning the time-machine backward and being restored to an old civilization that I understand.

Los Angeles is only 400 miles away from where I live and so close by jet that I can breakfast at home, give a noon lecture at one of the universities in LA, and be back in time to prepare dinner. But it's the city of the future, and I am more a stranger there than in a foreign country. In a foreign country people don't expect you to be just like them, but in Los Angeles, which is infiltrating the world, they don't consider that you might be different because they don't recognize any values except their own. And soon there may not be any others.

Feeling rather seedy in the black and brown Italian suit which had seemed quite decent in San Francisco, I arrived at the pool of the Beverly Hills Hotel, sans bathing suit or change of clothes. And as I walked past the recumbent forms to the producer, also recumbent, who was limply waving to me, I remembered Katharine Hepburn as poor Alice Adams in her simple organdy frock among the plushly overdressed rich girls at the party. Only here it was I who was overdressed; they were expensively undressed. They didn't look young, and they didn't act old, these people eating and drinking and sunning themselves around the pool. They seemed to be ageless like crocodiles; and although they weren't fat, they were flabby.

Despite the narcissism of their attitudes, and the extraordinary amount of loving care they lavished on their bodies, each giving way to the sun-blessed fantasy of himself, stretching this way and that to catch or avoid the rays, it was impossible to feel superior to them. They could afford to make this spectacle of themselves.

In San Francisco, vulgarity, "bad taste," ostentation are regarded as a kind of alien blight, an invasion or encroachment from outside. In Los Angeles, there is so much money and power connected with ostentation that it is no longer ludicrous: it commands a kind of respect. For if the mighty behave like this, then quiet good taste means that you can't *afford* the conspicuous expenditures, and you become a little ashamed of your modesty and propriety. *Big* money and its way of life is exciting; the vulgarity of the powerful is ugly, but not boring. This, you begin to feel, is how people behave when they're strong enough to act out their fantasies of wealth. In this environment, if you're not making it in a big way, you're worse than nothing — you're a failure. But if you can still pass for young, maybe there's still time to make it; or, at least, you can delay the desperation and self-contempt that result from accepting these standards that so few can meet. It's easy to reject all this when I'm back in San Francisco. But not here. You can't really laugh at the Beverly Hills Hotel and people who pay $63 a day for a suite that's like a schoolboy's notions of luxury. It's too impressive. Laughter would stick in the throat — like sour grapes.

What "sensible" people have always regarded as the most preposterous, unreal and fantastic side of life in California — the sun palace of Los Angeles and its movie-centered culture — is becoming embarrassingly, "fantastically" actual, not just here but almost anywhere. It embodies the most common, the most widespread dream — luxury in the sun, a state of permanent vacation. And as it is what millions of people want and will pay money for, the Hollywood fantasy is economically practical. Across the country, homes become as simple, bare and convenient as simulated motels, and motels are frequently used as residences.

But pioneers suffer from stresses we don't know about, and the people I met in Los Angeles seem to have developed a terrible tic: they cannot stop talking about their "cultural explosion." The producer went on and on about it, about their new museums, and their concerts, and their galleries, and their "legitimate" collegiate theater. It was like my first trip to New York, when I wanted to see skyscrapers and go to shows and hear jazz, and New Yorkers wanted me to admire the flowers blooming in Rockefeller Plaza. I wanted to talk about the Los Angeles that fascinated and disturbed me, and about movies and why there were fewer good movies in 1963 than in any year in my memory. He discussed the finer things in life, trying to convince me and maybe himself that Los Angeles, in its cultural boom, was making phenomenal strides toward becoming like other cities — only, of course, more so.

I dutifully wrote in my notebook but not about what he was saying. Perhaps, because the whole scene was so nightmarish, with all the people spending their ordinary just-like-any-other-day at the pool, conducting business by the telephones whose wires stretched around them like lifelines, and this earnest man in wet trunks ordering me double Bourbons on the rocks and talking culture while deepening his tan, I began to think about horror movies.

Zeitgeist and Poltergeist; Or, Are Movies Going to Pieces?

The week before, at home, some academic friends had been over and as we talked and drank we looked at a television showing of Tod Browning's 1931 version of *Dracula*. Dwight Frye's appearance on the screen had us suddenly squealing and shrieking, and it was obvious that old vampire movies were part of our common experience. We talked about the famous ones, Murnau's *Nosferatu* and Dreyer's *Vampyr*, and we began to get fairly involved in the lore of the genre — the strategy of the bite, the special earth for the coffins, the stake through the heart versus the rays of the sun as disposal methods, the cross as vampire repellent, et al. We had begun to surprise each other by the affectionate, nostalgic tone of our mock erudition when the youngest person present, an instructor in English, said, in a clear, firm tone, "*The Beast with Five Fingers* is the greatest horror picture I've ever seen." Stunned that so bright a young man could display such shocking taste, preferring a Warner Brothers forties mediocrity to the classics, I gasped, "But why?" And he answered, "Because it's completely irrational. It doesn't make any sense, and that's the true terror."

Upset by his neat little declaration — existentialism in a nutshell — by the calm matter-of-factness of it, and by the way the others seemed to take it for granted, I wanted to pursue the subject. But O. Henry's remark "Conversation in Texas is seldom continuous" applies to California, too. *Dracula* had ended, and the conversation shifted to other, more "serious" subjects.

But his attitude, which had never occurred to me, helped to explain some of my recent moviegoing experiences. I don't mean that I agree that *The Beast with Five Fingers* is a great horror film, but that his enthusiasm for the horror that cannot be rationalized by the mythology and rules of the horror game related to audience reactions that had been puzzling me. Last year I had gone to see a famous French film, Georges Franju's *Eyes Without a Face*, which had arrived in San Francisco in a dubbed version called *The Horror Chamber of Dr. Faustus* and was playing on a double-horror bill in a huge Market Street theater. It was Saturday night and the theater, which holds 2646, was so crowded I had trouble finding a seat.

Even dubbed, *Eyes Without a Face*, which Franju called a "poetic fantasy," is austere and elegant: the exquisite photography is by the great Shuftan, the music by Maurice Jarre, the superb gowns by Givenchy. It's a symbolist attack on science and the ethics of medicine, and though I thought this attack as simpleminded in its way as the usual young poet's denunciation of war or commerce, it is in some peculiar way a classic of horror.

Pierre Brasseur, as a doctor, experiments systematically, removing the faces of beautiful young kidnaped women, trying to graft them onto the ruined head of his daughter. He keeps failing, the girls are destroyed and yet he persists — in some terrible parody of the scientific method. In the end, the daughter — still only eyes without a face — liberates the dogs on which he also experiments and they tear off *his* head.

It's both bizarrely sophisticated (with Alida Valli as his mistress doing the kidnaping in a black leather coat, recalling the death images from Cocteau's *Orpheus*) and absurdly naive. Franju's style is almost as purified as Robert Bresson's, and although I dislike the mixture of austerity and mysticism with blood and gore, it produced its effect — a vague, floating, almost lyric sense of horror, an almost abstract atmosphere, impersonal and humorless. It has nothing like the fun of a good old horror satire like *The Bride of Frankenstein* with Elsa Lanchester's hair curling electrically instead of just frizzing as usual, and Ernest Thesiger toying with mandrake roots and tiny ladies and gentlemen in glass jars. It's a horror film that takes itself very seriously, and even though I thought its intellectual pretensions silly, I couldn't shake off the exquisite, dread images.

But the audience seemed to be reacting to a different movie. They were so noisy the dialogue was inaudible; they talked until the screen gave promise of bloody ghastliness. Then the chatter subsided to rise again in noisy approval of the gory scenes. When a girl in the film seemed about to be mutilated, a young man behind me jumped up and down and shouted encouragement. "Somebody's going to *get* it," he sang out gleefully. The audience, which was, I'd judge, predominantly between fifteen and twenty-five, and at least a third feminine, was as pleased and excited by the most revolting, obsessive images as that older, mostly male audience is when the nudes appear in *The Immoral Mr. Teas* or *Not Tonight, Henry*. They'd gotten what they came for: they hadn't been cheated. But nobody seemed to care what the movie was about or be interested in the logic of the plot — the reasons for the gore.

And audiences have seemed indifferent to incomprehensible sections in big expensive pictures. For example, how is it that the immense audience for *The Bridge on the River Kwai*, after all those hours of watching a story unfold, didn't express discomfort or outrage or even plain curiosity about what exactly happened at the end — which through bad direction or perhaps sloppy editing went by too fast to be sorted out and understood. Was it possible that audiences no longer cared if a film was so untidily put together that information crucial to the plot or characterizations was obscure or omitted altogether? *What Ever Happened to Baby Jane?* was such a mess that *Time*, after calling it "the year's scariest, funniest and most sophisticated thriller," got the plot garbled.

In recent years, largely because of the uncertainty of producers about what will draw, films in production may shift from one script to another, or may be finally cut so that key sequences are omitted. And the oddity is that it doesn't seem to matter to the audience. I couldn't tell what was going on in parts of *55 Days at Peking*. I was flabbergasted when Cleopatra, with no hint or preparation, suddenly demonstrated clairvoyant powers, only to dispense with them as quickly as she had

acquired them. The audience for *The Cardinal* can have little
way of knowing whose baby the priest's sister is having, or of
understanding how she can be in labor for days, screaming in
a rooming house, without anybody hearing her. They might
also be puzzled about how the priest's argument against her
marriage, which they have been told is the only Catholic position, can, after it leads to her downfall and death, be casually
dismissed as an error.

It would be easy to conclude that people go to see a "show"
and just don't worry if it all hangs together so long as they've
got something to look at. But I think it's more complicated than
that: audiences used to have an almost rational passion for
getting the story straight. They might prefer bad movies to good
ones, and the *Variety* list of "all-time top grossers" (such as
The Greatest Show on Earth and *Going My Way*) indicates that
they did, but although the movies might be banal or vulgar,
they were rarely incoherent. A movie had to tell some kind of
story that held together: a plot had to parse. Some of the
appreciation for the cleverness of, say, Hitchcock's early thrillers
was that they distracted you from the loopholes, so that, afterwards, you could enjoy thinking over how you'd been tricked
and teased. Perhaps now "stories" have become too sane, too
explicable, too commonplace for the large audiences who want
sensations and regard the explanatory connections as mere
"filler" — the kind of stuff you sit through or talk through
between jolts.

It's possible that television viewing, with all its breaks and
cuts, and the inattention, except for action, and spinning the
dial to find some action, is partly responsible for destruction of
the narrative sense — that delight in following a story through
its complications to its conclusion, which is perhaps a child's
first conscious artistic pleasure. The old staples of entertainment
— inoffensive genres like the adventure story or the musical or
the ghost story or the detective story — are no longer commercially safe for moviemakers, and it may be that audiences

don't have much more than a TV span of attention left: they want to be turned on and they spend most of their time turning off. Something similar and related may be happening in reading tastes and habits: teen-agers that I meet have often read Salinger and some Orwell and *Lord of the Flies* and some Joyce Cary and sometimes even Dostoyevsky, but they are not interested in the "classic" English novels of Scott or Dickens, and what is more to the point, they don't read the Sherlock Holmes stories or even the modern detective fiction that in the thirties and forties was an accepted part of the shared experience of adolescents. Whatever the reasons — and they must be more than TV, they must have to do with modern life and the sense of urgency it produces — audiences can no longer be depended on to respond to conventional forms.

Perhaps they want much more from entertainment than the civilized, but limited rational pleasures of genre pieces. More likely, and the box-office returns support this, they want something different. Audiences that enjoy the shocks and falsifications, the brutal series of titillations of a *Mondo Cane*, one thrill after another, don't care any longer about the conventions of the past, and are too restless and apathetic to pay attention to motivations and complications, cause and effect. They want less effort, more sensations, more knobs to turn.

A decade ago, *The Haunting*, an efficient, professional and to all appearances "commercial" genre piece, might have made money. By the end of 1963, its grosses in the United States and Canada, according to *Variety*, were $700,000. This may be compared with $9,250,000 for *Irma La Douce*, $4,600,000 for *The Birds*, $3,900,000 for *55 Days at Peking* — all three, I think, much less enjoyable movies, or to be more exact, terrible movies, and in varying degrees pointless and incomprehensible. A detective genre piece, *The List of Adrian Messenger*, also incomparably better than the three films cited, and with a tricky "star" selling campaign, grossed only $1,500,000. It's easy to imagine that Robert Wise, after the energetic excesses of *West Side Story*, turned to *The Haunting* for a safe, sane respite, and that

John Huston, after wrestling with *Freud*, turned to an intriguing detective story like *Adrian Messenger* for a lucrative, old-fashioned holiday. But what used to be safe seems now to be folly. How can audiences preoccupied with identity problems of their own worry about a case of whodunit and why and how? Following clues may be too much of an effort for those who, in the current teen-age phrase, "couldn't care less." They want shock treatment, not diversion, and it takes more than ghosts to frighten them.

The Haunting is set in that pleasantly familiar "old dark house" that is itself an evil presence, and is usually inhabited by ghosts or evil people. In our childhood imaginings, the unknowable things that have happened in old houses, and the whispers that someone may have died in them, make them mysterious, "dirty"; only the new house that has known no life or death is safe and clean. But so many stories have used the sinister dark house from-which-no-one-can-escape and its murky gardens for our ritual entertainment that we learn to experience the terrors as pleasurable excitations and reassuring reminders of how frightened we used to be before we learned our way around. In film, as in story, the ambiance is fear; the film specialty is gathering a group who are trapped and helpless. (Although the women are more easily frightened, the men are also powerless. Their superior strength doesn't count for much against unseen menaces: this may explain why the genre was often used for a male comedian — like Bob Hope in *The Ghost Breakers*. Russ Tamblyn serves a similar but feeble cowardly-comic function in *The Haunting*.) The action is confined to the house and grounds (the maze); the town is usually far away, just far enough away so that "nobody will hear you if you scream."

In recent years film festivals and art houses have featured a peculiar variant of the trapped-in-the-old-dark-house genre (Buñuel's *The Exterminating Angel* is the classic new example), but the characters, or rather figures, are the undead or zombies of the vampire movies. "We live as in coffins frozen side by side in a garden" — *Last Year at Marienbad*. "I'm dead"

— the heroine of *Il Mare*. "They're all dead in there" — the hostess describing the party of *La Notte*. Their vital juices have been sucked away, but they don't have the revealing marks on the throat. We get the message: alienation drains the soul without leaving any marks. Or, as Bergman says of his trilogy, "Most of the people in these three films are dead, completely dead. They don't know how to love or to feel any emotions. They are lost because they can't reach anyone outside of themselves." This "art" variant is a message movie about failure of communication and lack of love and spiritual emptiness and all the rest of that. It's the closest thing we've got to a new genre but it has some peculiarities. The old dark house was simply *there*, but these symbolic decadent or sterile surroundings are supposed to reflect the walking death of those within the maze. The characters in the old dark house tried to solve the riddle of their imprisonment and tried to escape; even in *No Exit* the drama was in *why* the characters were there, but in the new hotel-in-hell movies the characters don't even want to get out of the maze — nor one surmises do the directors, despite their moralizing. And audiences apparently respond to these films as modern and relevant just because of this paralysis and inaction and minimal story line. If in the group at the older dark house, someone was not who we thought he was, in the new dull party gatherings, it doesn't matter who anybody is (which is a new horror).

Although *The Haunting* is moderately elegant and literate and expensive, and the director gussies things up with a Marienbadish piece of statuary that may or may not be the key to something or other, it's basically a traditional ghost story. There is the dedicated scientist who wants to contribute to science in some socially unacceptable or scientifically reproachable area — in this case to prove the supernatural powers of the house. (The scientist is, somewhat inexplicably, an anthropologist; perhaps Margaret Mead has set the precedent for anthropologists to dabble in and babble on anything — so that the modern concept of the anthropologist is like the old concept of the philosopher or, for that matter, the scientist.) And, in the expository style traditional for the genre, he explains the lore and jargon of psychic research, meticulously separating out ghost from poltergeist and so on. And of course the scientist, in the great tradition of *Frankenstein*, must have the abnormal or mad assistant: the role that would once have belonged to Dwight Frye is here modernized and becomes the Greenwich Village lesbian, Claire Bloom. And there is the scientist's distraught wife who fears that her husband's brilliant career will be ruined, and so on. The chaste heroine, Julie Harris (like an updated Helen Chandler, Dracula's anemic victim), is the movies' post-Freudian concept of the virgin: repressed, hysterical, insane — the source of evil.

It wasn't a great movie but I certainly wouldn't have thought that it could offend anyone. Yet part of the audience at *The Haunting* wasn't merely bored, it was hostile — as if the movie, by assuming interests they didn't have, made them feel resentful or inferior. I've never felt this kind of audience hostility toward crude, bad movies. People are relaxed and tolerant about ghoulish quickies, grotesque shockers dubbed from Japan, and chopped-up Italian spectacles that scramble mythologies and pile on actions, one stupidity after another. Perhaps they prefer incoherent, meaningless movies because they are not required to remember or connect. They can feel superior, contemptuous — as they do toward television advertising. Even when it's a virtuoso triumph, the audience is contemptuous toward advertising, because, after all, they see through it — they know somebody is trying to sell something. And because, like a cheap movie obviously made to pry money out of them, that is all advertising means, it's OK. But the few, scattered people at *The Haunting* were restless and talkative, the couple sitting near me arguing — the man threatening to leave, the woman assuring him that something would happen. In their terms, they were cheated: nothing happened. And, of course, they missed what was happening all along, perhaps because of nervous impatience or a primitive notion that the real things are physical, perhaps because people take from art and from popular entertainment only what they want; and if they are indifferent to story and motive and blank out on the connections, then a movie without physical action or crass jokes or built-in sentimental responses has nothing for them. I am afraid that the young instructor in English spoke for his times, that there is no terror for modern audiences if a story is carefully worked out and follows a tradition, even though the tradition was developed and perfected precisely to frighten entertainingly.

No wonder that studios and producers are unsure what to do next, scan best-seller lists for trends, consult audience-testing polls, anxiously chop out what a preview audience doesn't like. The New York *Times* chides the representatives of some seven companies who didn't want to invest in *What Ever Happened to Baby Jane?* but how could businessmen, brought up to respect logic and a good commercial script, possibly guess that this confused mixture of low camp and Grand Guignol would delight the public?

And if I may return for a moment to that producer whom I left sunning himself at the side of the pool — "Did you know that *Irma La Douce* is already the highest-grossing comedy in film history?" he asked me at one point, not in the droning voice of the civic-minded man discussing the cultural development of the community, but in the voice of someone who's really involved in what he's saying. "Yes," I said, "but is it even a comedy? It's a monstrous mutation." The producer shrugged his dark round shoulders helplessly: "Who knows what's a comedy any more?"

It is not just general audiences out for an evening's entertainment who seem to have lost the narrative sense, or become indifferent to narrative. What I think are processes of structural disintegration are at work in all types of movies, and though it's obvious that many of the old forms were dead and had to be broken through, it's rather scary to see what's happening — and not just at the big picture-palaces. Art-house films are even more confusing. Why, at the end of Godard's *My Life to Live,* is the heroine shot, rather than the pimp that the rival gang is presumably gunning for? Is she just a victim of bad marksmanship? If we express perplexity, we are likely to be told that we are missing the existentialist point: it's simply fate, she had to die. But a cross-eyed fate? And why is there so little questioning of the organization of *My Name Is Ivan* with its lyric interludes and patriotic sections so ill assembled that one might think the projectionist had scrambled the reels? (They often do at art houses, and it would seem that the more sophisticated the audience, the less likely that the error will be discovered. When I pointed out to a theater manager that the women in *Brink of Life* were waiting for their babies after they had miscarried, he told me that he had been playing the film for two weeks and I was his first patron who wasn't familiar with Bergman's methods.)

The art-house audience accepts lack of clarity as complexity, accepts clumsiness and confusion as "ambiguity" and as style. Perhaps even without the support of critics, they would accept incoherence just as the larger audience does: they may feel that movies as incomprehensible as *Viridiana* are more relevant to their experience, more true to their own feelings about life, and more satisfying and complex than works they can understand.

I trust I won't be mistaken for the sort of boob who attacks ambiguity or complexity. I am interested in the change from the period when the meaning of art and form in art was in making complex experience simple and lucid, as is still the case in *Knife in the Water* or *Bandits of Orgosolo,* to the current acceptance of art as technique, the technique which in a movie like *This Sporting Life* makes a simple, though psychologically confused, story look complex, and modern because inexplicable.

It has become easy — especially for those who consider "time" a problem and a great theme — to believe that fast editing, out of normal sequence, which makes it difficult, or impossible, for the audience to know if any action is taking place, is somehow more "cinematic" than a consecutively told story. For a half century movies have, when necessary, shifted action in time and place and the directors generally didn't think it necessary to slap us in the face with each cut or to call out, "Look what I can do!" Yet people who should know better will tell you how "cinematic" *The Loneliness of the Long Distance Runner* or *This Sporting Life* is — as if fiddling with the time sequence was good in itself, proof that the "medium" is really being used. Perhaps, after a few decades of indoctrination in high art, they are convinced that a movie is cinematic when they don't understand what's going on. *This Sporting Life*, which Derek Hill, among others, has called the best feature ever made in England, isn't gracefully fragmented, it's smashed. The chunks are so heavy and humorless and, in an odd way, disturbing, that we can tell the film is meant to be bold, powerful, tragic.

There's a woman writer I'd be tempted to call a three-time loser: she's Catholic, Communist, and lesbian; but she comes on more like a triple threat. She's in with so many groups that her books are rarely panned. I thought of her when I read the reviews of *This Sporting Life*: this film has it made in so many ways, it carries an identity card with all the outsiders. The hero is "bewildered," the heroine "bruised" and "afraid of life," the brutal rugby games are possibly a "microcosm of a corrupt society," and the film murkily suggests all sorts of passion and protest, like a group of demonstrators singing "We Shall Overcome" and leaving it to you to fill in your own set of injustices. For *Show* magazine, "The football scenes bear the aspect of a savage rite, with the spectators as participants hungry for sacrifice. The love story . . . is simply another kind of scrimmage, a battle between two people who cannot communicate . . ." For the New York *Times*, the film "translates the confusions and unrequited longings of the angry young men and women of our time into memorable universal truths." (I wish the reviewer would spell out one or two of them for us.) The *Times* has an unusual interpretation of the love story: "The woman . . . only succumbs to him physically and the real roots he seeks are unattainable." This reminds me of my confusion as a schoolgirl when a jazz musician who had been introduced to me during the break called out "Dig you later" as he went back to the stand.

In the *Observer*, Penelope Gilliatt offers extraordinary praise: "*This Sporting Life* is a stupendous film. It has a blow like a fist. I've never seen an English picture that gave such expression to the violence and the capacity for pain that there is in the English character. It is there in Shakespeare, in Marlowe, in Lawrence and Orwell and Hogarth, but not in our cinema like this before. *This Sporting Life* is hard to write about because everything important about it is really subverbal." But then so are trees and animals and cities. Isn't it precisely the artist's task to give form to his experience and the critic's task to verbalize on how this has been accomplished? She goes on to write of the hero, "The events almost seem to be happening to him in the dark. Half of them are told while he is under dentist's gas, in flashback, which is a clumsy device if one is telling a story but the natural method if one is searching around a character." English dental hygiene is notorious; still, isn't telling a story, with or without gas and flashbacks, a pretty good "natural" method of searching around a character? But something *more* seems to be involved: "The black subjective spirit of the film is overpowering. It floods the sound track, which often has a peculiar resonance as though it were happening inside one's own head." Sort of a sunken cathedral effect? The bells are clanging in the reviewers' heads, but what's happening on the screen?

In one way or another, almost all the enthusiasts for a film like this one will tell you that it doesn't matter, that however you interpret the film, you will be right (though this does not prevent some of them from working out elaborate interpretations of *Marienbad* or *The Eclipse* or *Viridiana*). Walter Lassally says that "Antonioni's oblique atmospheric statements and Buñuel's symbolism, for example, cannot be analyzed in terms of good or bad . . . for they contain, in addition to any obvious meanings, everything that the viewer may read into them." Surely he can read the most onto a blank screen?

There's not much to be said for this theory except that it's mighty democratic. Rather pathetically, those who accept this Rorschach-blot approach to movies are hesitant and uneasy about offering reactions. They should be reassured by the belief that whatever they say is right, but as it refers not to the film but to them (turning criticism into autobiography) they are afraid of self-exposure. I don't think they really believe the theory — it's a sort of temporary public convenience station. More and more people come out of a movie and can't tell you what they've seen, or even whether they liked it.

An author like David Storey may stun them with information like "[This Sporting Life] works purely in terms of feeling. Only frivolous judgments can be made about it in conventional terms of style." Has he discovered a new method of conveying feeling without style? Or has he simply found the arrogance to frustrate normal responses? No one wants to have his capacity for feeling questioned, and if a viewer tries to play it cool, and discuss This Sporting Life in terms of corrupt professional football, he still won't score on that muddy field: there are no goal-posts. Lindsay Anderson, who directed, says, "This Sporting Life is not a film about sport. In fact, I wouldn't really call it a story picture at all. . . . We have tried to make a tragedy . . . we were making a film about something unique." A tragedy without a story is unique all right: a disaster.

In movies, as in other art forms, if you are interested only in technique or if you reject technique, the result is just about the same: if you have nothing to express it is very much like thinking you have so much to express that you don't know how to say it. Something related to absorption in technique is involved in the enthusiasm of young people for what is called "the New American Cinema," though these films are often made by those who reject craftsmanship as well as meaning. They tend to equate technique with science and those who produced the Bomb. This approach, which is a little like the attack on scientific method in Eyes Without a Face, is used to explain why they must make movies without taking time to learn how.

They're in a hurry, and anyway, technique might corrupt them.

The spokesmen for this cinema attack rationality as if it were the enemy of art ("as/ the heavy Boots of Soldiers and Intellect/ march across the/ flowerfields of subconscious" and so forth by Jonas Mekas). They have composed a rather strange amalgam in which reason = lack of feeling and imagination = hostility to art = science = the enemy = Nazis and police = the Bomb. Somewhere along the line, criticism is also turned into an enemy of art. The group produces a kind of euphoric publicity which is published in place of criticism, but soon it may have semi-intellectually respectable critics. In the *Nation* of April 13, 1964, Susan Sontag published an extraordinary essay on Jack Smith's *Flaming Creatures* called "A Feast for Open Eyes" in which she enunciates a new critical principle: "Thus Smith's crude technique serves, beautifully, the sensibility embodied in *Flaming Creatures* — a sensibility based on indiscriminateness, without ideas, beyond negation." I think in treating indiscriminateness as a *value*, she has become a real swinger. Of course we can reply that if anything goes, nothing happens, nothing works. But this is becoming irrelevant. In Los Angeles, among the independent film makers at their midnight screenings I was told that I belonged to the older generation, that Agee-alcohol generation they called it, who could not respond to the new films because I didn't take pot or LSD and so couldn't learn just to *accept* everything. This narcotic approach of torpid acceptance, which is much like the lethargy of the undead in those failure-of-communication movies, may explain why those films have seemed so "true" to some people (and why the directors' moralistic messages sound so false). This attitude of rejecting critical standards has the dubious advantage of accepting everyone who says he is an artist as an artist and conferring on all his "noncommercial" productions the status of art. Miss Sontag is on to something and if she stays on and rides it like Slim Pickens, it's the end of criticism — at the very least.

It's ten years since Dylan Thomas answered Maya Deren's call for a new poetry of film with "I'm not at all sure that I want such a thing, myself, as a poetic film. I think films fine as they are, if only they were better! . . . I like stories, you know — I like to see something going on." Movies have changed in these ten years, disastrously in the last few years; they have become "cinema."

At the art-house level, critics and audiences haven't yet discovered the beauty of indiscriminateness, but there's a lot of talk about "purely visual content" — which might be called the principle of ineffability. *Time* calls Resnais's *Muriel* "another absorbing exercise in style." Dwight Macdonald calls *Marienbad* " 'pure' cinema, a succession of images enjoyable in themselves." And Richard Roud, who was responsible (and thus guilty) for the film selection at the New York Film Festivals, goes all the way: films like *La Notte*, he says, provide an "experience in pure form."

Once matters reach this plane, it begins to seem almost unclean to raise issues about meaning and content and character, or to question the relevance of a sequence, the quality of a performance. Someone is sure to sneer, "Are you looking for a paraphrasable content? A film, like a poem, *is*." Or smile pityingly and remind you that Patroni Griffi had originally intended to call *Il Mare* "Landscape with Figures"; doesn't that tell you how you should look at it? It does indeed, and it's not my idea of a good time. After a few dismal experiences we discover that when we are told to admire a film for its pure form or its structure, it is going to exhibit irritating, confusing, and ostentatious technique, which will, infuriatingly, be all we can discover in it. And if we should mention that we *enjoy* the dramatic and narrative elements in movies, we are almost certain to be subjected to the contemptuous remark, "Why does cinema have to *mean* something? Do you expect a work by Bach to *mean* something?"

The only way to answer this is by some embarrassingly basic analysis, pointing out that words, unlike tones, refer to something and that movie images are rarely abstract or geometric designs, and that when they include people and places and actions, they have implications, associations. Robbe-Grillet, the scenarist of *Marienbad*, may say that the film is a pure construction, an object without reference to anything outside itself, and that the existence of the two characters begins when the film begins and ends ninety-three minutes later, but, of course, we are not born when we go in to see a movie — though we may want to die by the time we leave. And we can't even leave *Marienbad* behind because, although it isn't particularly memorable (it isn't even particularly offensive), a kind of creeping Marienbadism is the new aesthetics of "poetic" cinema. This can only sound like pedantry to those interested in "pure" art who tend to consider analysis as an enemy, anyway (though many of them are in it). The very same people who say that a movie shouldn't mean anything, that art is beyond meaning, also say that it must be seen over and over again because it reveals more meaning with subsequent viewings. And although the structure of many of the new films is somehow supposed to be the art, we are frowned upon if we question the organization of the material. There is nothing, finally, that we are allowed to question or criticize. We are supposed only to interpret — and that as we wish.

The leaders of this new left-wing formalism are Resnais, who gives us his vision of a bomb-shattered, fragmented universe, and Antonioni, the master practitioner of the fallacy of expressive form, who sets out to demonstrate that boredom (and its accompanying eroticism) is the sickness of our time (but doesn't explain how it helps to add to it). If their characters have a curious way of using their sophisticated vacuity as a come-on, are they not in their creators' image? They make assignations (as in *The Eclipse*), but nobody comes.

The movie houses may soon look as desolate as *Il Mare* — set in Capri in winter. I've never seen so many people sleeping through movies as at Lincoln Center: no wonder there is talk of "cinema" achieving the social status of opera. A few more seasons of such art and it will be evidence of your interest in culture and your sense of civic responsibility if you go to the movies.

The "techniques" of such films are so apparent, so obtrusive, that they may easily be assumed to be "advanced," "modern," "new." It's perfectly true you don't come out of an older movie like Renoir's *La Grande Illusion*, or Flaherty's *Man of Aran*, or Bergman's *Smiles of a Summer Night* saying, "What technique!" Nor do you come out of a concert by Serkin exclaiming about his technique — you're thinking of the music. But those who adore José Iturbi always say, "What technique!"; what *else* is there to respond to? And the comment — which means how fast he can play or how ostentatiously — is not so very far from the admiration for Antonioni or Torre Nilsson or Bresson's *Trial of Joan of Arc* (though they are generally admired for how slow they can play).

My attitude to what is happening to movies is more than a little ambivalent. I don't think that my own preferences or the preferences of others for coherence and wit and feeling are going to make much difference. Movies are going to pieces; they're disintegrating, and the something called cinema is not movies raised to an art but rather movies diminished, movies that look "artistic." Movies are being stripped of all the "nonessentials" — that is to say, faces, actions, details, stories, places — everything that makes them entertaining and joyful. They are even being stripped of the essentials — light (*The Eclipse*), sound (*The Silence*), and movement in some of the New American Cinema films (there is sure to be one called *Stasis*). It's obvious that the most talented film artists and the ones most responsive to our time and the attitudes of Camus and Sartre are the ones moving in this direction. The others, those trying to observe the older conventions, are usually (though not always) banal, trivial, ludicrously commercial, and out of touch, somehow. It is the highest talents, the most dedicated, who are driven to the dead end of "pure" cinema — just as our painters are driven to obliterate the image, and a dramatist like Beckett to reduce words to sounds.

Cinema, I suspect, is going to become so rarefied, so private in meaning, and so lacking in audience appeal that in a few years the foundations will be desperately and hopelessly trying to bring it back to life, as they are now doing with theater. The parallel course is, already, depressingly apparent. Clancy Sigal's (admiring) account of Beckett's *Endgame* might have been written of Bergman's *The Silence*:

Endgame's two main characters . . . occupy a claustrophobic space and a deeply ambiguous relationship. . . . Outside, the world is dead of some great catastrophe. . . . The action of the play mainly comprises anxious bickering between the two principal characters. Eventually, Clov dresses for the road to leave Hamm, and Hamm prepares for death, though we do not see the moment of parting . . . none of the actors is quite sure what the play is about, Beckett affects complete ignorance of the larger implications. "I only know what's on the page," he says with a friendly gesture.

Is Beckett leading the way or is it all in the air? His direction that the words of *Play* should be spoken so fast that they can't be understood is paralleled by Resnais's editing of *Muriel* so fast that you can't keep track of what's going on. Penelope Gilliatt writes, "You may have to go to the film at least twice, as I did, before the warmth of it seeps through . . ."; Beckett has already anticipated the problem and provided the answer with the stage direction, "Repeat play exactly."

When movies, the only art which everyone felt free to enjoy and have opinions about, lose their connection with song and dance, drama, and the novel, when they become cinema, which people fear to criticize just as they fear to say what they think of a new piece of music or a new poem or painting, they will become another object of academic study and "appreciation," and will soon be an object of excitement only to practitioners of the "art." Although *L'Avventura* is a great film, had I been present at Cannes in 1960, where Antonioni distributed his explanatory statement, beginning, "There exists in the world today a very serious break between science on the one hand . . . ,"

I might easily have joined in the hisses, which he didn't really deserve until the following year, when *La Notte* revealed that he'd begun to believe his own explanations — thus making liars of us all.

When we see Dwight Macdonald's cultural solution applied to film, when we see the prospect that movies will become a product for "Masscult" consumption, while the "few who care" will have their High Culture cinema, who wants to take the high road? There is more energy, more originality, more excitement, more *art* in American kitsch like *Gunga Din, Easy Living,* the Rogers and Astaire pictures like *Swingtime* and *Top Hat,* in *Strangers on a Train, His Girl Friday, The Crimson Pirate, Citizen Kane, The Lady Eve, To Have and Have Not, The African Queen, Singin' in the Rain, Sweet Smell of Success,* or more recently, *The Hustler, Lolita, The Manchurian Candidate, Hud, Charade,* than in the presumed "High Culture" of *Hiroshima Mon Amour, Marienbad, La Notte, The Eclipse,* and the Torre Nilsson pictures. As Nabokov remarked, "Nothing is more exhilarating than Philistine vulgarity."

Regrettably, one of the surest signs of the Philistine is his reverence for the superior tastes of those who put him down. Macdonald believes that "a work of High Culture, however inept, is an expression of feelings, ideas, tastes, visions that are idiosyncratic and the audience similarly responds to them as individuals." No. The "pure" cinema enthusiast who doesn't react to a film but feels he should, and so goes back to it over and over, is not responding as an individual but as a compulsive good pupil determined to appreciate what his cultural superiors say is "art." Movies are on their way into academia when they're turned into a matter of duty: a mistake in judgment isn't fatal, but too much anxiety about judgment is. In this country, respect for High Culture is becoming a ritual.

If debased art is kitsch, perhaps kitsch may be redeemed by honest vulgarity, may become art. Our best work transforms kitsch, makes art out of it; that is the peculiar greatness and strength of American movies, as Godard in *Breathless* and Truffaut in *Shoot the Piano Player* recognize. Huston's *The Maltese Falcon* is a classic example. Our first and greatest film artist D. W. Griffith was a master of kitsch: the sentiment and melodrama in his films are much more integral to their greatness than the critics who lament Griffith's lack of mind (!) perceive.

The movies are still where it happens, not for much longer perhaps, but the movies are still the art form that uses the material of our lives and the art form that we use. I am not suggesting that we want to see new and bigger remakes of the tired old standbys of the film repertory: who wants to see the new *Cimarron*, another *Quo Vadis?* And meanings don't have to be spread out for us like a free-lunch counter. There are movies that are great experiences like *Long Day's Journey into Night*, and just a few years back there were movies which told good stories — movies like *The Treasure of Sierra Madre, From Here to Eternity, The Nun's Story.*

People go to the movies for the various ways they express the experiences of our lives, and as a means of avoiding and postponing the pressures we feel. This latter function of art — generally referred to disparagingly as escapism — may also be considered as refreshment, and in terms of modern big city life and small town boredom, it may be a major factor in keeping us sane.

In the last few years there has appeared a new kind of filmgoer: he isn't interested in movies but in cinema. A great many of the film makers are in this group: they've never gone to movies much and they don't care about them. They're interested in what they can do in the medium, not in what *has* been done. This is, of course, their privilege, though I would suggest that it may explain why they have such limited approaches to film. I'm more puzzled by the large numbers of those who are looking for *importance* in cinema. For example, a doctor friend called me after he'd seen *The Pink Panther* to tell me I needn't "bother" with that one, it was just slapstick. When I told him I'd already seen it and had a good time at it, he was irritated; he informed me that a movie should be more than a waste of time, it should be an exercise of taste that will enrich your life. Those looking for importance are too often contemptuous of the crude vitality of American films, though this crudity is not always offensive, and may represent the only way that energy and talent and inventiveness can find an outlet, can break through the planned standardization of mass entertainment. It has become a mark of culture to revere the old slapstick (the Mack Sennett two-reelers and early Chaplins that aren't really as great as all that) and put down the new. But in a movie as shopworn as *Who's Been Sleeping in My Bed?* there is, near the end, an almost inspired satirical striptease by Carol Burnett. *The Nutty Professor* is too long and repetitive, but Jerry Lewis has some scenes that hold their own with the silent classics. I enjoyed *The Prize*, which opens badly but then becomes a lively, blatant entertainment; but there's no point in recommending it to someone who wants his life enriched. I couldn't persuade friends to go see *Charade*, which although no more than a charming confectionery trifle was, I think, probably the best American film of last year — as artificial and enjoyable in its way as *The Big Sleep*. The word had got around that it isn't *important*, that it isn't *serious*, that it doesn't do anything for you.

Our academic bureaucracy needs something alive to nourish it and movies still have a little blood which the academics can drain away. In the West several of the academic people I know who have least understanding of movies were suddenly interested by Laurence Alloway's piece called "Critics in the Dark" in *Encounter*. By suggesting that movie criticism had never gotten into the right hands — i.e., theirs, and by indicating *projects*, and by publishing in the prestigious *Encounter*, Alloway indicated large vistas of respectability for future film critics. Perhaps also they were drawn to his condescending approach to movies as a pop art. Many academics have always been puzzled that Agee could *care* so much about movies. Alloway, by taking the position that Agee's caring was a maladjustment, re-established their safe, serene worlds in which if a man gets excited about an idea or an issue, they know there's something the matter with him. It's not much consolation, but I think the cinema the academics will be working over will be the cinema they deserve.

[1964]

I

Broadsides

Fantasies of the Art-House Audience

For several decades now educated people have been condescending toward the children, the shopgirls, all those with "humdrum" or "impoverished" lives — the mass audience — who turned to movies for "ready-made" dreams. The educated might admit that they sometimes went to the movies designed for the infantile mass audience — the number of famous people who relax with detective fiction makes this admission easy — but presumably they were not "taken in"; they went to get away from the tensions of their complex lives and work. But of course when they really want to enjoy movies as an art, they go to foreign films, or "adult" or unusual or experimental American films.

I would like to suggest that the educated audience often uses "art" films in much the same self-indulgent way as the mass audience uses the Hollywood "product," finding wish fulfillment in the form of cheap and easy congratulation on their sensitivities and their liberalism. (Obviously any of my generalizations are subject to numerous exceptions and infinite qualifications; let's assume that I know this, and that I use large generalizations in order to be suggestive rather than definitive.)

By the time Alain Resnais's *Hiroshima Mon Amour* reached American art houses, expectations were extraordinarily high. Dwight Macdonald in *Esquire* had said: "It is the most original, moving, exciting and important movie I've seen in years, somehow managing to combine a love story with propaganda against war and the atomic bomb without either losing its full force." The rest of the press seemed to concur. The *Saturday Review* considered it "a masterpiece." The New York *Herald Tribune* decided that "it establishes beyond any man's cavilling the potentialities of the film as an art" — something one might have thought already established. *Time* decided that the theme was that "Hiroshima, like God, is love. It is the Calvary of the atomic age. It died for man's sins . . ." I met a couple who had seen the film five nights in a row; a University of California professor informed me that if I didn't like *this* one, he would never speak to me again. Dwight Macdonald wrote more and went further:

It is as stylised as *Potemkin* or *Ten Days that Shook the World*, as pure and powerful as cinema . . . It is also a novelistic exploration of memory, a *recherche du temps perdu* comparable to Proust. . . . For the first time since Eisenstein — we have a cinematic intelligence so quick, so subtle, so original, so at once passionate and sophisticated that it can be compared with Joyce, with Picasso, with Berg and Bartok and Stravinsky. The audience was extraordinarily quiet — no coughing, whispering, rustling of paper; a hypnotic trance. . . . It was oddly like a religious service, and if someone had made a wisecrack, it would have seemed not an irritation but a blasphemy.

Surely movies — even the greatest movies — are rarely received in such an atmosphere of incense burning. *Breathless* and *L'Avventura* were to be either admired or disliked or ignored, but *Hiroshima Mon Amour* was described in hushed tones; it was some sort of ineffable deep experience. Why?

The picture opened with those intertwined nude bodies — this could be symbolic of a true intermingling, but it irresistibly set off some lewd speculations about just *what* was going on. And what was that stuff they were covered with? Beach sand? Gold dust? Ashes? Finally, I accepted it as symbolic bomb ash, but I wasn't happy with it. (Later I discovered that it was supposed to be "sweat, ashes and dew.") Then the French girl said she had seen everything in Hiroshima, and the Japanese man told her she had seen nothing in Hiroshima. Then they said the same things over again, and again, and perhaps again. And I lost patience. I have never understood why writers assume that repetition creates a lyric mood or underlines meaning with profundity. My reaction is simply, "OK, I got it the first time, let's get on with it." Now, this is obviously not how we are supposed to react to Marguerite Duras's dialogue, which is clearly intended to be musical and contrapuntal, and I was going to try to get in the right, passive, receptive mood for a ritual experience, when some outright fraud made me sit up and pay attention. The action — or inaction — in bed was intercut with what purported to be documentary shots of the effect of the bomb on Hiroshima. Only I had seen some of the footage before in a Japanese atrocity movie that was about as documentary as *Peyton Place*. This clumsily staged imposture made me suspect that the Japanese man didn't know Hiroshima either, and I began to look askance at the truth he was supposed to represent. Where did he get this metaphysical identity with Hiroshima? As the film went on, and the heroine recounted her first love for a German soldier, how he had been killed on the last day of fighting, how she had been dragged away and her head shaved, how she had gone mad and been hidden away in the cellar by her shamed parents, I began to think less and less of the movie and more about why so many people were bowled over by it.

Was it possibly an elaborate, masochistic fantasy for intellectuals? Surely both sexes could identify with the girl's sexual desperation, her sensitivity and confusion — and had anyone dreamed up worse punishments for sexuality? Only a few years ago it had looked as if James Dean in *East of Eden* and *Rebel Without a Cause* had gone just about as far as anybody could in being misunderstood. But this heroine not only had her head shaved by people who didn't understand her love and need of the German, but she went *crazy* and was locked in a cellar. You can't go much further in being misunderstood. And, at the risk of giving offense, is this not what sends so many people to analysts — the fear that they'll go crazy if they don't get love?

The Japanese, it may be noted, is rather dull and uninteresting: he says no more than an analyst might; he is simply a sounding board. And if, being Japanese, he is supposed to represent the world's conscience, he brings an unsuitably bland, professionally sympathetic and upper-class manner to the function. But everybody who has suffered sexual deprivation — and who hasn't? — can identify with her and perhaps fantasize brutal parents and cellars. Even her insanity can be equated with those rough nights when a love affair fell apart or that nervous exhaustion at the end of the academic year that sends so many to the hospital or the psychiatric clinic.

It seemed to be a woman's picture — in the most derogatory sense of the term. And still she went on talking: her feelings, her doubts, her memories, kept pouring out. It began to seem like True Confession at the higher levels of spiritual and sexual communion; and I decided the great lesson for us all was to shut up. This woman (beautifully as Emmanuelle Riva interpreted her) was exposing one of the worst faults of intelligent modern women: she was talking all her emotions out — as if bed were the place to demonstrate sensibility. It's unfortunate that what people believe to be the most important things about themselves, their innermost truths and secrets — the real you or me — that we dish up when somebody looks sympathetic, is very likely to be the driveling nonsense that we generally have enough brains to forget about. The real you or me that we conceal because we think people won't accept it is slop — and why *should* anybody want it?

But here was the audience soaking it up — audiences of social workers, scientists, doctors, architects, professors — living and loving and suffering just like the stenographer watching Susan Hayward. Are the experiences involved really so different? Few of us have seen our lovers killed by partisan bullets, but something kills love anyway — something always does — and it's probably highly gratifying for many people to identify with a heroine who isn't responsible: it is the insane world that has punished her for her sexual expression. Emmanuelle Riva's sexual expression is far more forthright than a Hollywood heroine's, which makes it more appealing to an educated audience, and, of course, her character and her manner of indicating her emotional problems have a higher "tone." (It may be relevant to note that the educated audience, which generally ignores Miss Hayward, did turn out for *I Want to Live,* in which the character of Barbara Graham was turned into a sort of modern Tess of the d'Urbervilles — not only innocent of crime but horribly sinned against and *nobler* than anybody else.)

But what does her sad story have to do with Hiroshima and the bomb? Would not some other psychosexual story of deprivation (say, *Camille* or *Stella Dallas*) be just as relevant to the horrors of war if it were set in Hiroshima? It would seem so. However, the setting itself explains another aspect of the film's strong appeal, particularly to liberal intellectuals. There is a crucial bit of dialogue: "They make movies to sell soap, why not a movie to sell peace?" I don't know how many movies you have gone to lately that were made to sell soap, but American movies *are* like advertisements, and we can certainly assume that indirectly they sell a way of life that includes soap as well as an infinity of other products. But what makes the dialogue crucial is that the audience for *Hiroshima Mon Amour* feels virtuous because they want to buy peace. And the question I want to ask is: who's selling it?

Recently, at a cocktail party of artists and professors, I noticed displayed on a table right next to the pickled Jerusalem artichokes, two French publications — Lo Duca's new volume on *Eroticism in the Cinema* and Kenneth Anger's *Hollywood Babylon.* Both books are like more elegantly laid-out issues of *Confidential* and all those semi-nameless magazines which feature hideously outsized mammary glands, only these books are supposed to be chic — the latest intellectual camp. The Lo Duca book features stills from a Kenneth Anger movie in which nude ladies are wrapped in chains. Anger, you may recall, made his reputation with a film called *Fireworks,* in which a roman candle explodes inside a sailor's fly. His own book has a dust jacket photograph of Jayne Mansfield — an aerial view down her dress that makes her breasts look like long strips of cooked tripe. The book itself is a recounting of the legends (that is to say the dirty stories, scandals, and gossip) that Anger heard while growing up in southern California.

What struck me about these books, which function as entertainment to what might be called highbrows, was that their chic seemed to consist largely in a degradation of the female image. The stars and starlets are displayed at their most grotesque, just as they are in the cheapest American publications (in fact the photos are probably derived from those sources). This female image is a parody of woman — lascivious face, wet open mouth, gigantic drooping breasts. She has no character, no individuality: she's blonde or brunette or redhead, as one might consume a martini, an old-fashioned, or a gin and tonic.

Now I am told that even the junior-high-school boys of America use photographs like these as pinups, and that this is their idea of the desirable female. I don't believe it. I would guess that they pretend to this ideal because they're afraid they won't be considered manly and sexy if they admit they find this image disgusting. I don't believe that these photographs are erotic in any ordinary sense. I think that the grotesqueness of this female image is what people enjoy. Here are some possible reasons. First, these spongy, subhuman sex images reduce women to the lowest animal level. And in the modern world, where women are competent, independent, and free and equal, the men have a solid, competitive hostility — they want to see women degraded even lower than they were in the Victorian era. Here is woman reduced to nothing but a blob that will gratify any male impulse. And, of course, a woman who has no interest in life but love presents no challenge to the male ego. Second, there's the old split between sacred and profane love — and many men feel that the more degraded the female, the more potent they would become. Third, there's the vast homosexual audience which enjoys derision of the female. I would guess, and here's a big generalization, that more homosexuals than heterosexuals love to chortle over the nude photos of Anita Ekberg. She's so preposterous — a living satire of the female. It's my guess that the audience for nudie-cutie magazines uses them in much the same way the wealthy and educated use expensive French publications on the same theme: they want to laugh at the subjects and/or feel superior to them.

When the parodied female becomes known, becomes a "personality," derision gives way to admiration and sympathy and "understanding." In publications like the British *Sunday Times* you will find discussions with passages like "Marilyn Monroe grew up without affection and at times she was near suicide. When she talks about herself the awareness of her bitter past is never quite absent." *Time* and *Life* present her psychoanalytical comments on herself. And Dwight Macdonald in *Esquire* explains that "the expensive difficulties she makes for her employers are not so much prima donna assertiveness as symptoms of resentment and boredom." Sociologists read Zolotow's book on her character changes, and Cecil Beaton rhapsodizes that "she was born the postwar day we had need of her. Certainly she has no knowledge of the past. Like Giraudoux's Ondine, she is only fifteen years old; and she will never die." He's right, at least, about her not having knowledge of the past: she seems to have swallowed all the psychoanalytical clichés about maltreated children, and when she talks about her past she simply spews them up. And the educated public loves these burbling bits of Freudian "insight" when they come out of the mouths of "babes." In *The Misfits*, our heroine, with the sure instincts of the faithful dog, and the uncorrupted clarity of the good clean peasant, looks at each character in the film and knows him for what he is. The innocent eye can see the inner man — she's the female of the species of the strong, silent hero, but she's also the traditional whore with the heart of gold. Her performance in *The Misfits* appears uncontrollably nervous, but it's almost as if her confused state were the final proof of her sincerity. The public loves her the more because life seems too much for her.

La Vérité is a tired and trite and mechanical piece of slick moviemaking. Conceptually, it's rather like *Of Human Bondage*

— seen from Mildred's point of view. Although the title and the film's structure suggest that we are going to see the relativity of truth, the movie seems designed to show us the truth about Brigitte Bardot, just as *The Misfits* was written around Monroe. (These ladies are then congratulated for their histrionic achievements in playing themselves; certainly they are perfect in the roles — no one else could play them so well — but then, could they play anyone else?) This confusion of art and life which takes the form of sensationalism is becoming very popular in this Freudianized period. (Clouzot coyly plays with this confusion by having Bardot, the subject of a book by Simone de Beauvoir, accused in the courtroom of *La Vérité* of having read a book by de Beauvoir.)

It is supposed to be daring and modern to make these messed-up accounts of messed-up lives — though they may seem very much like the old Sunday supplements with their daring exposés. In this new form, however, the appeal is not only to the mass audience but also to the more literate, who are led to believe that they are getting some inside psychological dope.

Apparently these screen incarnations of male fantasies, Monroe (once a calendar girl come to comic strip life, an implausible but delicious affront to respectability) and Bardot (the distillation of all those irresponsible, petulant teen-agers who may never know that human experience has depth and expressiveness and potentialities beyond their immediate range of impulses) are objects of enthusiasm not so much for their (former or present) polymorphous-perverse physical charms and their (former or present) comedy talents, as for their messy, confused public-private lives — the nervous breakdowns, miscarriages, over-weight problems, husband troubles, and all those mental and physical ills which now comprise the image of a great star. The new heroine of our films is becoming the wretched star herself. In the pre-Freudian age, the exploitation of personal ailments in films like *The Misfits* and *La Vérité* would have been regarded as disgusting. It *is* disgusting, and the condescending type of sympathetic "understanding" which is now widely purveyed is an insult to Freud and man. In the frivolous, absurd old days, stars were photographed in their bubble baths: now they bathe in tears of self-pity — while intellectual critics tap their understanding typewriters.

The "mass" audience looks up at the "stars"; the educated audience looks down sympathetically, as if reading a case history. They all stew in their own narcissism. The mass audience is beginning to catch up. On a recent television program Ed Sullivan clucked sympathetically at Brigitte Bardot and told her how much he sympathized with the hard life of glamour girls like her and Monroe and Taylor, and, final irony, told her how much he admired the way she had "handled herself."

The educated American is a social worker at heart: he feels especially sympathetic toward these slovenly ladies because their slovenliness marks them as misfits who couldn't function in his orderly world. The same man who is enchanted with Monroe in the seduction scene of *Some Like It Hot* — crawling all over Tony Curtis while hanging out of her dress both fore and aft — expects his girl friends or wife to be trim, slender and well-groomed. The decor in the homes and offices of the American professional classes is clean and functional — Scandinavian with a guilty dash of Japanese (as reparation for the bomb, we sit close to the earth). Upon occasion, the American will desert the art house for an American picture, particularly if it is advertised with the intellectually fashionable decor. For this decor is an article of faith: it is progressive and important; it calls businessmen and artists to conferences at Aspen, where it is linked with discussions of such topics as "Man the Problem Solver." And so American movies now often come, packaged as it were, with several minutes of ingenious, abstract, eye-catching titles. This send-off — the graphics look provided by Saul Bass and other designers — has virtually nothing to do with the style or mood of the picture, but it makes the movie look more *modern*. (How can the picture be dismissed as trash when it looks like your own expensive living room?) This type of design, using basic colors and almost no soft lines, was, of course, devised so that advertising would be clear and effective with a minimum of cost. In movies, a photographic medium, complexity and variety and shadings of beauty are no more expensive than simplification. But modern graphic design, which has built an aesthetic on advertising economics, has triumphed: new big productions (like *The Misfits*) open with such a proud array of flashy designs that the movie itself comes on rather apologetically.

The advertising campaign for new films often uses a motif that appears again at the opening of the film: presumably, if the ad was good enough to get you there, you'll appreciate having it amplified. Perhaps the next Hollywood "genius" will be the man who can design the whole movie to look like a high-powered ad. At present, the movie that begins when the packaging is out of the way is in a different, and older, style of advertising art. This style was summed up by a member of the audience a few weeks ago when I was looking at a frightfully expensive, elaborately staged movie. The beautiful heroine, in pale blue, was descending an elegant beige staircase, when a voice from the dark piped up — "Modess, because . . . " When the beautiful heroine in pale blue finally got into her creamy white lace and the properly nondenominational clergyman intoned, "Wilt thou, Robert, take this woman . . . ," another voice in the theater groaned, "I wilt."

The social worker-at-heart finds true reassurance when the modern-designed movie also has modern design built into the theme: a movie like *Twelve Angry Men*. Ask an educated American what he thought of *Twelve Angry Men* and more likely than not he will reply, "That movie made some good points" or "It got some important ideas across." His assumption is that it carried these ideas, which also happen to be his ideas, to the masses. Actually, it didn't: this tense, ingenious juryroom melodrama was a flop with the mass audience, a success only at revivals in art houses.

The social psychology of *Twelve Angry Men* is perfectly attuned to the educated audience. The hero, Henry Fonda — the one against the eleven — is lean, intelligent, gentle but strong; this liberal, fair-minded architect is *their* hero. And the boy on trial is their dream of a victim: he is of some unspecified minority, he is a slum product who never had a chance, and, to clinch the case, his father didn't love him. It isn't often that professional people can see themselves on the screen as the hero — in this case the Lincolnesque architect of the future — and how they love it! They are so delighted to see a movie that demonstrates a proposition they have already accepted that they cite *Twelve Angry Men* and *The Defiant Ones* as evidence that American movies are really growing up.

It is a depressing fact that Americans tend to confuse morality and art (to the detriment of both), and that, among the educated, morality tends to mean social consciousness. Not implicit social awareness (Antonioni isn't "saying anything," they complain of *L'Avventura*) but explicit, machine-tooled, commercialized social consciousness. "The old payola won't work any more," announces the hero of *The Apartment*, and even people who should know better are happy to receive the message. How reassuring *The Apartment* is, with its cute, soft-hearted Jewish doctor and his cute, soft-hearted, fat, mama-comic Jewish wife — so unworldly and lovable that they take the poor frustrated sap for a satyr (almost as deadly in its "humor" as Rock Hudson being mistaken for a homosexual in *Pillow Talk*). In *The Apartment*, the little people are little dolls; the guys at the top are vicious and corrupt and unfaithful to their wives as well. The moral is, stick at the bottom and you don't have to do the dirty. This is the pre-bomb universe; and its concept of the "dirty" is so old-fashioned and irrelevant, its notions of virtue and of vice so smugly limited, that it's positively cozy to see people for whom deciding to quit a plushy job is a big moral decision. The "social consciousness" of the educated is so unwieldy, so overstuffed, that the mass audience may well catch up before the intellectuals have found any grounds to move on to — though surely many should be happy to vacate the premises of Freud and Marx.

The art-house audience is at its dreamiest for Russian films like *Ballad of a Soldier* and *The Cranes Are Flying*. How eager they are to believe the best about the Soviet Union, to believe that love is back, propaganda is out, and it's all right to like Russian movies because the Russians are really nice people, very much like us, only better. These sentiments have been encouraged by the theaters and by the cultural exchange agreement, and at showings of *The Cranes Are Flying* there was a queasy little prefatory note: "At the same time you are watching this Soviet film, Soviet audiences are watching an American motion picture." I was happy for the voice in the theater which piped up, "But it's six A.M. in the Soviet Union."

The Cranes Are Flying and *Ballad of a Soldier* are both good examples of nineteenth-century patriotism and nineteenth-century family values; neither seems to belong to the Communist period at all — they're reminiscent of American war epics of the silent era. And sophisticated Americans love the simple, dutiful characters that they would laugh at in American movies. It's a long time since audiences at art houses accepted the poor, ravished unhappy heroine who has to marry the cad who rapes her. They go even farther toward primitivism at *Ballad of a Soldier*: they love the "touching" and "charming" hero and heroine who express such priggish repugnance at a soldier's unfaithful wife (how would these two react if they caught the wife sleeping with a German, like the heroine of *Hiroshima Mon Amour?*). *Ballad of a Soldier* takes us back to the days when love was sweet and innocent, authority was good, only people without principles thought about sex, and it was the highest honor to fight and die for your country. These homely values, set in handsome, well-photographed landscapes, apparently are novel and refreshing — perhaps they're even exotic — to art-house audiences. It's a world that never was, but hopeful people would love to associate it with life in the Soviet Union.

Are these recruiting posters so morally superior to American lingerie ads like *Butterfield 8*? Are they as effective in the U.S.S.R. as in the outside world? We can see the results of *Butterfield 8*:

half the junior-high-school girls in America are made up to look like Elizabeth Taylor, and at the Academy Award Show it was hard to tell the stars apart — there were so many little tin Lizzies. It's more difficult to gauge the effects of Russia's antique middle-class morality. Perhaps educated Americans love the Russians more than the Russians do. All over America people are suddenly studying Russian; and they sometimes give the impression that the first word they want to learn is "Welcome."

A congressional subcommittee headed by Kathryn Granahan, a Democrat from Pennsylvania who is known as America's leading lady smut-hunter, is exploring the possibility that the influx of foreign films, most especially the French film *Les Liaisons Dangereuses*, may be a Communist plot to undermine American moral structure — that is to say that Americans are being offered a preoccupation with sex so that they will become degenerate, corrupt, too weak to combat the Communist threat. Mrs. Granahan has stated that the social, cultural and moral standards of France are among the greatest impediments to a strong NATO stand against international Communism.

In other words, she takes the position that a strong state, a state capable of defending itself, must be a Puritan state, and that individual freedom and the loosening of sexual standards threaten the state. This is, of course, the present Communist position: even American jazz is regarded as a threat. Nothing could be *cleaner* — in nineteenth-century terms — than Russian movies. Observers at the Moscow Film Festival reported that the Russians were quite upset after the showing of *The Trials of Oscar Wilde*: they had been under the impression that Wilde was imprisoned for his revolutionary politics — for socialism, not for sodomy. Russians have been protected from just such information, discussion and art as Mrs. Granahan would protect us from. Apart from what appears to be a wholly unfounded notion that the Russians are trying to poison us via French sexual standards, there is an interesting issue here. For absurd as the Granahan position seems to be, I have heard a variant of it from many people who would scoff at the way she puts it.

Everywhere in the United States enthusiasts for *La Dolce Vita* explain that it's a great lesson to us — that Rome fell because of sexual promiscuity and high living, and we will too — that the Communists are going to win because of our moral laxity, our decay. It's as if poor old Gibbon had labored in vain, and the churches' attitudes have triumphed. Even those who no longer believe in God seem to accept the idea that European and American habits and values are loose and sinful and will bring destruction down upon us.

May I suggest that this is just as nonsensical as the Granahan line? If all Europeans and all Americans suddenly became heterosexual and monogamous — if everyone took the pledge and there were no more drinking, if all nightclubs were closed, and if the rich turned their wealth over to the poor — I cannot see that our *power* position in this nuclear age would in any way be affected. And it's astonishing that sensible people can get so sentimental about Russian movies with their Puritan standards, the bourgeois morality that developed out of the rising salaried classes and the Stalinist drive to stamp out individual freedom. Queen Victoria squats on the Kremlin; and Americans who fought to rid themselves of all that repressive Victorianism now beat their breasts and cry, look how *good* they are, look how *terrible* we are — why, we don't *deserve* to win. Has Puritanism so infected our thinking that we believe a nuclear war would be won by the pure in heart?

[1961]

The Glamour of Delinquency
On the Waterfront, East of Eden,
Blackboard Jungle . . .

A "regular" movie says yes to the whole world or it says not much of anything. What is there in *The Long Gray Line,* A

Man Called Peter, The Prodigal or *Not as a Stranger* that can stir an audience out of its apathy — an exposed beating heart, a man fighting a vulture — and who cares? And who really cares about the bland prosperity that produces these entertainments? The United States has now achieved what critics of socialism have always posited as the end result of a socialist state: a prosperous, empty, uninspiring uniformity. (If we do not have exactly what Marx meant by a classless society, we do have something so close to it that the term is certainly no longer an alluring goal.) What promises does maturity hold for a teen-ager: a dull job, a dull life, television, freezers, babies and baby sitters, a guaranteed annual wage, taxes, social security, hospitalization insurance, and death. Patriotism becomes a series of platitudes; even statements that are true seem hypocritical when no longer informed with fire and idealism. It may be because this culture offers nothing that stirs youthful enthusiasm that it has spewed up a negative reaction: for the first time in American history we have a widespread nihilistic movement, so nihilistic it doesn't even have a program, and, ironically, its only leader is a movie star: Marlon Brando.

Our mass culture has always been responsive to the instincts and needs of the public. Though it exploits those needs without satisfying them, it does nonetheless throw up images that indicate social tensions and undercurrents. Without this responsiveness, mass culture would sink of its own weight. But it doesn't sink — there *is* a kind of vitality in it. Even the most routine adventure pictures, with Jeff Chandler or Rory Calhoun or Randolph Scott or John Wayne, empty and meaningless as they are, cater to unsatisfied appetites for action and color and daring — ingredients that are absent from the daily lives of patrons. But if films and other areas of mass culture did not produce anything that moved us more directly, they would become as rigid and formalized as ballet — a series of repeated gestures for a limited audience of connoisseurs (the western has reached this point). When more ambitious film makers want to make a film with dramatic conflict, they draw upon the hostility to conformity embodied in the crazy, mixed-up kid.

The phenomenon of films touching a social nerve is not new. The gangster films in the thirties expressed a fundamental hostility to society and authority; the gangsters made their own way, even if they paid for it by prison or death. But in the thirties the gangsters were not the only rebels, there was a large active body of political rebellion, given partial expression in films by the dispossessed heroes who asked for a job, a home, and a life. In the fifties there is no American political rebellion, there is not even enough political theory to give us a feasible explanation of delinquency itself — the new dissidents who say that a job, a home, and the life that goes with them aren't worth the trouble. One thing seems evident: when the delinquent becomes the hero in our films, it is because the image of instinctive rebellion expresses something in many people that they don't dare express. These kids seem to be the only ones who are angry about apathy: they seem to be the only ones with guts enough, or perhaps they are the only ones irresponsible enough, to act out a *no* to the whole system of authority, morality and prosperity.

The depth of Brando's contact with some sections of the public may be gauged by the extraordinary resentments expressed toward James Dean for what was considered an imitation of Brando in *East of Eden* (though Dean's acting suggests Montgomery Clift as much as it does Brando, while his facial qualities suggest Gregory Peck); and the jeers and walkouts on *Blackboard Jungle* because Vic Morrow employed a Brando style. The reaction is quite archaic — as if Brando fans feared that other actors were trying to take some power away from their god, that the public might worship graven images instead of the true god.

Alienation

Alienation, the central theme of modern literature, has, like everything else, entered mass culture. Films borrow the artist-hero of literature only to turn him into the boob of A *Song to Remember, Rhapsody in Blue, Moulin Rouge, Limelight;* the alienation of a Stephen Daedalus or a Marcel, the heroic expense of extending consciousness, becomes inexplicable, but glamorous, misery. (The artist suffers because he can't get the girl; she, lacking the audience's hindsight, doesn't know that he's so good a catch that one day a movie will solemnize his life. The irony of the artist's suffering is his inability to guess that Hollywood will make him immortal.) Those at work in films have, however, to one degree or another, projected alienated non-artist heroes and heroines in some of the best, though not always commercially successful, films of recent years: *The Stars Look Down, Odd Man Out, An Outcast of the Islands, The Men, The Member of the Wedding, A Streetcar Named Desire, From Here to Eternity.* In these films, alienation is not merely the illusion of cynicism or cowardice which is dispelled in the rousing finish of a *Casablanca* or a *Stalag 17.*

The subject matter of *On the Waterfront* is alienation at the lowest social level. In *From Here to Eternity* Prewitt had formulated his position ("If a man don't go his own way, he's nothin'") and was willing to take the risks. Terry Malloy, the hero of *On the Waterfront*, is alienated at the instinctive level of the adolescent and the bum, and the drama, as those who made the film see it, is in his development of consciousness and responsibility, his taking his place as a man.

The attempt to create a hero for the mass audience is a challenge and a great big trap. *On the Waterfront* meets the challenge, falls into the trap. The creation of a simple hero is a problem that doesn't come up often in European films, where the effort is to create characters who move us by their humanity — their weaknesses, their wisdom, their complexity — rather than by their heroic dimensions. Our films, however, deny the human weaknesses and complexities that Europeans insist upon. It's as if we refused to accept the human condition: we don't want to see the image of ourselves in those cheats and cuckolds and cowards. We want heroes, and Hollywood produces them by simple fiat. Robert Taylor or John Wayne is cast as the hero and that's that; any effort to relate the hero's actions to his character is minimal or routine. Real heroism is too dangerous a subject for Hollywood — for there is no heroism without failure risked or faced, and failure, which is at the heart of drama, is an unpopular subject in America.

On the Waterfront succeeds brilliantly in creating a figure out of the American lower depths, a figure simple in reasoning power but complicated in motivation and meaning; it fails to win complete assent when it attempts to make this figure into a social and symbolic hero — by fiat. But how should we interpret the view of Harper's that, "if the makers of On the Waterfront had chosen to have it merely a decadently sophisticated underworld travelogue, a kind of American 'Quai des Brumes,' they would have been truer to themselves, their subject and their art. Still better, they could of stood in bed." If I read this right, the implication is that if the film dealt with defeat, it would be more honest, but it would be decadent. This is a view which quite possibly has affected those who made the film, and Harper's, inadvertently and revealingly, justifies the artists' fear of "decadence" by its contempt for "decadence."

It's likely that those who made the film — Kazan, Schulberg, Spiegel, Brando, Bernstein — share in the American fantasy of success, a fantasy which they spectacularly act out in their own careers, and want to believe that their material fits into a drama of man's triumph. A drama of man's defeat would seem somehow antisocial, un-American, "arty," and even decadent. It's quite likely also that art to them is a call to action as much as a reach into consciousness, so that they feel bound to demonstrate a victory of good over evil; they want the film to "come out right" politically, though this demonstration probably moves the audience much less than if it had to take home an unresolved, disturbed recognition of social difficulties. (The motive power behind much of our commercial entertainment is: give the public a happy ending so they won't have to think about it afterwards.) Perhaps the artists of On the Waterfront fear the reality of failure not only for their hero but for themselves. If the film did not resolve its drama in triumph, it might not reach the mass audience, and if it reached a smaller audience, that — in America — would be failure.

From Here to Eternity did not convert its hero into a socially accepted leader, did not reduce issues to black and white, and it was a huge popular success. But a curious displacement occurred in the course of the film: Prewitt's fate as hero got buried in the commotion of the attack on Pearl Harbor, and it was easy to get the impression that it didn't really matter what happened to him as he would probably have gotten killed anyway. And, as a related phenomenon, Montgomery Clift's fine performance as Prewitt was buried in the public praise for Frank Sinatra and Burt Lancaster. It was almost as if Prewitt wasn't there at all, as if the public wanted to forget his troublesome presence. Lancaster, an amazingly kinesthetic actor, has built-in heroism; his Sergeant Warden was closer to the conventional hero stereotype, and he had managed to stay alive. Or perhaps Prewitt wasn't troublesome enough: there was no mystery or confusion about why he behaved as he did. He had his own value system, and perhaps his clarity prevented him from stirring the audience. *Formulated* alienation seems already part of the past; Prewitt is the last Hollywood representative of depression-style alienation.

On the Waterfront is a more ambitious film, though its moral scheme is that battle of good versus evil which is a film commonplace. No doubt those who made the film, and many of those who see it, view the conflict in the film not as a commonplace, but as a rendering of the "supreme" theme. But this "supreme" theme has never been the theme of great drama because it tends to diminish man's humanity, rather than to illuminate it. Working with this theme, it is natural for the artists to take the next step and to employ the most easily accessible symbols that are ready-to-hand to the artists and perfectly familiar to the widest audience. The priest stands for conscience and humanity; the pure, selfless girl is the hero's reward; the union boss represents brutal avarice. And crucifixion is used in the broadest sense as an equivalent for suffering.

The center of the dramatic structure, the priest's speech over Dugan's body in the hold, is the poorest scene of the film. The priest speaks with such facility that the ideological mechanics become distressingly obvious, and the re-enactment of the stoning of saints is an embarrassing contrivance, an effort to achieve a supremely powerful effect by recall rather than creation. The scene appeals not only to Catholic interest but to what we have come to recognize as Catholic taste as well. And although the concept of crucifixion in the film is scarcely the Catholic Church's concept, in using the figure of the priest the artists acquire a certain amount of unearned increment by making the film more acceptable to Catholics. When Terry tells the priest to go to hell, the patent intention is to shock the religious audience, and, of course, to cue us all: we know that such sacrilege is possible only for one who will shortly be redeemed.

On the theatrical level, most of the Christian symbolism functions well in the film. The artists have not further debased it; compared to what we are accustomed to in Hollywood pictures, they have given it considerable dignity. But theatricality can too easily be confused with dramatic strength and Christian mythology provides an all too convenient source of theatrical devices — the jacket, for example, that passes from one crucified figure to another. Such devices do not give meaning, they give only dramatic effect, the *look* of meaning.

The director, Elia Kazan, is undoubtedly a master of what is generally regarded as "good theater": all those movements, contrasts, and arrangements which have been developed to give inferior material the look of drama. "Good theater" is an elaborate set of techniques for throwing dust in the eyes of the audience, dust, which to many theater-trained minds, is pure gold. When Kazan has real dramatic material in *On the Waterfront*, his staging is simple and he lets the actors' faces and voices do the work; but when the material is poor or unrealized, he camouflages with "effective staging" — the theater term for what is really high pressure salesmanship. Your theater instinct tells you that these effects are supposed to do something for you, but you may be too aware of the manipulation to feel anything but admiration (or resentment) for the director's "know-how."

The advantages of Kazan's direction are in his fine eye for living detail (for example, in Terry's first interchange with the men from the crime commission); the disadvantages are that the best things are often overpowered by the emphasis given to the worst. Rod Steiger's fine performance as the brother stays within its own framework, while Malden's priest is so overburdened with reference and effect that it disintegrates. Though this priest is not cut from the same cloth as Paramount's priests, at times (and he has his coy moments) he adopts a similar protective coloration. The musical score is excellent; then at a crucial moment it stops, and the silence compels awareness of the music. There are a few places where Kazan's dexterity fails completely: moving the union men around as a herd is too "staged" to be convincing. And even "good theater" doesn't allow for elements that are tossed in without being thought out (the ship owner, an oddly ambiguous abstraction, possibly cartooned in obeisance to the labor-union audience) or tossed in without being felt (the complacent, smiling faces of the priest and the girl at the end — converted, by a deficiency of artistic sensibility, into pure plaster). Many weaknesses go back to the script, of course (for example, the failure to show the reasons for the union men's loyalty to the boss), but Kazan, by trying to make assets out of liabilities, forces consideration of his responsibility.

If one feels bound to examine the flaws and facilities of *On the Waterfront* it is because, intermittently, and especially in Brando's scenes with the girl in the saloon and with his brother in the cab, the film is great. Brando's performance is the finest we have had in American films since Vivien Leigh's Blanche DuBois. Marlon Brando has that ability shared by most great actors: he can convey the multiple and paradoxical meanings in a character.

Brando makes contact with previously untapped areas in American social and psychological experience. If one had doubts about the authenticity of Terry's character, audience manifestations would confirm its truth. Brando's inarticulate wise guy attracts a startling number of its kind; there they are in the theater, gratified by their image, shouting at the screen and guffawing at Brando. Their derision is just like Terry's derisive compliments to the girl; they, too, are afraid to expose their vulnerability. They are exhibitionistic in their excitement when Terry gestures and voices disbelief in social values: it is not Terry as a candidate for redemption who excites them, but Terry the tough. They have a truer sense of Terry and themselves than those who conceived the film.

The writer and director placed this imaginatively compelling figure in a structure which, while theatrically fairly sound, is not the dramatic complement the figure deserves. Terry has his own kind of consciousness; he is *too* compelling to act out *their* consciousness and to fit the social role they assign him. Terry is credible until he becomes a social hero. Does moral awakening for a Terry mean that he acquires the ability to change the external situation, or does it mean simply an intensification and a broadening of his alienation? We know that movie heroes can always conquer evil, but in the early sequences we didn't know that Terry was going to be turned into this kind of "regular" hero. The other protagonists have been oversimplified until they seem to be mere symbols rather than human beings who might have some symbolic meaning. As dramatic characters they lack dimensions, as symbolic representations of the waterfront struggle they are inadequate. Our social problems are much too complex to be dramatically rendered in a Christian parable. The artists who made the film have a remarkable negative similarity: they do not risk alienation from the mass audience. And they do not face up to the imaginative task — nor to the social risk — of creating fresh symbols. Have they earned the right to show their hero risking his life in order to save his soul?

The myth of the creation of a saint (or, indeed, a multiplicity of saints) which cripples the dramatic development of Terry's character, does an even more obvious disservice to the social questions the film raises. The myth structure forces a superficial answer to questions for which no one has a satisfactory answer. The honest union posited at the end is an abstraction, which could not even be dramatically posited if the film had not already abstracted the longshore local it treats from the total picture of waterfront unionism and American business. An item in *Time* for September 27, 1954, is to the point:

John Dwyer, a brawny hiring boss on the brawling New York City docks (and a prototype of Marlon Brando's movie role in *On the Waterfront*), quit his $10,000-a-year job last year to fight the racket-ridden International Longshoremen's Association. As vice president of the A.F.L.'s new rival dock union, he won thousands of dock-wallopers away from the I.L.A. But last month the I.L.A. won a Labor Relations Board election (by a scant 263 votes out of 18,551), and thereby held on to control of waterfront jobs.

The A.F.L. brasshats, retreating from their attempt to reform the docks, cut their organizing losses (about $1,000,000), ended their all-out campaign and fired John Dwyer. When Dwyer protested, they ignored his letters and hung up on phone calls. Last week Dwyer bitterly told his men to "forget about the A.F.L. and go back to the I.L.A." Brusquely, the I.L.A. snubbed Dwyer and said A.F.L. rank-and-filers could come back only if they paid up back dues. For a happy ending dockers could go to the movies.

This kind of data suggests why alienation is such a powerful theme in our art: if, for the individual, efforts to alter a situation end in defeat, and adjustment (with decency) is impossible, alienation may be all that's left. Would Terry seem so compelling if his behavior and attitudes did not express a profound mass cynicism and a social truth? More goes into his alienation than the activities of a John Friendly, and his character is powerful because it suggests much more — the desire of adolescents to find an acceptable ethic, quasi-homosexual elements in this ethic, adolescent hostility toward adult compromises, the identification with an antisocial code, the intensity of aspirations. Terry's scene with his brother in the cab is drama because these accumulated elements explode. These elements and many more derive, not merely from a corrupt union, but from the dislocation of youth in our society, and ultimately, if one takes a pessimistic view, they derive from the human condition. The betrayal experienced by the boy who kills the pigeons is not altogether mistaken. With *On the Waterfront* alienation reaches the widest audience at the level of the raw unconscious hero who suggests the unconscious alienation experienced at all social levels. The artists who wanted to affect everybody just about did.

Artists who aim at nobility may achieve something pretentious and overscaled, but their aim tells us something about the feeling and tone of American life that is not wholly to be deprecated. Abroad, it *is* deprecated, and the excesses of *On the Waterfront* gave European critics a gloating edge of triumph. Is it perhaps evidence of cultural condescension that the festival committees which had passed over *From Here to Eternity* and *On the Waterfront* honored *Marty*, a thin, mechanical piece of sentimental realism — as if to say, "Stick to little things, you Americans, when you try to do something bigger, you expose your dreadful vulgarity."

On the Waterfront came as a public shock in 1954 because Hollywood films have stayed away from the real America, just as, while feeding Christians to the lions, they have stayed away from the real Rome. According to *Harper's*, "The things movies 'say' are so much better stated through indirect suggestion, and Hollywood has developed so many techniques of skillful evasion, that the burden of censorship and the pressure groups has always been more apparent than real. Art thrives on limitations." One wonders if *Harper's* goes to movies often enough to see Hollywood's "techniques of skillful evasion" in operation. If there is anything "skillful" in our films, it is merely in product differentiation — in making each new film just like the others that have sold, yet with some little difference in casting or locale or extra costliness that can give it special appeal. Within the temples of *The Egyptian* you can see the shape of the lowest theater, mouldy in motive and manner. When you hear the whore of Babylon ask the hero for "the greatest gift any man can give a woman — his innocence — that he can give only once" you know that those responsible for the film have long since surrendered their greatest gift. A bad film can be a good joke, as *Duel in the Sun* once so delightfully demonstrated; but *Valley of the Kings, Garden of Evil, The High and the Mighty* are not even very good jokes. Despite its defects, and they are major, *On the Waterfront* provides an imaginative experience. If one regrets that the artists, having created an authentic image of alienation, failed to take that image seriously enough, one remembers also that most films provide no experience at all.

Romance

The alienated hero acquires a new dimension in *East of Eden*: James Dean's Cal, even more inarticulate and animalistic than Terry, is a romantic figure, decorated with all sorts of charming gaucheries, and set, anachronistically, in a violent reverie of pre-World War I youth. At one level he's the All-American boy (and the reverse of the usual image of the artist as a youth): he's not too good at school, he's sexually active, he's not interested in politics but has a childlike responsiveness to parades, he doesn't care about words or ideas. Yet this lack of intellectual tendencies is projected as evidence of sensitivity and purity of feeling; the strangled speech, the confused efforts at gesture, as poetry. This is a new image in American films: the young boy as beautiful, disturbed animal, so full of love he's defenseless. Maybe his father doesn't love him, but the camera does, and we're supposed to; we're thrust into upsetting angles, caught in infatuated close-ups, and prodded, "Look at all that beautiful desperation."

The film is overpowering: it's like seeing a series of teasers — violent moments and highly charged scenes without structural coherence (one begins to wonder if the teaser is Kazan's special genre?). When Cain strikes Abel, the sound track amplifies the blow as if worlds were colliding; a short heavy dose of expressionism may be followed by a pastoral romp or an elaborate bit of Americana; an actor may suddenly assume a psychotic stance, another actor shatter a train window with his head. With so much going on, one might forget to ask why. The explanation provided (Cal wants his father to love him) is small reason for the grotesque melodramatic flux. But from a director's point of view, success can be seen as effectiveness, failure as dullness — and *East of Eden* isn't dull.

If, after the film, the air outside the theater seems especially clean and fresh, it is not only from relief at escaping the cracker-barrel humanism, it's the restorative power of normal, uncoerced perspective: it's a little like coming out of a loony bin. A boy's agonies should not be dwelt on so lovingly: being misunderstood may easily become the new and glamorous lyricism. With *East of Eden*, Hollywood has caught up with the main line of American avant-garde cinema — those embarrassingly autoerotic twelve-minute masterpieces in which rejected, inexplicable, and ambiguous figures are photographed in tortured chiaroscuro, films which exude symbolism as if modern man were going to find himself by chasing the shadow of an alter ego in a dark alley. When alienation is exploited for erotic gratification, film catches up with the cult realities of city parks and Turkish baths; clear meanings or definite values would be too grossly explicit — a vulgar intrusion on the Technicolor night of the soul.

The romance of human desperation is ravishing for those who wish to identify with the hero's amoral victory: everything he does is forgivable, his crimes are not crimes at all, because he was so terribly *misunderstood*. (And who in the audience, what creature that ever lived, felt he was loved enough?) This is the victory that we used to think of as a child's fantasy: now it is morality for nursery school and theater alike. The concept of Terry was a little behind the times: he was posited as heroic because he acted for the social good. Cal is the hero simply and completely because of his *need*, and his frenzied behavior, the "bad" things that he does, establish him as a hero by demonstrating his need. (When Peter Lorre as *M* said he couldn't help what he did, who would have thought him heroic? We have come a slippery distance.) This is a complete negation of previous conceptions of heroism: the hero is not responsible for his actions — the crazy, mixed-up kid becomes a romantic hero by being treated on an infantile level. And the climax of the film is not the boy's growing up beyond this need or transferring it to more suitable objects, but simply the satisfaction of an infantile fantasy: he displaces his brother and is at last accepted by his father.

In theater and film, the mixed-up kid has evolved from the depression hero, but the explanation from the thirties (poverty did this) no longer works, and the refinement of it in *On the Waterfront* (corruption did this) didn't work. It gives way in *East of Eden* to something even more facile and fashionable: the psychiatric explanation (lack of love did this). Although it's rather bizarre to place this hyped-up modern type in the setting of a historical novel, the reminiscent haze has some advantages: the basic incoherence of motive would probably be even more apparent in a modern setting. Cal's poetry of movement would be odd indeed if he were leaping and careening in the streets of 1955.

The type of heroism entrenched in most older and routine films is based on the obscenity: "right makes might and might makes right." (The hero can back up his moral and ethical edge on the villain with stronger fists.) And an absurd corollary is attached: the girl loves the man who fights for the right. *East of Eden* introduces a rather dismaying new formula: need for love makes right, and the girl loves the boy who most needs to be loved.

Films can, and most of them do, reduce all the deprivations and coercions, desires and hopes of social and individual experience, to the simple formula of needing love. In *The Young at Heart*, the bitter depression hero once played by John Garfield is brought up to date: the young composer (Frank Sinatra) is simply an oddball, bitter because he is an orphan and the world has never made a place for him. But Doris Day accepts him and when he feels all warm and cozy in her middle-class family, his bitterness melts. (Most artists are, of course, bitter against precisely the middle-class coziness that Doris Day and her family represent.) In a more sophisticated version, we get Gloria Grahame in *The Cobweb*: she is all fixed-up and able to save her marriage (and square the Production Code) once she knows her husband really needs her. (Lauren Bacall gives her no real competition: she has been analyzed — she is mature and doesn't need anybody.) The convenient Hollywood explanation for alienation — for failure to integrate in the economy, for hostility to authority and society — is, then, lack of love and acceptance. You're bland and happy when you're loved, and if you're unhappy, it's not really your fault, you just haven't been loved. This is the language of the jukebox, and when Freud is reduced to this level, psychoanalysis becomes the language of idiocy. (In a few years, films will probably reflect the next national swing: so I got love, now what?)

Snow Jobs in Sunshine Land

Nobody is satisfied with Hollywood's approach to delinquency, but who has a better one? The psychiatrically-oriented social workers and teachers are advised that they will be included in the delinquent's hostility to authority and that they must get through to the boy. But is the boy mistaken in feeling that they are trying to give him a snow job and that they are part of the apparatus of deadly adjustment to what he is reacting against? *Blackboard Jungle* says that the boy *is* mistaken, and though in many ways a good film, like *The Wild One* it's a snow job. *The Wild One* had taken a news story as the basis for a nightmare image: the leather-jacketed pack of motorcyclists take over a town; their emblem is a death's head and crossed pistons and rods, and Brando is their leader, Lee Marvin his rival. But the movie seemed to be frightened of its subject matter and reduced it as quickly as possible to the trivial meaninglessness of misunderstood boy meets understanding girl; the audience could only savor the potentialities. *Blackboard Jungle* lifts a group of mixed-up kids from the headlines and tries to devise a dramatic structure for them out of the social problem drama. Delinquency is treated as a problem with a definite solution: the separation of the salvageable from the hopeless, and the drama is in the teacher's effort to reach the salvageable. (Like the newspapers, both films avoid discussion of why the boys form their own organizations, with rigid authority, strict codes, and leaders.) Although the script of *Blackboard Jungle* is sane and intelligible, the thematic resolution (like the end of *The Wild One*) is an uneasy dodge — not because it isn't well worked out, but because the film draws its impact from a situation that can't be so easily worked out. It's hard to believe in the good teacher's idealism; audiences audibly assent to the cynical cowardice of the other teachers — even though it's rather overdone. Somehow it's no surprise when we excavate the short story on which the rather shoddy novel was based to find that in the original version, "To Break the Wall," the teacher did *not* break through. This, like Dwyer's "forget about the A.F.L. and go back to the I.L.A.," has the ring of truth — what *Harper's* might call "decadence."

If a film deals with boys rejecting society and ignores *what* they reject, it's easy to pretend there are no grounds for rejection — they're just mixed-up. In denying that there are reasons for not wanting to adjust, the films are left to wrestle clinically, rather than dramatically, with the boys' anger, dealing with the boys at face value, just as the newspapers do. The strongest film element is always the truculent boy, whose mixture of shyness, fear and conceit has a peculiarly *physical* assertiveness: there's bravado in his display of energy. That energy — which adjusted, genteel types subdue or have had drained away or never had — is itself an assault upon the society that has no use for it. He can be invited to work it off only in games, or in leathercraft in some youth center.

The delinquent is disturbing because he is delinquent from values none of us really believe in; he acts out his indifference to what we are all somewhat indifferent to. And in acting it out, he shocks us by making us realize that *necessary* values are endangered. When he is moody and uncooperative and suspicious of the adult, official world we understand something of what he is reacting against and we think we perceive values that he must be struggling for. But when he attacks the weak, when he destroys promiscuously, when, as in *Mad at the World*, he wantonly throws a whisky bottle and kills a baby, we become possible targets and victims of a moral indifference that we both share and do not share.

In the gangster films we knew where we were: if we identified with the small businessmen trying to protect their livelihoods and their pride against extortion, the gangster was an enemy; and if the gangster rubbed out a rival or, when cornered, shot a policeman, these were occupational hazards for gangsters and police, and they were rational. But in the delinquent films we who feel ourselves to be innocent, and even sympathetic, become as vulnerable as a cop. Just as Negro hatred of whites includes even the whites who believe in equality, so the delinquent's violence may strike any one of us. The hold-up victim who offers no resistance is as likely to be beaten as the one who resists, and despised for his cowardice as well.

Confused feelings of identification and fear turn us into the mixed-up audience. There's been plenty of violence in Hollywood films for many years, but it did not stir up the violent audience reactions produced by *On the Waterfront* and *Blackboard Jungle* (many theaters have had, for the first time, to call in police to keep order). In these films the violence means something, it's not just there to relieve the boredom of the plot as in *The Prodigal*, and pressure groups are right in seeing it as a threat. This violence is discharged from boredom with American life, and we have no available patterns into which it fits, no solutions for the questions it raises, and, as yet, no social or political formulations that use indifference toward prosperity and success as a starting point for new commitments.

Though films take up social discontent only to dissolve it in unconvincing optimism, the discontent has grown out of that optimism. A Polynesian coming to an industrial country for the first time might see a technological civilization as a state of nature; Americans who have lost the passion for social involvement see the United States almost the same way (we have lost even the passion for technology). Our economic system, our social order, are accepted, not with respect, but as facts, accepted almost at the same level on which "regular" films are accepted — a convictionless acceptance which is only a hair's breadth away from violent negation. When language is debased to the level of the pitch man, why not use animal grunts? They're more honest, and they say more. Why respect authority which is weak, uncertain, and corrupt? Why care about social relations when they have reached such interpersonal virtuosity that no one shows off or presses an opinion too hard? Why care about acquiring the millionaire's equipment of the middle-class home; does anyone really enjoy a power-driven lawn mower? Everything in America makes life easier, and if Americans are not really happy, they're not really unhappy either. If they feel some pangs of dissatisfaction, what can they blame it on? Only themselves — guiltily — and so the IBM operator who begins to fantasize, the file clerk who can't fight off sleep, hie themselves to the analyst. What a relief to go to the movies and hear mixed-up kids say it out loud. They don't always say it in attractive ways, but it is a no and *somebody* has to say it. It's explosively present.

Though the expressions of the mixed-up kids are antisocial, in a society which insists that all is well, these expressions are interpreted as a psychological disorder. It's a social lie to pretend that these kids are only in conflict with themselves or that they merely need love or understanding. Instinctively, the audience knows better. Pressures can emasculate the theme and remove it from the screen: this exploitation and destruction of every theme is the history of American movies. Marlon Brando can be cleaned up and straightened out for the approval of the family magazines, just as he is in his movie roles; he can become a model of affirmation, impersonating baseball players or band leaders in "regular" pictures. But won't his fans want to kill his pigeons?

[1955]

〰〰〰〰〰〰

Commitment and the Straitjacket

Room at the Top, Look Back in Anger, The Entertainer, Sons and Lovers, Saturday Night and Sunday Morning . . .

The new look in English films is reality: the streets, the factories and towns, houses and backyards of grim, modern, industrialized England. The young English authors and directors are striking at social problems of every type; but the backgrounds, the environment, show us a larger theme: the ugliness, the fatalism, the regimentation of daily life. In Hollywood, in the thirties, Warner Brothers produced the socially conscious gangster and depression melodramas that starred Paul Muni, James Cagney, Edward G. Robinson. Viewed today, most of those films don't look like much. But they were an angry reaction to the frustrations, poverty, and injustices of the thirties, and they had tremendous impact at the time. That English moviemaking should now become just about the most socially conscious in the world is amazing when you consider that, as the critic-director Tony Richardson put it, "It is a frightening and disturbing comment on British democracy that certain institutions — the monarchy, the army, the church, the public school, the prisons, the police — are guarded from any candid presentation with as hard and tough an iron curtain as the Russian bloc has ever imposed." How can you produce social criticism when you can't criticize the official organs of power? You look at the way people live.

The new English movement got its impetus and much of its style from the documentaries made under the group title "Free Cinema." In the mid-fifties, these short explorations of the modern cities, with their jazz clubs, night life, seaside resorts, factories, and markets were the first films shot by a group of young critics — Richardson, Karel Reisz, Lindsay Anderson.

But unlike the French New Wave group of critics who became both directors and scenarists, when the English critics began to make features, they did not prepare their own scenarios. They joined with some of the new English literary figures — John Braine, John Osborne, Alan Sillitoe, Wolf Mankowitz, and others. Their features are not so cheap as the French ones — nor so individual in style and subject matter. They share the documentary look of the Free Cinema shorts; in fact, the five big films are all the work of two cameramen — Freddie Francis photographed *Room at the Top*, the first feature by Jack Clayton, *Sons and Lovers* by Jack Cardiff, and *Saturday Night and Sunday Morning*, the first feature by Karel Reisz; Oswald Morris did *Look Back in Anger*, the first feature by Tony Richardson, and his second, *The Entertainer*.

The semidocumentary surface of these films is linked to an ideology which is in its way peculiar to English film critics — the ideology of commitment. If you read *Sight and Sound*, in which so many films are appraised for the degree of the director's commitment to a social point of view (good if left wing, bad if not), you will discover that in this ideology, location shooting, particularly around working-class locations, is, in itself, almost a proof of commitment. In judging works from other countries, the English will overestimate a film like *Marty*, and they'll suggest that a film that is stylized or that deals with upper-class characters is somehow "evasive" — that it doesn't want to come to terms with the material. This attitude gives the critics an extraordinarily high moral tone. They are always pecking away at failures of conviction or commending a show of conviction. A few issues back, the editor, Penelope Houston, praised some new actors in these terms: "This kind of purposeful acting is something encouragingly new on the British screen; and the cinema cannot be allowed to imagine it can continue to do without it." Doesn't that sound a bit like a high-minded social worker addressing her charges? As a result of this rigid and restrictive critical vocabulary, *Sight and Sound*, still the finest magazine in the film world, is becoming monotonous. The critics are too predictable — and this is a danger for the new movement in English films as well.

Look what happens to these critics when they confront a picture like *I'm All Right, Jack* — a cynical slapstick farce about the Welfare State. Wherever the innocent hero turns, he sees corruption, and when he tries to expose it, he is considered insane. The big businessmen are the villains in the plot, and they indulge in all kinds of familiar skullduggery, but the film also shows the trade unionists as smug and self-centered. And though the satire of union practices is much more affectionate, it is so accurately aimed — and we are so unused to it — that it comes off much the better. As the shop steward, Peter Sellers is avid to protect the workers' rights — he's earnest, he's monstrously self-serious. He wears a little Hitler mustache — that mustache was always an oddly lower-middle-class adornment on Hitler; this shop steward is lower middle class in his habits, but he's a fanatical proletarian in theory. He speaks in a self-educated jargon that derives from political pamphlets. The movie satirizes this little stuffed shirt and the featherbedding practices of his union.

Now, we may assume that the English workers know what their unions are, but the committed critics still regard them as both underdogs and sacred cows. The reviewer for *Films and Filming* said, "Something rather frightening has happened to the Boulting Brothers. They have turned sour. *I'm All Right, Jack* is the latest in their run of social comedies. I hope it is the last. . . ." Earlier satires by the Boultings, the critic went on, were innocent fun, but this was "malicious, and worse, depressingly cynical."

In its guide to filmgoers, *Sight and Sound* dismissed *I'm All Right, Jack* as "more jaundiced than stimulating," and Penelope Houston wrote, ". . . this is a picture made from no standpoint, other than from the shoulder-shrugging confidence that 'everything is fair game.' It looks like the work of sour liberals, men who have retired from the contest and are spending their time throwing stones at the players." Doesn't that make you wonder what the "contest" is that moviemakers are supposed to be involved in? The only possible interpretation is that it's all right to see human folly on the right, but that it's not fair game if you find it on the left. It's a little like the old argument that you shouldn't point out anything wrong with the Soviet Union, or you were giving aid to the reactionaries. How long does it take for liberal film journals to catch up with what, as Stanley Kauffmann pointed out, Shaw indicated long ago, that trade unionism would be the capitalism of the working class? Miss Houston goes on to say of the Boultings, ". . . they are not social satirists because they too overtly revel in the dislocations that give them something to laugh at. One would hate to share all their laughter." Isn't that a preposterously prissy approach to satire — as if to say that if you really laugh at the social scene, there must be something the matter with you. The critic's jargon isn't far removed from the shop steward's.

There are other recent lightweight English films that deal with the contemporary scene that are worth a look. *Expresso Bongo*, a satire on entertainment crazes, specifically rock-'n-roll, is the best British musical comedy since the days of Jessie Matthews, Sonnie Hale, and Jack Buchanan. The script is by Wolf Mankowitz, who has an ear for the poetry of unlikely places. You may have heard his fine dialogue in the short film, *The Bespoke Overcoat*; in *Expresso Bongo*, he stylizes theatrical sentimentality and vulgarity. The talent-agent hero — a liar and pretender who is more likable and humane than many honest heroes — is the closest relative in these films to Archie Rice, The Entertainer.

Sapphire is a thriller about a light-skinned Negro girl found dead on Hampstead Heath. The manhunt involves going into the Negro sections of London, and going also into the psychological areas of the antagonism of Negroes and whites. Although the movie has its self-conscious preachments, it goes much farther in some ways than American movies. There is an amusingly haughty barrister with a little beard — a Negro bishop's son, played by Gordon Heath. When asked if he had intended to marry Sapphire, he explains that he couldn't possibly — "She was part white."

You may note that the movie itself falls into a prejudicial racial cliché: nobody wastes any tears over high-yellow Sapphire — she was trying to pass, and so, presumably, she earned her fate as a corpse. But her dark brother is a physician in the Midlands. He's not ashamed of his skin; he wears a philosophic smile, and he's intelligent, understanding, and "dignified" — the type of Negro who's always praised for bringing credit to his people. He's a bore, but we see a lot of him, probably to offset some of the location shots of Negro streets and the view we get of jazz dives. Most of the Negroes I know aren't happy about looking Negro, but on the screen it's certainly a blessing that Negro parts must almost always be played by Negroes. In the movies, the unfortunate fact that Anne Frank was Jewish, and hence, not acceptable as the heroine of an expensive production, was rectified by casting Millie Perkins in the role. Soon, Jeffrey Hunter, like H. B. Warner before him, will make Jesus Christ more socially acceptable. (You may have observed that, although Christ is always played by a Gentile, a Jew is frequently cast as Judas.)

Another thriller, *Tiger Bay*, has good performances by Hayley Mills and Horst Bucholtz, and excellent use of locale — the dockland of Cardiff in Wales. Here, too, there is a large concentration of Negroes in the overcrowded tenements. Until this last year, British pictures scarcely gave any evidence that there were Negroes on the island.

Room at the Top is the good old story of the bright, ambi-tious boy from the provinces who wants to make good in the big city. Stendhal set it in the post-Napoleonic period in *The Red and the Black*; Theodore Dreiser set it in the beginnings of industrialization in *An American Tragedy*. In *Room at the Top*, the boy comes from the modern industrial slums of York-shire; he has acquired a cynical education in a German prison camp; and he has become a civil servant. Like Julien Sorel and Clyde Griffiths, Joe Lampton is on the make; unlike them, he doesn't get killed for his sexual transgressions, though he does get beaten up in a manner which suggests a ritual punishment. *Room at the Top*, like its predecessors, is about class, money and power — and about how sex, which is used to get them, traps the user. The theme of the opportunistic social climber is a good, solid theme; the surprise of *Room at the Top* is the English setting. We wouldn't be surprised by a costume picture which had, in a bit part, a comic parvenu whom the elegant nobleman could put down. But an aggressive, unfunny young parvenu, a slum-bred man who wants to break through the class structure and get into the Establishment — that's new. In this country, it would be a rags-to-riches story, the birth of a tycoon — but in English films it's the sort of thing that just isn't done.

The movie tells a story, and it's absorbing, and, for the most part, convincing in a way that few recent American films have been. In this country, it helped bring adults back into the movie houses. This was partly because of the superb love scenes, and partly, no doubt, because of the unusually blunt dialogue. "Frank," or "gamy" are, I think, the words the advertisers prefer. The movie has the look, and occasionally the sound, of four-letter words.

Look Back in Anger doesn't need four-letter words: the hero's polysyllabic discourse is infinitely more abusive and shocking.

British understatement is gone; the case is marvelously over-stated. I'm afraid it's almost at the level of confession that I must state that although *Look Back in Anger* is obviously a mess in any number of ways, I think this mess — and *The Entertainer*, also a mess — are the most exciting films to have come out of England in this period.

During the years when I was programming for the Berkeley Cinema Guild, I developed some pride in being able to get people to come to see a picture I thought ought to be seen. But I couldn't convince any great number of people to look at *Look Back in Anger*. I wrote that it was like a blazing elaboration of that one stunning interchange in *The Wild One* when Brando is asked, "What are you rebelling against?" and he replies, "What have you got?" But the audiences that packed the theater for *The Wild One* didn't show up for the intellectual wild one.

Why did people who were so happy with *Room at the Top* ignore *Look Back in Anger*? It's true, Joe Lampton is a relatively simple man with a goal — he wants to get somewhere — and Jimmy Porter can't think of anyplace to go. But he tells us something about where we are — which Lampton is incapable of doing. Just as declamation, *Look Back in Anger* is exciting — and both it and *The Entertainer* are original in their dialogue and characters. And, after all, none of these English movies is great as a movie. Compared to the work of a great director like Renoir or De Sica, *Room at the Top*, or *Sons and Lovers*, or *Saturday Night and Sunday Morning* are a high-school girl's idea of cinema art. *Look Back in Anger* got the worst possible reception from the American press. The New York *Herald Tribune* really invited an audience with the statement: "The hero is probably the most unpleasant seen on film in years . . . it [the movie] dodges not one dreary issue." Bosley Crowther in the New York *Times* lured them further with the information that Jimmy Porter was " a conventional weakling, a routine cry-baby, who cannot quite cope with the problems of a tough environment, and so, vents his spleen in nasty words." I won't degrade you and me by attempting to quote the barbarous language of the local critics: they didn't distinguish themselves any more than usual. It's bad enough to look at the *New Yorker*: the masterly John McCarten opened with, "The hero of *Look Back in Anger*, a character called Jimmy Porter, is insufferable, and so is the film, of English origin, in which he figures." McCarten seems to judge characters on the basis of whether they'd be unassertive and amiable drinking companions. Wouldn't he find Hamlet insufferable, and Macbeth, and Othello, and Lear?

We tend to take for granted a certain level of awareness — the awareness that binds us to our friends, that draws us to new ones. If someone I knew said of *Look Back in Anger* what *Variety* did, I would feel as if the Grand Canyon had suddenly opened at my feet. On what basis could one go on talking with someone who said that "*Look Back in Anger*'s thin theme is merely an excuse for Osborne to vent his spleen on a number of conventions which have served the world fairly well for a number of years." Like colonialism, one supposes, and the class system, and segregation, and a few other conventions. How can good movies reach an audience when they're filtered through minds like these? We need some angry young critics; we particularly need them in San Francisco, where a large audience for good films depends on the judgments of one not very gifted man who can virtually make or break a foreign film.

Look Back in Anger is a movie about the intellectual frustrations of a man who feels too much — an idealist who hasn't lost his ideals: they're festering. It is about the way his sensitivity turns into pain and suffering and into torture of others. It is about the failures of men and women to give each other what they need, with the result that love becomes infected. And it is about class resentments, the moral vacuity of those in power, the absence of courage. It's about humanity as a lost cause — it's about human defeat. Richard Burton brings to the role the passion his countryman put into the lines: "Do not go gentle into that good night. Rage, rage, against the dying of the light."

And the sordid flat Jimmy Porter lives in becomes a fiery landscape when he cries out against ugliness, injustice, stupidity. "Will Mummy like it?" he taunts his wife. Her "Mummy" stands for all the stale conventions of class society; and it is the "Mummy" in her that he keeps striking at.

Much of the movie is in terrible taste — the hero crows like a rooster; but perhaps just because nobody seems worried about the excesses, something breaks through. If we're going to have talking pictures, let us acknowledge the glory of talk, and be grateful for rhetoric which has the splendor of wrath and of wit.

It was Osborne who once remarked that "The British Royal Family is the gold filling in a mouthful of decay." His play *The Entertainer* — also filmed by Tony Richardson — is a study of decay and desperation. *The Entertainer* is what *Death of a Salesman* tried to be. Please don't misunderstand: I'm not suggesting they're on the same level. Osborne is immensely talented.

The Entertainer reached wider audiences than *Look Back in Anger*. But that doesn't mean it was well received. The *New Yorker* gave it a great send-off: Brendan Gill took care of it in a single paragraph, beginning with, "*The Entertainer* is a very good and a very depressing picture, and I hope you'll be brave enough to go and see it." Somehow one knows that few will. Everybody has heard that it's "depressing," but it's bad movies that are depressing, not good ones. The rejection of both these films as "depressing" seems to stem from the critical school which regards all art as entertainment for tired businessmen — and theatrical and cinematic art as after-dinner entertainment. The tired businessman doesn't want to get involved in the work or to care about it — it's just supposed to aid his digestion. But suppose the play or film tells you why your stomach is sour — or excites or upsets you so that you can't rest easily that night. Well, most critics, wanting to keep you just as you are — whether you're a tired businessman or not — will caution you against it. They have a whole stock of cautionary terms. They will point out that it is "slow" or "turgid" or deals with "dismal" or "squalid" life or "makes demands on the audience" or is "full of talk." You may have noticed that critics regard talk as something that is only acceptable in very small amounts — too much talk, one might think, like too much alcohol, cannot be absorbed in the bloodstream. If tired businessmen find *Look Back in Anger* or *The Entertainer* negative or depressing, who cares? No doubt, they find the plots of Shakespeare too complicated and the speeches ever so long. Is it the function of critics to congratulate them on their short span of attention by suggesting that all Shakespearean plays should be simplified and cut? The critic who does that has become a tired businessman. Archie Rice, the Entertainer, was described by the dean of American film critics, the colosssus of the New York *Times*, as "a hollow, hypocritical heel . . . too shallow and cheap to be worth very much consideration." In this country, the movie reviewers are a destructive bunch of solidly, stupidly respectable mummies — and it works either way, maternal or Egyptian.

Archie Rice is no hypocrite; he is a man in a state of utter despair — but he is too sane and too self-aware to ask for pity or sympathy. He is one of the few really created characters in modern drama or films. And the movie, if it gave us nothing but Olivier's interpretation of this character, would be a rare and important experience. *The Entertainer* is not a satisfying whole work. Tony Richardson may not be the film director people hoped he was: in both these Osborne films, he tries to set stylized theater pieces in documentary, Free Cinema-type locations. And though the locations are in themselves fascinating, and although the material of the drama has grown out of these locations and is relevant to them, Richardson can't seem to achieve a unity of style. The locations seem rather arbitrary: they're too obviously selected because they're "revealing" and photogenic.

It is, by the way, something of a shock to discover that the overwhelmingly literate Osborne didn't attend a university; his

mother was a barmaid. Which leads us to another author from
the working classes.

Sons and Lovers was made with American money, but it was
made in England, with outdoor shooting in the industrial Midlands. The director, Jack Cardiff, was formerly known as one of
the finest cameramen in England. The script is mainly by Gavin
Lambert, formerly the editor of *Sight and Sound,* and easily the
best of the English film critics; and the cast, except for Dean
Stockwell, is also English. *Sons and Lovers* is one of the best
movie adaptations of a major novel — still, when you think it
over, that isn't saying as much as it might seem to.

The camera work by Freddie Francis, in black-and-white
CinemaScope, is extraordinarily beautiful; the pictorial qualities, particularly of the outdoor scenes, make a stronger impression than the story line. It's a curiously quiet, pastoral sort of
film; the rhythm is off — the pictorial style, exquisite as it is, is
neither Lawrentian nor a visual equivalent or even approximation of Lawrence's prose. The visual beauties aren't informed
by Lawrence's passionate sense of life. The artist's fire simply
isn't there — the movie is temperate, earnest, episodic. Perhaps
the writer and director are too gentlemanly for Lawrence, too
hesitant. They seem afraid of making some terrible mistake,
and so they take no chances. But it's like *The Beast in the
Jungle* — nothing happens, and that's the most terrible thing
of all. The movie becomes a rather tepid series of scenes illus-
trating Lawrence's themes, carefully thought out and, mostly,
in very good taste.

The movie fulfills a genuine function if it directs people to
the book — but this is a boomerang. Pick up the book again at
almost any point, and the movie simply disappears. There's a
richness and a fullness in the novel. So many of us for years have
been referring to it casually as great, then you start reading again
— and it really *is* great. But the movie has beauty for the eye,
and the image of Trevor Howard as Mr. Morel is something to
carry in memory forever.

From the sublime to the ridiculous: can the movies grant us a few years' moratorium on post-coital discussions? There are two sequences of this type in *Sons and Lovers* — and they're the worst scenes in the movie — embarrassing, even grotesque. The first is with the frightened, inhibited girl who has submitted sacrificially — and the young hero then accuses her of having hated it. The second is with the emancipated older woman who accuses the hero of not having given all of himself. Lawrence *does* have scenes like this, but they're the culminations of relationships that have been developed over hundreds of pages; they're not really adaptable to the theatrical convention which speeds them up. In the film, it's as if, as soon as two people hit the sack, they know exactly what's wrong with their relationship and why it's got to end. What happens to the crucial love affairs in the film version of *Sons and Lovers* is rather like what happened to the Crusades in the Cecil B. De-Mille version — they became one quick, decisive battle.

In fairness to *Sons and Lovers*, I should point out that the worst of the current post-coital sequences is in another film — the very fine experimental American film, *Shadows*. The despoiled virgin sits up, and with eyes swimming with tears, says, "I didn't know it would be so awful." Show me the man *that* won't reduce to insect size. If all these sequences from recent films could be spliced together, a good title might be "Quo Vadis."

The press treated *Sons and Lovers* quite respectfully; it's a very respectful movie. *Time* even announced that "this production, in only 103 minutes, includes everything important in Lawrence's 500-page novel." An incredible statement! Was it perhaps a deliberate suggestion to *Time*'s readers that there was no reason to read Lawrence? But then, it's a little difficult to know what *Time*'s reviewer thought was important in the novel — he tells us that "Wendy Hiller is repellently pitiable as the carnivorous mother who entraps D. H. Lawrence's hero." The *New Yorker* provided a further simplification. Paul Morel's struggle for freedom of spirit and for sexual expression — his problems with the two women — are summed up by Whitney Balliett as "short-lived alliances" with a girl who "devours only his spirit" and a woman who "devours only his flesh." Lawrence, it would appear, was writing a nice old-fashioned novel about sacred and profane love.

It was left to *Life* magazine to supply the final word: according to *Life*, "As in most of Lawrence's works, the villain in *Sons and Lovers* is overindustrialization, which in the process of reducing its victims to slavery, also subverts their healthy passion. Although the message is dated, the film is given immediacy and sharp reality . . ." and so forth.

Just how "dated" this message is you can see in *Saturday Night and Sunday Morning* — set in those same Midlands a half-century later. Industrialization has swallowed up the whole working class. The movie is supposed to be a young man's coming of age and accepting adult responsibility — becoming, to use the wretched new cant — "mature." But when you look at what he's going to accept, your heart may sink. He has spirit and vitality, and he has a glimmer that there should be some fun in life, and maybe a little action. What does he do to express his dissatisfaction? He throws a few spitballs, he has an affair with a married woman, and he announces that he's not going to become like his parents. But he picks a proper, porcelain bride with an uplift so high it overreaches her mind. Caught in this gigantic penal colony of modern industrial life, she looks ahead to the shiny appliances of a housing tract — for her, it's the good life. "Why are you always throwing things?" she asks him primly. The film ends sweetly and happily, but what future can the hero have when the movie is over but to fall into the stinking stupor of his parents, get drunk, quarrel with his wife, and resign himself to bringing up little working-class brats?

It's easy to see why *Saturday Night and Sunday Morning* is a big box-office success in England: it expresses honest working-class attitudes and its characters are mass audience characters. Unlike the people of *Look Back in Anger* and *The Entertainer*

— both financial failures — they don't talk about anything outside the working-class range of experiences. They're concerned
with the job, the pint, the telly, the house with plumbing inside.
But it's hard to know why the American critics should be so
enthusiastic about this rather thin film — in this country, it's
playing to art-house audiences who, one might suppose, would
be more excited by a wider range of emotion and experience.

Saturday Night and Sunday Morning goes about as far as a
movie can toward satisfying the requirement for "commitment."
It is entirely set in working-class locations, the hero is a Nottingham factory worker, and the film is all told from his point of
view. That may explain why English critics have been calling it
everything from "the finest picture of the year" to "the greatest
English picture of all time," and describing the hero as the most
revolutionary hero the British screen has had. I don't know what
they're talking about. The film is brilliantly photographed —
once again by Freddie Francis — and Albert Finney is very good
as the hero. But the calculation is all too evident in the composition and timing. Everything is held in check; every punch is
called and then pulled. When the hero and his cousin are fishing, the caught fish signals the end of the scene; a dog barks for
a fade-out. The central fairground sequence is like an exercise
in cinematography, and the hero's beating is just another mechanical plot necessity. (Couldn't we also have a long-lasting
moratorium on the hero's being beaten up as a punishment for
adultery? We had it in *Room at the Top,* in *Sons and Lovers,*
and now in *Saturday Night and Sunday Morning.* I don't care if
I never see another man beaten up.)

What we see in this "committed" movie makes hash of the
whole theory of commitment. When we look at the way people
live, what we see raises questions that go beyond the scope of
the "committed" answers. This reality of working-class life is the
dehumanization that the anarchist theoreticians predicted. The
concept of creative labor or satisfaction in work would be a
howling joke in these great factories — and a howling joke to

the union men — a complacent mass of Philistines. How can anyone take pride even in honest labor? Featherbedding is an essential part of the system. Further advances in welfare — guaranteed annual wages, pensions — are rational social advances; but these lives are so impoverished that more material comforts are like the satin quilting in a casket. The workers are well paid and taken care of — and nobody's out to break any chains. The chains of industrialism are so vast, so interlocking, so unyielding that they have become part of the natural landscape.

The hero has no push, either intellectual or economic, to get out of his environment. He's a worker who's going to remain a worker — unless the final stage of mechanization gives way to automation — then the state may support him for not working. He knows that if he stays where he is, he has protection, security, medical care.

But Prometheus wasn't a hero by virtue of being chained to a rock. And what is revolutionary about showing us working-class life if the rebellious hero is shown as just young and belligerent — a man who needs to marry and settle down? How is he different from his fellows? Most of them aren't aware that their lives lack anything. We rally around his poor little spark — but there's no fire. It's the old Warner Brothers trick: you identify with Humphrey Bogart, the cynic who sneers at hollow patriotism; then he comes through for his country and his girl. It turns out that he always really believed in the official values; he just didn't like the tone, the bad form of officialdom. Our worker hero tells us his acceptance of the conventions is somehow different from his parents' acceptance.

An artist's commitment must be to a fuller vision of life than simply a commitment to the improvement of working-class living standards; conceivably this fuller vision may encompass an assault on working-class values. There is a crude kind of sense in the notion that working-class life is reality: the lives of the privileged rich never seem quite real. But this often ties in with left-wing sentimentality and the assumption that the artist who attempts to deal with the desperate and dissatisfied offshoots of industrialism — those trying to find some personal satisfaction in life or in art — is somehow dodging the *real* issues. The English dress up their theory of commitment — but sometimes the skeleton of Stalinism seems to be sticking out.

Time magazine, perhaps by the use of God's eye, sees *Saturday Night and Sunday Morning* as a "stirring tribute to the yeoman spirit that still seems to survive in the . . . redbrick eternities of working life in England. After 900 years, if Sillitoe is right, the Saxons are still unconquered." If that's unconquered man, how does conquered man live? The indomitable Bosley Crowther says, "Unlike *L'Avventura* and other pictures about emptiness and despair, this one is clear-eyed and conclusive. It is strong and optimistic. It is 'in.' " Crowther has never been farther out.

Isn't this Welfare State life just about what the Soviet worker looks forward to? Greater comfort, more material goods, less work. This endpoint of controlled, socialized capitalism doesn't seem very different from the ideals of industrialized life under the Soviet system — except that in the Welfare State one is not officially required to be enthusiastic. The worker feeds the machine, and if he doesn't want more material goods then what does he want? He may, one has the nagging suspicion, begin to want the romance and adventure of wars and catastrophes. Nobody in this parody of the good society is neglected or mistreated. Nobody cries out. We must supply our own cry of rage.

These films, even *I'm All Right, Jack, Expresso Bongo, Sapphire*, and *Tiger Bay* share a true horror — the people live without grace. They live in little ugly rooms, and they get on each other's nerves, and their speech is charged with petty hostilities. The main difference between the English working class and the American working class experience may be the miracle of space — our space and the privacy it affords us — which allows for day-to-day freedom of thought and action.

Thinking about the attitudes toward life in this group of films, I became aware of a lack they have in common. For years, I've been making fun of the way the movies use love as the great healer, the solution to everything. And I suddenly realized that in these films, for all their sex, the only satisfactory love affair is in *Room at the Top* — and the hero sacrifices *that* for position. I'm not sure what conclusions can be drawn from this desolate view of the human spirit — but it's rather scary. Life without beauty, without hope, without grace, without art, without love — and Crowther finds it "strong and optimistic."

[1961]

❧❧❧❧❧❧❧

Hud, Deep in the Divided Heart of Hollywood

As a schoolgirl, my suspiciousness about those who attack American "materialism" was first aroused by the refugees from Hitler who so often contrasted their "culture" with our "vulgar materialism" when I discovered that their "culture" consisted of their having had servants in Europe, and a swooning acquaintance with the poems of Rilke, the novels of Stefan Zweig and Lion Feuchtwanger, the music of Mahler and Bruckner. And as the cultural treasures they brought over with them were likely to be Meissen porcelain, Biedermeier furniture, oriental carpets, wax fruit, and bookcases with glass doors, it wasn't too difficult to reconstruct their "culture"and discover that it was a stuffier, more middle-class materialism and sentimentality than they could afford in the new world.

These suspicions were intensified by later experience: the most grasping Europeans were, almost inevitably, the ones who leveled the charge of American materialism. Just recently, at a film festival, a behind-the-iron-curtain movie director, who interrupted my interview with him to fawn over every Hollywood dignitary (or supposed dignitary) who came in sight, concluded the interview with, "You Americans won't understand this, but I don't make movies just for money."

Americans are so vulnerable, so confused and defensive about prosperity — and nowhere more so than in Hollywood, where they seem to feel they can cleanse it, justify their right to it, by gilding it with "culture," as if to say, see, we're not materialistic, we appreciate the finer things. ("The hunting scene on the wall of the cabana isn't wallpaper: it's handpainted.") Those who live by making movies showing a luxurious way of life worry over the American "image" abroad. But, the economics of moviemaking being what they are, usually all the producers do about it is worry — which is probably just as well because films made out of social conscience have generally given an even more distorted view of America than those made out of business sense, and are much less amusing.

The most conspicuous recent exception is *Hud* — one of the few entertaining American movies released in 1963 and just possibly the most completely schizoid movie produced anywhere anytime. *Hud* is a commercial Hollywood movie that is ostensibly an indictment of materialism, and it has been accepted as that by most of the critics. But those who made it protected their material interest in the film so well that they turned it into the opposite: a celebration and glorification of materialism — of the man who looks out for himself — which probably appeals to movie audiences just because it confirms their own feelings. This response to *Hud* may be the only time the general audience has understood film makers better than they understood themselves. Audiences ignored the cant of the makers' liberal, serious intentions, and enjoyed the film for its vital element: the nihilistic "heel" who wants the good things of life and doesn't give a damn for the general welfare. The writers' and director's "anti-materialism" turns out to be a lot like the refugees' anti-materialism: they had their Stefan Zweig side — young, tender Lon (Brandon de Wilde) and Melvyn Douglas's Homer, a representative of the "good" as prating and tedious as Polonius; and they had their protection, their solid salable property of Meissen and Biedermeier, in Paul Newman.

Somehow it all reminds one of the old apochryphal story conference — "It's a modern western, see, with this hell-raising, pleasure-loving man who doesn't respect any of the virtues, and, at the end, we'll fool them, he doesn't get the girl and he doesn't change!"

"But who'll want to see *that*?"

"Oh, that's all fixed — we've got Paul Newman for the part."

They could cast him as a mean man and know that the audience would never believe in his meanness. For there are certain actors who have such extraordinary audience rapport that the audience does not believe in their villainy except to relish it, as with Brando; and there are others, like Newman, who in addition to this rapport, project such a traditional heroic frankness and sweetness that the audience dotes on them, seeks to protect them from harm or pain. Casting Newman as a mean materialist is like writing a manifesto against the banking system while juggling your investments so you can break the bank. Hud's shouted last remark, his poor credo, "The world's so full of crap a man's going to get into it sooner or later, whether he's careful or not," has, at least, the ring of *his* truth. The generalized pious principles of the good old codger belong to no body.

The day *Hud* opened in San Francisco the theater was packed with an audience that laughed and reacted with pleasure to the verve and speed and economy, and (although I can't be sure of this) enjoyed the surprise of the slightly perverse ending as much as I did. It was like the split movies of the war years — with those cynical heel-heroes whom we liked because they expressed contempt for the sanctimonious goody guys and overstuffed family values, and whom we still liked (because they were played by actors who *seemed* contemptuous) even when they reformed.

It's not likely that those earlier commercial writers and directors were self-deceived about what they were doing: they were trying to put something over, and knew they could only go so far. They made the hero a "heel" so that we would identify with his rejection of official values, and then slyly squared everything by having him turn into a conventional hero. And it seems to me that we (my college friends) and perhaps the audience at large didn't take all this very seriously, that we enjoyed it for its obvious hokum and glamour and excitement and romance, and for the wisecracking American idiom, and the tempo and rhythm of slick style. We enjoyed the *pretense* that the world was like this — fast and funny; this pretense which was necessary for its enjoyment separated the good American commercial movie — the good "hack" job like *Casablanca* or *To Have and Have Not* — from film art and other art. This was the best kind of Hollywood *product*: the result of the teamwork of talented, highly paid professional hacks who were making a living; and we enjoyed it as a product, and assumed that those involved in it enjoyed the money they made.

What gave the Hollywood movie its vitality and its distinctive flavor was that despite the melodramatic situations, the absurd triumphs of virtue and the inordinate punishments for trivial vice — perhaps even because of the stale conventions and the necessity to infuse some life that would make the picture seem new within them — the "feel" of the time and place (Hollywood, whatever the locale of the story) came through, and often the attitudes, the problems, the tensions. Sometimes more of American life came through in routine thrillers and prison-break films and even in the yachting-set comedies than in important, "serious" films like *The Best Years of Our Lives* or *A Place in the Sun*, paralyzed, self-conscious imitations of European art, or films like *Gentleman's Agreement*, with the indigenous paralysis of the Hollywood "problem" picture, which is morally solved in advance. And when the commercial film makers had some freedom and leeway, as well as talent, an extraordinary amount came through — the rhythm of American life that gives films like *She Done Him Wrong*, *I'm No Angel*, the Rogers-Astaire musicals, *Bringing Up Baby*, *The Thin Man*, *The Lady Eve*, *Double Indemnity*, *Strangers on a Train*, *Pat and Mike*, *The Crimson Pirate*, *Singin' in the Rain*, *The Big Sleep*, or the more recent *The Manchurian Candidate* and

Charade a freshness and spirit that makes them unlike the films of any other country. Our movies are the best proof that Americans are liveliest and freest when we don't take ourselves too seriously.

Taking *Hud* as a commercial movie, I was interested to see that the audience reacted to Hud as a Stanley Kowalski on the range, laughing with his coarseness and sexual assertiveness, and sharing his contempt for social values. Years before, when I saw the movie version of *A Streetcar Named Desire*, I was shocked aud outraged at those in the audience who expressed their delight when Brando as Stanley jeered at Blanche. At the time, I didn't understand it when they laughed their agreement as Stanley exploded in rage and smashed things. It was only later, away from the spell of Vivien Leigh's performance, that I could reflect that Stanley was clinging to his brute's bit of truth, his sense that her gentility and coquetry were intolerably fake. And it seemed to me that this was one of the reasons why *Streetcar* was a great play — that Blanche and Stanley upset us, and complicated our responses. This was no Lillian Hellman melodrama with good and evil clay pigeons. The conflict was genuine and dramatic. But Hud didn't have a dramatic adversary; his adversaries *were* out of Lillian Hellmanland.

The setting, however, wasn't melodramatic, it was comic — not the legendary west of myth-making movies like the sluggish *Shane* but the modern West I grew up in, the ludicrous real West. The comedy was in the realism: the incongruities of Cadillacs and cattle, crickets and transistor radios, jukeboxes, Dr. Pepper signs, paperback books — all emphasizing the standardization of culture in the loneliness of vast spaces. My West wasn't Texas; it was northern California, but our Sonoma County ranch was very much like this one — with the frame house, and "the couple's" cabin like the housekeeper's cabin, and the hired hands' bunkhouse, and my father and older brothers charging over dirt roads, not in Cadillacs but in Studebakers, and the Saturday nights in the dead little town with its movie house and ice cream parlor. This was the small-town West I and so many of my friends came out of — escaping from the swaggering small-town hotshots like Hud. But I didn't remember any boys like Brandon de Wilde's Lon: he wasn't born in the West or in anybody's imagination; that seventeen-year-old blank sheet of paper has been handed down from generations of lazy hack writers. His only "reality" is from de Wilde's having played the part before: from *Shane* to *Hud*, he has been our observer, our boy in the West, testing heroes. But in *Hud*, he can't fill even this cardboard role of representing the spectator because Newman's Hud has himself come to represent the audience. And I didn't remember any clean old man like Melvyn Douglas's Homer: his principles and rectitude weren't created either, they were handed down from the authors' mouthpieces of the socially conscious plays and movies of the thirties and forties. Occupied towns in the war movies frequently spawned these righteous, prophetic elder citizens.

Somewhere in the back of my mind, Hud began to stand for the people who would vote for Goldwater, while Homer was clearly an upstanding Stevensonian. And it seemed rather typical of the weakness of the whole message picture idea that the good liberals who made the film made their own spokesman a fuddy-duddy, worse, made him inhuman — except for the brief sequence when he isn't a spokesman for anything, when he follows the bouncing ball and sings "Clementine" at the movies. Hud, the "villain" of the piece, is less phony than Homer.

In the next few days I recommended *Hud* to friends (and now "friends" no longer mean college students but academic and professional people) and was bewildered when they came back indignant that I'd wasted their time. I was even more bewildered when the reviews started coming out; what were the critics talking about? Unlike the laughing audience, they were taking *Hud* at serious message value as a work of integrity, and, even in some cases, as a tragedy. In the New York *Herald Tribune*, Judith Crist found that "Both the portraits and the people are completely without compromise — and therein is not only the

foundation but also the rare achievement of this film." In the
Saturday Review, Arthur Knight said that "it is the kind of
creative collaboration too long absent from our screen . . . by
the end of the film, there can be no two thoughts about Hud:
he's purely and simply a bastard. And by the end of the film, for
for all his charm, he has succeeded in alienating everyone, including the audience." According to Bosley Crowther in the
New York *Times*:

Hud is a rancher who is fully and foully diseased with all the germs
of materialism that are infecting and sickening modern man . . .
And the place where he lives is not just Texas. It is the whole
country today. It is the soil in which grows a gimcrack culture that
nurtures indulgence and greed. Here is the essence of this picture.
While it looks like a modern Western, and is an outdoor drama,
indeed, *Hud* is as wide and profound a contemplation of the
human condition as one of the New England plays of Eugene
O'Neill. . . . The striking, important thing about it is the clarity
with which it unreels. The sureness and integrity of it are as crystal-
clear as the plot is spare . . . the great key scene of the film, a
scene in which [the] entire herd of cattle is deliberately and dutifully destroyed . . . helps fill the screen with an emotion that I've
seldom felt from any film. It brings the theme of infection and
destruction into focus with dazzling clarity.

As usual, with that reverse acumen that makes him invaluable,
Crowther has put his finger on a sore spot. The director carefully builds up the emotion that Crowther and probably audiences in general feel when the cattle, confused and trying to
escape, are forced into the mass grave that has been dug by a
bulldozer, and are there systematically shot down, covered with
lime, and buried. This is the movie's big scene, and it can be
no accident that the scene derives some of its emotional power
from the Nazis' final solution of the Jewish problem; it's inconceivable that these overtones would not have occurred to the
group — predominantly Jewish — who made the film. Within
the terms of the story, this emotion that is worked up is wrong,
because it is not Hud the bad man who wants to destroy the

herd; it is Homer the good man who accedes to what is necessary to stop the spread of infection. And is all this emotion appropriate to the slaughter of animals who were, after all, raised to be slaughtered and would, in the normal course of events, be even more *brutally* slaughtered in a few weeks? What's involved is simply the difference in money between what the government pays for the killing of the animals and their market value. It would not have been difficult for the writers and director to arrange the action so that the audience would feel quick relief at the destruction of the herd. But I would guess that they couldn't resist the opportunity for a big emotional scene, a scene with *impact*, even though the emotions don't support the meaning of the story. They got their big scene: it didn't matter what it meant.

So it's pretty hard to figure out the critical congratulations for clarity and integrity, or such statements as Penelope Gilliatt's in the *Observer*, "Hud is the most sober and powerful film from America for a long time. The line of it is very skillfully controlled: the scene when Melvyn Douglas's diseased cattle have to be shot arrives like the descent of a Greek plague." Whose error are the gods punishing? Was Homer, in buying Mexican cattle, merely taking a risk, or committing hubris? One of the things you learn on a ranch, or any other place, is that nobody is responsible for natural catastrophes; one of the things you learn in movies and other dramatic forms is the symbolic use of catastrophe. The locusts descended on Paul Muni in *The Good Earth* because he had gotten rich and *bad*: a farmer in the movies who neglects his humble wife and goes in for high living is sure to lose his crops. *Hud* plays it both ways: the texture of the film is wisecracking naturalism, but when a powerful sequence is needed to jack up the action values, a disaster is used for all the symbolic overtones that can be hit — and without any significant story meaning. I don't think the line of *Hud* is so much "controlled" as adjusted, set by conflicting aims at seriousness and success.

It hardly seems possible but perhaps Crowther thought the

cattle were symbolically "fully and foully diseased with all the germs of materialism that are infecting and sickening modern man." Those sick cattle must have *something* to do with the language he uses in describing the film. "It is a drama of moral corruption — of the debilitating disease of avaricious self-seeking — that is creeping across the land and infecting the minds of young people in this complex, materialistic age. It is forged in the smoldering confrontation of an aging cattleman and his corrupted son." Scriptwriters have only to toss in a few bitter asides about our expense-account civilization and strew a few platitudes like, "Little by little the country changes because of the men people admire," and the movie becomes "a drama of moral corruption."

The English critics got even more out of it: Derek Prouse experienced a "catharsis" in *The Sunday Times*, as did Peter John Dyer in *Sight and Sound*. Dyer seems to react to cues from his experience at *other* movies; his review, suggesting as it does a super-fan's identification with the film makers' highest aspirations, is worth a little examination. "From the ominous discovery of the first dead heifer, to the massacre of the diseased herd, to Homer's own end and Hud's empty inheritance of a land he passively stood by and watched die, the story methodically unwinds like a python lying sated in the sun." People will be going to *Hud*, as Charles Addams was reported to have gone to *Cleopatra*, "to see the snake." Dyer squeezes out more meaning and lots more symbolism than the film makers could squeeze in. (A) Homer just suddenly up and died, of a broken heart, one supposes. It wasn't prepared for, it was merely convenient. (B) Hud's inheritance isn't empty: he has a large ranch, and the land has oil. Dyer projects the notion of Hud's emptiness as a human being onto his inheritance. (C) Hud didn't passively stand by and watch the land die. The *land* hasn't changed. Nor was Hud passive: he worked the ranch, and he certainly couldn't be held responsible for the cattle becoming infected — unless Dyer wants to go so far as to view that infection as a symbol of or a punishment for Hud's sickness. Even Homer, who blamed Hud for just about everything else, didn't accuse him of infecting the cattle. Dyer would perhaps go that far, because somehow "the aridity of the cattle-less landscape mirrors his own barren future." Why couldn't it equally mirror Homer's barren past? In this scheme of symbolic interpretation, if there was a dog on the ranch, and it had worms, Hud the worm would be the reason. Writing of the "terse and elemental polarity of the film," Dyer says, "The earth is livelihood, freedom and death to Homer; an implacably hostile prison to Hud" — though it would be just as easy, and perhaps more true to the audience's experience of the film, to interpret Hud's opportunism as love of life and Homer's righteousness as rigid and life-destroying — and *unfair*. The scriptwriters give Homer principles (which are hardly likely to move the audience); but they're careful to show that Hud is misunderstood and rejected when he makes affectionate overtures to his father.

Dyer loads meaning onto Hud's actions and behavior: for example, "Instead of bronco-busting he goes in for a (doubtless) metaphorical bout of pig-wrestling." Why "instead of" — as if there were bronco-busting to do and he dodged it — when there is nothing of the kind in the film? And what would the pig-wrestling be a metaphor for? Does Dyer take pigs to represent women, or does he mean that the pig-wrestling shows Hud's swinishness? Having watched my older brothers trying to catch greased pigs in this traditional western small-town sport, I took the sequence as an indication of how boring and empty small-town life is, and how coarse the games in which the boys work off a little steam. I had seen the same boys who wrestled greased pigs and who had fairly crude ideas of sex and sport enter a blazing building to save the lives of panic-stricken horses, and emerge charred but at peace with the world and themselves.

Are the reviewers trying to justify having enjoyed the movie, or just looking for an angle, when they interpret the illustrative details *morally*? Any number of them got their tip on Hud's character by his taking advantage of a husband's absence to go to bed with the wife. But he couldn't very well make love to her when her husband was home — although that would be par for the course of "art" movies these days. The summer nights are very long on a western ranch. As a child, I could stretch out on a hammock on the porch and read an Oz book from cover to cover while my grandparents and uncles and aunts and parents didn't stir from their card game. The young men get tired of playing cards. They either think about sex or try to do something about it. There isn't much else to do — the life doesn't exactly stimulate the imagination, though it does stimulate the senses. Dyer takes as proof of Hud's bad character that "his appetites are reserved for married women." What alternatives are there for a young man in a small town? Would it be proof of a *good* character to seduce young girls and wreck their reputations? There are always a few widows, of course, and, sometimes, a divorcee like Alma, the housekeeper. (Perhaps the first female equivalent of the "white Negro" in our films: Patricia Neal plays Alma as the original author Larry McMurtry described the Negro housekeeper, the "chuckling" Halmea with "her rich teasing laugh.") But they can hardly supply the demand from the married men, who are in a better position to give them favors, jobs, presents, houses, and even farms. I remember my father taking me along when he visited our local widow: I played in the new barn which was being constructed by workmen who seemed to take their orders from my father. At six or seven, I was very proud of my father for being the protector of widows.

I assumed the audience enjoyed and responded to Hud's chasing women because this represented a break with western movie conventions and myths, and as the film was flouting these conventions and teasing the audience to enjoy the change, it didn't occur to me that in *this* movie his activity would be construed as "bad." But Crowther finds that the way Hud "indulges himself with his neighbor's wife" is "one of the sure, unmistakable tokens of a dangerous social predator." Is this knowledge derived from the film (where I didn't discover it) or from Crowther's knowledge of life? If the latter, I can only supply evidence against him from my own life. My father who was adulterous, and a Republican who, like Hud, was opposed to any government interference, was in no sense and in no one's eyes a social predator. He was generous and kind, and democratic in the western way that Easterners still don't understand: it was not out of guilty condescension that mealtimes were communal affairs with the Mexican and Indian ranchhands joining the family, it was the way Westerners lived.

If Homer, like my father, had frequented married women or widows, would Dyer interpret that as a symbol of Homer's evil? Or, as Homer voiced sentiments dear to the scriptwriters and critics, would his "transgressions" be interpreted as a touching indication of human frailty? What Dyer and others took for symbols were the clichés of melodrama — where character traits are sorted out and separated, one set of attitudes and behavior for the good characters, another for the bad characters. In melodrama, human desires and drives make a person weak or corrupt: the heroic must be the unblemished good like Homer, whose goodness is not tainted with understanding. Reading the cues this way, these critics missed what audiences were reacting to, just as Richard Whitehall in *Films and Filming* describes Newman's Hud as "the-hair-on-the-chest-male" — although the most exposed movie chest since Valentino's is just as hairless.

I suppose we're all supposed to react on cue to movie rape (or as is usually the case, attempted rape); rape, like a cattle massacre, is a box-office value. No doubt in *Hud* we're really supposed to believe that Alma is, as Stanley Kauffmann says, "driven off by his [Hud's] vicious physical assault." But in terms of the modernity of the settings and the characters, as well as the age of the protagonists (they're at least in their middle thirties), it was more probable that Alma left the ranch because a frustrated rape is just too sordid and embarrassing for all concerned — for the drunken Hud who forced himself upon her, for her for defending herself so titanically, for young Lon the innocent who "saved" her. Alma obviously wants to go to bed with

Hud, but she has been rejecting his propositions because she doesn't want to be just another casual dame to him; she wants to be treated differently from the others. If Lon hadn't rushed to protect his idealized view of her, chances are that the next morning Hud would have felt guilty and repentant, and Alma would have been grateful to him for having used the violence necessary to break down her resistance, thus proving that she *was* different. They might have been celebrating ritual rapes annually on their anniversaries.

Rape is a strong word when a man knows that a woman wants him but won't accept him unless he commits himself emotionally. Alma's mixture of provocative camaraderie plus reservations invites "rape." (Just as, in a different way, Blanche DuBois did — though Williams erred in having her go mad: it was enough, it was really *more*, that she was broken, finished.) The scriptwriters for *Hud*, who, I daresay, are as familiar as critics with theories of melodrama, know that heroes and villains both want the same things and that it is their way of trying to get them that separates one from the other. They impart this knowledge to Alma, who tells Hud that she wanted him and he could have had her if he'd gone about it differently. But this kind of knowingness, employed to make the script more clever, more frank, more modern, puts a strain on the credibility of the melodramatic actions it explicates — and embellishes. Similarly, the writers invite a laugh by having Alma, seeing the nudes Lon has on his wall, say, "I'm a girl, they don't do a thing for me." Before the Kinsey report on women, a woman might say, "They don't do a thing for me," but she wouldn't have prefaced it with "I'm a girl" because she wouldn't have known that erotic reactions to pictures are not characteristic of women.

The Ravetches have been highly praised for the screenplay: Penelope Gilliatt considers it "American writing at its abrasive best"; Brendan Gill says it is "honestly written"; *Time* calls it "a no-compromise script." Dyer expresses a fairly general view when he says it's "on a level of sophistication totally unexpected from their scripts for two of Ritt's least successful, Faulkner-inspired films." This has some special irony because not only is their technique in *Hud* a continuation of the episodic method they used in combining disparate Faulkner stories into *The Long Hot Summer*, but the dialogue quoted most appreciatively by the reviewers to illustrate their new skill (Alma's rebuff of Hud, "No thanks, I've had one cold-hearted bastard in my life, I don't want another") is lifted almost verbatim from that earlier script (when it was Joanne Woodward telling off Paul Newman). They didn't get acclaim for their integrity and honesty that time because, although the movie was entertaining and a box-office hit, the material was resolved as a jolly comedy, the actors and actresses were paired off, and Newman as Ben Quick the barn burner turned out not really to be a barn burner after all. They hadn't yet found the "courage" that keeps Hud what *Time* called him, "an unregenerate heel" and "a cad to the end." It may have taken them several years to learn that with enough close-ups of his blue, blue eyes and his hurt, sensitive mouth, Newman's Ben Quick could have burned barns all right, and audiences would have loved him more for it.

In neither film do the episodes and characters hold together, but Ritt, in the interim having made Hemingway's *Adventures of a Young Man* and failed to find a style appropriate to it, has now, with the aid of James Wong Howe's black and white cinematography, found something like a reasonably clean visual equivalent for Hemingway's prose. Visually *Hud* is so apparently simple and precise and unadorned, so skeletonic, that we may admire the bones without being quite sure of the name of the beast. This Westerner is part gangster, part *Champion*, part rebel-without-a-cause, part the traditional cynic-hero who pretends not to care because he cares so much. (And it is also part *Edge of the City*, at least the part about Hud's having accidentally killed his brother and Homer's blaming him for it. Ritt has plagiarized his first film in true hack style: the episode was integral in *Edge of the City* and the friendship of Cassavetes and Poitier — probably the most beautiful scenes Ritt has directed — drew meaning from it; in *Hud* it's a fancy "traumatic" substitute for explaining why Hud and Homer don't get along.)

When *Time* says *Hud* is "the most brazenly honest picture to be made in the U.S. this season" the key word is brazenly. The film brazens it out. In the *New Yorker* Brendan Gill writes, "It's an attractive irony of the situation that, despite the integrity of its makers, *Hud* is bound to prove a box-office smash. I find this coincidence gratifying. Virtue is said to be its own reward, but money is nice, too, and I'm always pleased to see it flowing toward people who have had other things on their minds." Believing in this coincidence is like believing in Santa Claus. Gill's last sentence lacks another final "too." In Hollywood, a "picture with integrity" is a moneymaking message picture. And that's what Crowther means when he says, "*Hud* is a film that does its makers, the medium and Hollywood proud." He means something similar when he calls his own praise of the film a "daring endorsement" — as if it placed him in some kind of jeopardy to be so forthright.

If most of the critics who acclaimed the film appeared as innocent as Lon and as moralistic as Homer, Dwight Macdonald, who perceived that "it is poor Hud who is forced by the script to openly practice the actual as against the mythical American Way of Life" regarded this perception as proof of the stupidity of the film.

But the movie wouldn't necessarily be a good movie if its moral message was dramatically sustained in the story and action, and perhaps it isn't necessarily a bad movie if its moral message is not sustained in the story and action. By all formal theories, a work that is split cannot be a work of art, but leaving the validity of these principles aside, do they hold for lesser works — not works of art but works of commerce and craftsmanship, sometimes fused by artistry? Is a commercial piece of entertainment (which may or may not aspire to be, or pretend to be, a work of art) necessarily a poor one if its material is confused or duplicit, or reveals elements at variance with its stated theme, or shows the divided intentions of the craftsmen who made it? My answer is no, that in some films the more ambivalence that comes through, the more the film may mean to us or the more fun it may be. The process by which an idea for a movie is turned into the product that reaches us is so involved, and so many compromises, cuts, and changes may have taken place, so much hope and disgust and spoilage and waste may be embodied in it or mummified in it, that the tension in the product, or some sense of urgency still left in it, may be our only contact with the life in which the product was processed. Commercial products in which we do not sense or experience divided hopes and aims and ideas may be the dullest — ones in which everything alive was processed out, or perhaps ones that were never alive even at the beginning. *Hud* is so astutely made and yet such a mess that it tells us much more than its message. It is redeemed by its fundamental dishonesty. It is perhaps an archetypal Hollywood movie: split in so many revealing ways that, like *On the Waterfront* or *From Here to Eternity*, it is the movie of its year (even though it's shallow and not nearly so good a film as either of them).

My friends were angry that I'd sent them to *Hud* because, like Macdonald, they "saw through it," they saw that Hud was not the villain, and they knew that though he expressed vulgar notions that offended *them*, these notions might not be unpopular. The film itself flirts with this realization: when Homer is berating Hud, Lon asks, "Why pick on Hud, Grandpa? Nearly everybody around town is like him."

My friends, more or less socialist, detest a crude Hud who doesn't believe in government interference because they believe in more, and more drastic, government action to integrate the schools and end discrimination in housing and employment. However, they are so anti-CIA that at Thanksgiving dinner a respected professor could drunkenly insist that he had positive proof that the CIA had engineered the murder of Kennedy with no voice but mine raised in doubt. They want centralized power when it works for their civil-libertarian aims, but they dread and fear its international policies. They hate cops but call them at the first hint of a prowler: they are split, and it shows in a million ways. I imagine they're very like the people who made *Hud*, and like them they do rather well for themselves. They're so careful to play the game at their jobs that if they hadn't told you that they're *really* screwing the system, you'd never guess it.

[1964]

II

**Retrospective Reviews:
Movies Remembered with Pleasure**

༄༅༄༅༄༅

The Earrings of Madame de . . .
(1953)

Madame de, a shallow, narcissistic beauty, has no more feeling for her husband than for his gifts: she sells the diamond earrings he gave her rather than confess her extravagance and debts. Later, when she falls in love with Baron Donati, he presents her with the same pair of earrings and they become a token of life itself. Once she has experienced love she cannot live without it: she sacrifices her pride and honor to wear the jewels, she fondles them as if they were parts of her lover's body. Deprived of the earrings and of the lover, she sickens . . . unto death.

This tragedy of love, which begins in careless flirtation and passes from romance, to passion, to desperation is, ironically, set among an aristocracy that seems too superficial and sophisticated to take love tragically. Yet the passion that develops in this silly, vain, idle society woman not only consumes her but is strong enough to destroy three lives.

The novella and the movie could scarcely be more unlike: the austere, almost mathematical style of Louise de Vilmorin becomes the framework, the logic underneath Ophuls's lush, romantic treatment. In *La Ronde* he had used Schnitzler's plot structure but changed the substance from a cynical view of sex as the plane where all social classes are joined and leveled (venereal disease is transmitted from one couple to another in this wry roundelay) — to a more general treatment of the failures of love. For Ophuls *La Ronde* became the world itself — a spinning carousel of romance, beauty, desire, passion, experience, regret. Although he uses the passage of the earrings as a plot motif in the same way that Louise de Vilmorin had, he deepens and enlarges the whole conception by the creation of a world in such flux that the earrings themselves become the only stable, recurrent element — and they, as they move through many hands, mean something different in each pair of hands, and something fatally different for Madame de because of the different hands they have passed through. It may not be accidental that the film suggests de Maupassant: between *La Ronde* and *The Earrings of Madame de . . .* Ophuls had worked (rather unsuccessfully) on three de Maupassant stories which emerged as *Le Plaisir*.

In these earlier films he had also worked with Danielle Darrieux; perhaps he was helping to develop the exquisite sensibility she brings to Madame de — the finest performance of her career. Her deepening powers as an actress (a development rare among screen actresses, and particularly rare among those who began, as she did, as a little sex kitten) make her seem even more beautiful now than in the memorable *Mayerling* — almost twenty years earlier — when, too, she had played with Charles Boyer. The performances by Danielle Darrieux, Charles Boyer, and Vittorio De Sica are impeccable — ensemble playing of the smoothness usually said to be achieved only by years of repertory work.

However, seeing the film, audiences are hardly aware of the performances. A novelist may catch us up in his flow of words; Ophuls catches us up in the restless flow of his images — and because he does not use the abrupt cuts of "montage" so much as the moving camera, the gliding rhythm of his films is romantic, seductive, and, at times, almost hypnotic. James Mason once teased Ophuls with the jingle: "A shot that does not call for tracks is agony for poor dear Max." The virtuosity of his camera technique enables him to present complex, many-layered material so fast that we may be charmed and dazzled by his audacity and hardly aware of how much he is telling us. It is no empty exercise in decor when Madame de and the Baron dance in what appears to be a continuous movement from ball to ball. How much we learn about their luxurious lives, the social forms of their society, and the change in their attitudes toward each other! By the end, they have been caught in the dance; the trappings of romance have become the trap of love.

The director moves so fast that the suggestions, the feelings, must be caught on the wing; Ophuls will not linger, nor will he *tell* us anything. We may see Madame de as a sort of Anna Karenina in reverse; Anna gets her lover but she finds her life shallow and empty; Madame de's life has been so shallow and empty she cannot get her lover. She is destroyed, finally, by the fact that women do not have the same sense of honor that men do, nor the same sense of pride. When, out of love for the Baron, she thoughtlessly lies, how could she know that he would take her lies as proof that she did not really love him? What he thinks dishonorable is merely unimportant to her. She places love before honor (what woman does not?) and neither her husband nor her lover can forgive her. She cannot undo the simple mistakes that have ruined her; life rushes by and the camera moves inexorably.

The very beauty of *The Earrings of Madame de . . .* is often used against it: the sensuous camerawork, the extraordinary romantic atmosphere, the gowns, the balls, the staircases, the chandeliers, the polished, epigrammatic dialogue, the preoccupation with honor are all regarded as evidence of lack of substance. Ophuls's reputation has suffered from the critics' disinclination to accept an artist for what he can do — for what he loves — and their effort to castigate him for not being a different *type* of artist. Style — great personal style — is so rare in moviemaking that critics might be expected to clap their hands when they see it; but, in the modern world, style has become a target, and because Ophuls's style is linked to lovely ladies in glittering costumes in period decor, socially-minded critics have charged him with being trivial and decadent. Lindsay Anderson, not too surprisingly, found him "uncommitted, unconcerned with profundities" (Anderson's *Every Day Except Christmas* is committed all right, but is it really so profound?) and, in his rather condescending review of *The Earrings of Madame de . . .* in *Sight and Sound,* he suggested that "a less sophisticated climate might perhaps help; what a pity he is not, after all, coming to make a film in England." It's a bit like telling Boucher or Watteau or Fragonard that he should abandon his pink chalk and paint real people in real working-class situations.

The evocation of a vanished elegance — the nostalgic fin de siècle grace of Ophuls's work — was perhaps a *necessary* setting for the nuances of love that were his theme. If his characters lived crudely, if their levels of awareness were not so high, their emotions not so refined, they would not be so vulnerable, nor so able to perceive and express their feelings. By removing love from the real world of ugliness and incoherence and vulgarity, Ophuls was able to distill the essences of love. Perhaps he cast this loving look backward to an idealized time when men could concentrate on the refinements of human experience because in his own period such delicate perceptions were as remote as the Greek pursuit of perfection.

Born Max Oppenheimer in Germany in 1902 (he changed his name because of family opposition to his stage career) he worked as an actor and then directed more than 200 plays before he turned to movies in 1930. His first film success, *Liebelei,* came in 1932; because he was Jewish, his name was removed from the credits. The years that might have been his artistic maturity were, instead, a series of projects that didn't materialize or, if started, couldn't be completed. He managed to make a few movies — in Italy, in France, in Holland; he became a French citizen; then, after the fall of France, he went to Switzerland, and from there to the United States, where, after humiliating experiences on such films as *Vendetta* he made *Letter from an Unknown Woman, Caught,* and *The Reckless Moment.* In 1950 in France he finally got back to his own type of material with *La Ronde;* the flight from Hitler and the chaos of the war had lost him eighteen years. Working feverishly, with a bad heart, he had only a few years left — he died in 1957. No wonder the master of ceremonies of *La Ronde* says, "J'adore le passé"; the past of Ophuls's films is the period just before he was born. There was little in his own lifetime for which he could have been expected to feel nostalgia. Perhaps the darting, swirling, tracking camerawork for which he is famous is an expression of the evanescence of all beauty — it must be swooped down on, followed. It will quickly disappear.

[1961]

*The Golden Coach**
(1953)

At his greatest, Jean Renoir expresses the beauty in our common humanity — the desires and hopes, the absurdities and follies, that we all, to one degree or another, share. As a man of the theater (using this term in its widest sense to include movies) he has become involved in the ambiguities of illusion and "reality," theater and "life" — the confusions of identity in the role of man as a role-player. The methods and the whole range of ideas that were once associated with Pirandello and are now associated with Jean Genet are generally considered highly theatrical. But perhaps it is when theater becomes the most theatrical — when the theater of surprise and illusion jabs at our dim notions of reality — that we become conscious of the roles we play.

Jean Renoir's *The Golden Coach* is a comedy of love and appearances. In her greatest screen performance, Anna Magnani, as the actress who is no more of an actress than any of us, tries out a series of love roles in a play within a play within a movie. The artifice has the simplest of results: we become caught up in a chase through the levels of fantasy, finding ourselves at last

* Based on Prosper Merimée's one-act play, *Le Carrosse du Saint Sacrement*, which was derived from the same Peruvian story that served as source material for an episode in Thornton Wilder's *The Bridge of San Luis Rey*.

with the actress, naked in loneliness as the curtain descends, but awed by the wonders of man's artistic creation of himself. Suddenly, the meaning is restored to a line we have heard and idly discounted a thousand times: "All the world's a stage."

The commedia dell'arte players were actors who created their own roles. They could trust in inspiration and the free use of imagination, they could improvise because they had an acting tradition that provided taken-for-granted situations and relationships, and they had the technique that comes out of experience. *The Golden Coach,* Renoir's tribute to the commedia dell'arte, is an improvisation on classic comedy, and it is also his tribute to the fabulous gifts, the inspiration, of Anna Magnani. At her greatest, she, too, expresses the beauty in our common humanity. It is probably not coincident with this that Renoir is the most sensual of great directors, Magnani the most sensual of great actresses. Though he has taken Prosper Merimée's vehicle and shaped it for her, it will be forever debatable whether it contains her or is exploded by her. But as this puzzle is parallel with the theme, it adds another layer to the ironic comedy.

Perhaps only those of us who truly love this film will feel that Magnani, with her deep sense of the ridiculous in herself and others, Magnani with her roots in the earth so strong that she can pull them out, shake them in the face of pretension and convention, and sink them down again stronger than ever — the actress who has come to be the embodiment of human experience, the most "real" of actresses — is the miraculous choice that gives this film its gusto and its piercing beauty. If *this* woman can wonder who she is, then all of us must wonder. Renoir has shaped the material not only for her but out of her and out of other actresses' lives. Talking about the production, he remarked, "Anna Magnani is probably the greatest actress I have ever worked with. She is the complete animal — an animal created completely for the stage and screen . . . Magnani gives so much of herself while acting that between scenes . . . she collapses and the mask falls. Between scenes she goes into a deep state of depression . . ." Like the film itself, the set for the film is an unreal world where people suffer. In *The Golden Coach* we see Magnani in a new dimension: not simply the usual earthy "woman of the people," but the artist who exhausts her resources in creating this illusion of volcanic reality.

The work has been called a masque, a fairy tale, and a fable — each a good try, but none a direct hit: the target shimmers, our aim wavers. *The Golden Coach* is light and serious, cynical and exquisite, a blend of color, wit, and Vivaldi. What could be more unreal than the time and place — a dusty frontier in Renaissance Peru. (You can't even fix the time in the Renaissance — the architecture is already Baroque.) A band of Italian players attempts to bring art to the New World. Magnani is Camilla, the Columbine of the troupe; among her lovers is the Spanish viceroy, who, as the final token of his bondage — the proof of his commitment to love over position and appearances — presents her with the symbol of power in the colony, the golden coach. Through this formal "taken-for-granted" situation, life (that is to say, art) pours out — inventive, preposterous, outrageous, buoyant. And in the midst of all the pleasures of the senses, there is the charging force of Magnani with her rumbling, cosmic laughter, and her exultant cry — "Mama mia!"

The script has its awkward side, and those who don't get the feel of the movie are quick to point out the flaws. Some passages of dialogue are clumsily written, others embarrassingly over-explicit ("Where does the theatre end and life begin?" — which isn't even a respectable question). Much of the strained rhythm in the dialogue may be blamed on the fact that Renoir's writing in English doesn't do justice to Renoir the film artist. And, though Magnani herself, in her first English-speaking role, is vocally magnificent, some of the others speak in dreary tones and some of the minor characters appear to be dubbed. The "international" cast — in this case, largely Italian, English and French — never really seems to work; at the basic level they don't speak the same language. And Renoir allows some of the performers more latitude than their talent warrants; though Duncan Lamont and Ricardo Rioli are marvelous love foils, Paul Campbell is shockingly inept, and the scenes in which he figures go limp. Another defect is in the directorial rhythm. This was Renoir's second color film, and as in his first, *The River*, which was also a collaboration with his great cinematographer-nephew, Claude Renoir, static patches of dialogue deaden the movement; his sense of film rhythm seems to falter when he works in color. Instead of indulging in the fancy fool's game of Freudian speculation that he fails when he tries to compete with his father, it seems simpler to suggest that he gets so bemused by the beauty of color that he carelessly neglects the language of cinema which he himself helped to develop.

But in the glow and warmth of *The Golden Coach*, these defects are trifles. When the singing, tumbling mountebanks transform the courtyard of an inn into a playhouse, the screen is full of joy in creative make-believe. When, at a crucial point in the story, Magnani announces that it is the end of the second act, and the movie suddenly becomes a formalized stage set, we realize that we have been enchanted, that we had forgotten where we were. When the hand of the creator becomes visible, when the actor holds the mask up to view, the sudden revelation that this world we have been absorbed in is not life but theater brings us closer to the actor-characters. So many movies pretend to be life that we are brought up short, brought to consciousness, by this movie that proclaims its theatricality. And the presence of the artists — Renoir and Magnani — is like a great gift. When, in the last scene of *The Golden Coach*, one of the most exquisitely conceived moments on film, the final curtain is down, and Magnani as the actress stands alone on stage, bereft of her lovers, listening to the applause that both confirms and destroys the illusion, the depth of her loneliness seems to be the truth and the pity of all roles played.

[1961]

Smiles of a Summer Night
(1955)

Late in 1955 Ingmar Bergman made a nearly perfect work — the exquisite carnal comedy *Smiles of a Summer Night*. It was the distillation of elements he had worked with for several years in the 1952 *Secrets of Women* (originally called *The Waiting Women*), the 1953 *A Lesson in Love,* and the early 1955 *Dreams;* these episodic comedies of infidelity are like early attempts or drafts. They were all set in the present, and the themes were plainly exposed; the dialogue, full of arch epigrams, was often clumsy, and the ideas, like the settings, were frequently depressingly middle class and novelettish. Structurally, they were sketchy and full of flashbacks. There were scattered lovely moments, as if Bergman's eye were looking ahead to the visual elegance of *Smiles of a Summer Night,* but the plot threads were still woolly. *Smiles of a Summer Night* was made after Bergman directed a stage production of *The Merry Widow,* and he gave the film a turn-of-the-century setting. Perhaps it was this distance that made it possible for him to create a work of art out of what had previously been mere clever ideas. He not only tied up the themes in the intricate plot structure of a love roundelay, but in using the lush period setting, he created an atmosphere that saturated the themes. The film is bathed in beauty, removed from the banalities of short skirts and modern-day streets and shops, and, removed in time, it draws us *closer*.

Bergman found a high style within a set of boudoir farce conventions: in *Smiles of a Summer Night* boudoir farce becomes lyric poetry. The sexual chases and the round dance are romantic, nostalgic: the coy bits of feminine plotting are gossamer threads of intrigue. The film becomes an elegy to transient love: a gust of wind and the whole vision may drift away.

There are four of the most beautiful and talented women

ever to appear in one film: as the actress, the great Eva Dahl-beck, appearing on stage, giving a house party and, in one in-spired suspended moment, singing "Freut Euch des Lebens"; the impudent love-loving maid, Harriet Andersson — as a blonde, but as opulent and sensuous as in her other great roles; Margit Carlquist as the proud, unhappy countess; Ulla Jacobsson as the eager virgin.

Even Bergman's epigrams are much improved when set in the quotation marks of a stylized period piece. (Though I must admit I can't find justification for such bright exchanges as the man's question, "What can a woman ever see in a man?" and her response, "Women are seldom interested in aesthetics. Be-sides, we can always turn out the light." I would have thought you couldn't get a laugh on that one unless you tried it in an old folks' home, but Bergman is a man of the theater — audi-ences break up on it.) Bergman's sensual scenes are much more charming, more unexpected in the period setting: when they are deliberately unreal they have grace and wit. How different it is to watch the same actor and actress making love in the stuck elevator of *Secrets of Women* and in the golden pavilion of *Smiles of a Summer Night*. Everything is subtly improved in the soft light and delicate, perfumed atmosphere.

In Bergman's modern comedies, marriages are contracts that bind the sexes in banal boredom forever. The female strength lies in convincing the man that he's big enough to act like a man in the world, although secretly he must acknowledge his dependence on her. (J. M. Barrie used to say the same thing in the cozy, complacent Victorian terms of plays like *What Every Woman Knows*; it's the same concept that Virginia Woolf raged against — rightly, I think — in *Three Guineas*.) The stray-ing male is just a bad child — but it is the essence of maleness to stray. Bergman's typical comedy heroine, Eva Dahlbeck, is the woman as earth-mother who finds fulfillment in accepting the infantilism of the male. In the modern comedies she is a strapping goddess with teeth big enough to eat you up and a jaw and neck to swallow you down; Bergman himself is said to refer to her as "The Woman Battleship."

But in *Smiles of a Summer Night*, though the roles of the sexes are basically the same, the perspective is different. In this vanished setting, nothing lasts, there are no winners in the game of love; all victories are ultimately defeats — only the game goes on. When Eva Dahlbeck, as the actress, wins back her old lover (Gunnar Bjornstrand), her plot has worked — but she hasn't really won much. She caught him because he gave up; they both know he's defeated. *Smiles* is a tragi-comedy; the man who thought he "was great in guilt and in glory" falls — he's "only a bumpkin." This is a defeat we can all share — for have we not all been forced to face ourselves as less than we hoped to be? There is no lesson, no moral — the women's faces do not tighten with virtuous endurance (the setting is too unreal for endurance to be plausible). The glorious old Mrs. Armfeldt (Naima Wifstrand) tells us that she can teach her daughter nothing — or, as she puts it, "We can never save a single person from a single suffering — and that's what makes us despair."

Smiles of a Summer Night was the culmination of Bergman's "rose" style and he has not returned to it. (*The Seventh Seal*, perhaps his greatest "black" film, was also set in a remote period.) The Swedish critic Rune Waldekranz has written that *Smiles of a Summer Night* "wears the costume of the fin de siècle period for visual emphasis of the erotic comedy's fundamental premise — that the step between the sublime and the ridiculous in love is a short one, but nevertheless one that a lot of people stub their toe on. Although benefiting from several ingenious slapstick situations, *Smiles of a Summer Night* is a comedy in the most important meaning of the word. It is an arabesque on an essentially tragic theme, that of man's insufficiency, at the same time as it wittily illustrates the belief expressed fifty years ago by Hjalmar Söderberg that the only absolutes in life are 'the desire of the flesh and the incurable loneliness of the soul.'"

[1961]

La Grande Illusion
(1937)

In form, *La Grande Illusion* is an escape story; yet who would think of it this way? It's like saying that *Oedipus Rex* is a detective story. The great work transcends the usual categories. *La Grande Illusion* is a perceptive study of human needs and the subtle barriers of class among a group of prisoners and their captors during World War I. The two aristocrats, the German prison commander von Rauffenstein (Erich von Stroheim) and the captured French officer de Boeldieu (Pierre Fresnay), share a common world of memories and sentiments. Though their class is doomed by the changes which have produced the war, they must act out the rituals of noblesse oblige and serve a nationalism they do not believe in. The Frenchman sacrifices his life for men he does not really approve of — the plebian Marechal (Jean Gabin) and the Jew Rosenthal (Marcel Dalio). These ironies and ambiguities give genuine depth to the theme — fraternization, and the illusions of nationality.

La Grande Illusion had an immediate, idealistic aim. Hitler was about to move into Austria and Czechoslovakia: another war was imminent. Renoir hoped to reawaken in the German people the spirit of comradeship that had developed toward the end of World War I, when he had been in a prison camp. "I made *La Grande Illusion* because I am a pacifist," Renoir said in 1938, but already his hopes for the film had been destroyed. The new Nazi nationalism was more frenzied and irrational than the nationalism he had argued against. Goebbels had already banned the movie in Germany; by the summer of 1940, the Nazis were in Paris, and the prints were confiscated.

By then Renoir had fled France, and he thought that *La Grande Illusion*, having failed in its purpose — to guide men toward a common understanding, having failed even to reach the men he was addressing — would be as ephemeral as so many other films. But *La Grande Illusion* is poetry: it is not limited to a specific era or a specific problem; its larger subject is the nature of man, and the years have not diminished its greatness.

Although the message of *La Grande Illusion* is in its hope for international brotherhood, compassion, and peace, it is also an elegy for the death of the old European aristocracy. It's rare for a man who aligns himself with the rising working classes to perceive the beauty and elegance of the decaying elite and the way of life that is finished no matter which countries win the war. Compare Renoir's treatment of the career officers with, say, Eisenstein's in *Potemkin*, and you have the measure of Renoir's humanity. Eisenstein idealizes the proletariat, and cruelly caricatures the military; Renoir isn't a sociologist or a historian who might show that there were heroes and swine in both groups — he simply isn't concerned with swine. His officers — von Rauffenstein and de Boeldieu — were at home in the international sportsmanship of the prewar world, but the skills, maneuvers, courage and honor that made military combat a high form of sportsmanship are a lost art, a fool's game, in this mass war. The war, ironically, has outmoded the military. These officers are commanding men who, in their terms, are not even soldiers; the fighting itself has become a series of base humiliations. They have lost sympathy with the world; they have lost even their self-respect. All they have left is their sense of the rules of the fool's game — and they play by them. Von Rauffenstein's grief at his slaughter of de Boeldieu is so moving and painful because von Rauffenstein knows the stupidity and waste of it. When he cuts the sprig of geranium, the only flower in the fortress, it is for the death of nobility — and his own manhood. (Von Stroheim had used the geranium in the fortress scene of *Queen Kelly* — but the flower wasn't cut off, the whole picture was.) Von Rauffenstein and de Boeldieu are in a great romantic tradition: Cyrano had his plume, they draw on their white gloves, perhaps the district officer in Kenya dressed for dinner even when his only guests might be Mau-Mau. They go in style.

Marechal, the mechanic who has become an officer, has no sense of style — he is uneasy in the presence of urbanity and polish; but he is the common man raised to his finest qualities: he has natural gallantry. Perhaps it is not going too far to suggest that Renoir is a bit like Marechal, with his joy in life, his survival power. Renoir gives more of himself than an aristocrat would think proper. He has none of that aristocratic reserve, the attitude that what you don't express is more important than what you express. But, unlike Marechal, Renoir is an artist: he celebrates the life that Marechal lives.

To a generation unfamiliar with the young Gabin and the young Fresnay, a generation that thinks of von Stroheim in terms of his legendary, ruined masterpieces, the performances of these three actors are fresh and exciting — three different styles of acting that illuminate each other. The miracle of Gabin's performance in this type of good, simple-hero role is that you're not aware of any performance. With Fresnay and von Stroheim, you *are*, and you should be; they represent a way of life that is dedicated to superbly controlled outer appearances. Try to imagine an exchange of roles between, say, Gabin and Fresnay, and you see how "right" the casting and acting are. This is true, also, for the lesser roles: a few words and we know the worlds of these characters, who speak in their own tongues — French, German, or English, and who embody their backgrounds, classes, and attitudes.

In cinema there is the artistry that brings the medium alive with self-conscious excitement (Eisenstein's *Potemkin*, Orson Welles's *Citizen Kane*) and there is the artistry that makes the medium disappear (*La Grande Illusion*, De Sica's *Shoeshine*). *La Grande Illusion* is a triumph of clarity and lucidity; every detail fits simply, easily, and intelligibly. There is no unnecessary camera virtuosity: the compositions seem to emerge from the material. It's as if beauty just happens (is it necessary to state that this unobtrusive artistry is perhaps the most difficult to achieve?). The characters, the dialogue, the fortress, the farm, the landscape, all fuse into the story and the theme. The result is the greatest achievement in narrative film. It's a little embarrassing to state this so baldly, but *La Grande Illusion,* like Renoir's earlier, but very different, *Partie de Campagne,* is just about a perfect work (in fact, I can't find a flaw in it). There was no reason for Renoir to tap this vein again. His next great work was the tragi-comic carnal chase, *La Règle du Jeu,* which accelerates in intensity until it becomes a macabre fantasy.

It is not difficult to assess Jean Renoir's position as a film director: he is the master of the French school of naturalistic cinema. Even the best works of Feyder, Carné, Duvivier, Pagnol, don't have the luminosity of the great Renoir films. (It is one of those ludicrous paradoxes of fame that, even in film reviews, Renoir is commonly identified as the son of the great Impressionist, as if his own light, which has filled the screen for almost four decades, were not strong enough to prevent confusion.) How can his special radiance be explained? Perhaps it's because Renoir is thoroughly involved in his films; he reaches out toward us, he gives everything he has. And this generosity is so extraordinary that perhaps we can give it another name: passion.

[1961]

Forbidden Games
(1952)

This is perhaps the greatest war film since *La Grande Illusion* — neither, it should be noted, deals with actual warfare. The director, René Clément, is well known for such films as *Battle of the Rails, Les Maudits, M. Ripois, Gervaise,* but none of these approaches the stature of *Forbidden Games.* Nor do his other films approach *Forbidden Games* in mood or style; the cold irony which is one of his strongest characteristics is here transformed by love and tenderness — it becomes lacerating. *Forbidden Games* is so fully felt that Clément's method of presentation — a series of harsh contrasts between the intuitive, almost lyric understanding of the two children and the ludicrous, bestial human comedy of the adults — is an act of kindness to the audience: without the contrasts we would dissolve in tears of pity for us all.

If you are one of those Americans who think that American taste is not up to European taste, may we point out that in Paris itself, this film was a commercial disaster until it was awarded the Grand Prix at Venice. Whatever your judgment of the work as film art (though a masterwork, it has many imperfections), *Forbidden Games* is one of that small body of film experiences that does not leave you quite the same. (If you "think you may have seen it, but aren't sure" — you haven't seen it.)

Forbidden Games begins in 1940 on a crowded highway outside Paris; suddenly, German planes swoop down and strafe the refugees. A delicately beautiful five-year-old girl (Brigitte Fossey) gets up and wanders away from the dead bodies of her parents, clutching her dead puppy in her arms. A farm boy (eleven-year-old Georges Poujouly) finds her and takes her home to his crude, backward peasant family. The two children become playmates: their game — their passion — is to collect dead animals for their private cemetery, and for this game, they steal crosses from churches and graveyards.

The film is a tragi-comic fable on the themes of love, innocence, Christianity, war, and death. Its methods are suggestive rather than explicit. For example, there is no explanatory voice to tell us that Paulette is displacing emotion from her dead parents to the dead dog, and then to other dead animals and insects — we *experience* the displacement. It is only if we wish to that we may interpret Paulette's discovery and attachment to the symbols of death as a parody of the Church's fixation on death; in this interpretation, Paulette's and Michel's game is secret and forbidden because the cemetery game has become the province — the monopoly — of the Church. As a parallel, we have the peasants' confused, helpless attitude toward death, which is revealed in the film's comic highpoint: a mother's attempt to give her dying son a purge.

These contrasting attitudes toward death arise from contrasting kinds of innocence — each illuminating the other. Paulette's purity contrasts with her coquetry toward Michel, her inflexible dedication to the game. It is a babes-in-the-woods kind of innocence — only the woods are a cemetery. She and Michel are gentle with each other, and though helpless when attacked by adults, they are impervious and wise: they know adults are enemies to be manipulated or feared. The peasants have their own horrifying innocence: they are not the warm, earthy characters of Marcel Pagnol; though well-intentioned, they are quarrelsome, animalistic, stupid, superstitious, ignorant. They take Christian rituals and symbols at the most literal level; they haven't enough mental range or religious feeling to understand other emotional uses for these symbols. Michel is betrayed by his father not from malignance but out of that true abyss in which parents don't think the promises they give to children count.

Nobody points out — even in an ironic aside — what is indeed an ironic aside to the whole conception: that the adults, so shocked by the theft of the burial crosses, are not at all shocked, or even much concerned, by the game of war and death happening a few miles away.

The film plays a subtle game in our imaginations — a game of lost and found. Paulette, the orphaned Parisian, is as lost with the peasant family a few miles from Paris as she would be with a tribe in deepest Africa; the peasants with their Christian symbols are as strange to her as witch doctors throwing ju-ju bones. To the peasants she is a charming toy, but irrelevant to their lives. With Michel, Paulette is happy and safe — emotionally she has been found. When is she more in contact with "reality": when she is with Michel or when she has been separated from him — when the "authorities" of the Red Cross have her marked (and incorrectly identified)? *Forbidden Games* ends in pure tragedy — in one of the most desperately painful of all closing sequences. The ending is an opening into chaos: our normal complacencies, our little reassurances, are stripped away, and we, with the child, are lost.   [1961]

Shoeshine
(1947)

When *Shoeshine* opened in 1947, I went to see it alone after one of those terrible lovers' quarrels that leave one in a state of incomprehensible despair. I came out of the theater, tears streaming, and overheard the petulant voice of a college girl complaining to her boyfriend, "Well I don't see what was so special about that movie." I walked up the street, crying blindly, no longer certain whether my tears were for the tragedy on the screen, the hopelessness I felt for myself, or the alienation I felt from those who could not experience the radiance of *Shoeshine*. For if people cannot feel *Shoeshine*, what *can* they feel? My identification with those two lost boys had become so strong that I did not feel simply a mixture of pity and disgust toward this dissatisfied customer but an intensified hopelessness about everything . . . Later I learned that the man with whom I had quarreled had gone the same night and had also emerged in tears. Yet our tears for each other, and for *Shoeshine* did not bring us together. Life, as *Shoeshine* demonstrates, is too complex for facile endings.

Shoeshine was not conceived in the patterns of romance or melodrama; it is one of those rare works of art which seem to emerge from the welter of human experience without smoothing away the raw edges, or losing what most movies lose — the sense of confusion and accident in human affairs. James Agee's immediate response to the film was, "*Shoeshine* is about as beautiful, moving, and heartening a film as you are ever likely to see." A few months later he retracted his evaluation of it as a work of art and wrote that it was not a completed work of art but "the raw or at best the roughed-out materials of art." I think he should have trusted his initial response: the greatness of *Shoeshine* is in that feeling we get of human emotions that have not been worked-over and worked-into something (a pattern? a structure?) and cannot really be comprised in such a structure. We receive something more naked, something that pours out of the screen.

Orson Welles paid tribute to this quality of the film when he said in 1960, "In handling a camera I feel that I have no peer. But what De Sica can do, that I can't do. I ran his *Shoeshine* again recently and the camera disappeared, the screen disappeared; it was just life . . ."

When *Shoeshine* came to this country, *Life* Magazine wrote, "New Italian film will shock the world . . . will act on U.S. audiences like a punch in the stomach." But few Americans felt that punch in the stomach. Perhaps like the college girl they need to be hit by an actual fist before they can feel. Or, perhaps, to take a more charitable view of humanity, they feared the pain of the film. Just about everybody has heard of *Shoeshine* — it is one of the greatest and most famous films of all time — but how many people have actually seen it? They didn't even go to see it in Italy. As De Sica has said, "*Shoeshine* was a disaster for the producer. It cost less than a million lire but in Italy few people saw it as it was released at a time when the first American films were reappearing . . ." Perhaps in the U.S. people stayed away because it was advertised as a social protest picture — which is a little like advertising *Hamlet* as a political study about a struggle for power.

Shoeshine has a sweetness and a simplicity that suggest greatness of feeling, and this is so rare in film works that to cite a comparison one searches beyond the medium — if Mozart had written an opera set in poverty, it might have had this kind of painful beauty. *Shoeshine*, written by Cesare Zavattini, is a social protest film that rises above its purpose. It is a lyric study of how two boys* betrayed by society betray each other and themselves. The two young shoeshine boys who sustain their friendship and dreams amid the apathy of postwar Rome are

* Rinaldo Smordoni (Guiseppe) became a baker; Franco Interlenghi (Pasquale) became a film star.

destroyed by their own weaknesses and desires when sent to prison for black-marketeering. This tragic study of the corruption of innocence is intense, compassionate, and above all, humane.

[1961]

༄༅༄༅༄༅

*The Beggar's Opera**
(1953)

The Beggar's Opera came to be written after a suggestion by Swift that a "Newgate pastoral might make an odd pretty sort of thing." (His coupling of Newgate, the notorious London prison which held its executions outside the prison walls — to the delight of huge crowds — with the term "pastoral" might be likened to a more recent usage. In her most famous song, Billie Holiday described a Negro body hanging from a poplar tree as a "pastoral scene of the gallant South.") John Gay worked out the idea in a new form: a musical play with the lyrics fitted to existing music. To Londoners, weary of the bombast of Italian opera (described by a character in a contemporary play as "squeaking Recitative, paltry Eunuchs . . . and trills of insignificant, outlandish Vowels") Gay's corrupt gang of thieves, highwaymen, whores, and informers were the fresh, sweet breath of England. And most of the music was already popular: Gay and the composer-arranger John Pepusch assembled and composed some 69 songs including the favorite carols, airs from operas, dances and tunes of the period, for which Gay wrote new words.

The English were happy with the form — the ballad–opera — in which dialogue is dialogue and songs are distinct and separate songs. (Probably more people than would care to admit it

* This is the only film version of John Gay's *The Beggar's Opera*. The Bertolt Brecht–Kurt Weill *The Threepenny Opera* which was filmed by Pabst in 1931 merely uses the John Gay original as source material for the characters and concepts.

feel the same way: the recitatives of "grand" opera are what drive us to drink in the intermissions.) *The Beggar's Opera*, produced in 1728, was so successful that it started what in Hollywood is known as a "cycle": there were about fifty ballad-operas produced in the next decade.

The Beggar's Opera is a many-leveled satire. John Gay satirized not only the familiar heroics and absurdities of Italian opera, but the politics of the day (Macheath the highwayman represented Robert Walpole, the most powerful man in England — famous for his talents and innovations in fiscal policy), as well as the foibles of well-known personalities (the rivalry of Polly and Lucy referred to the feud between two leading actresses). Those targets are now a matter for historians, but the large butt of the joke — the corruption and hypocrisy of mankind — still sits around. And by 1953, a new set of conventions, as tired and inflated as Italian opera, were ready for potshots: the conventions of the movies — the westerns, the swashbucklers, the musicals, the chaste heroines, the intrepid Robin Hood type heroes, the phony realism. Although the story is a mordant mixture of Hogarthian corruption and revels out of Breughel, this production does not emphasize what I suppose it's customary to call the latent savagery of the material. Arthur Bliss arranged the score so that we come out humming the light, sweet airs; Christopher Fry adapted the text freely, retaining the mocking, raffish spirit — but only for our pleasure. And the actors are having such a good time playing scoundrels that their zest for villainy is infectiously satiric. *The Beggar's Opera* is more fun than any other neglected movie of the past decade.

The only filmed opera that is light, playful, and sophisticated, it may have suffered at box offices from the (deservedly) bad reputations of the many filmed operas that use the stage-set like an embalming table. It may have suffered even more from its greatest virtues: it is unrealistic in style, and the brilliant, unabashed theatricality, the choreographed chases and betrayals and captures, the elegant march to the gallows, the dazzling, macabre ballet under the titles at the end as the prisoners and jailers whirl amidst their stocks and irons, may have been too much of a jolt for movie audiences. Most movie directors attempt to conceal their artifice in a realistic surface; here, artifice is used with the carefree delight and audacity of early Douglas Fairbanks films — delight in the film medium. Not even in Pirandello productions is there a more exquisite stylization of the derangements of art and life than in the hanging scene. We wait for the rescue, we know something must save Macheath, and something theatrically perfect does: Macheath as the actor playing Macheath simply refuses to be hanged. Only Filch, the obscene dwarf, holding a mirror on a long stick so that he can see the hanging, could be disappointed. Or perhaps movie audiences who expect to see vice exploited and then castigated, not satirized with grace and wit.

The star of *The Beggar's Opera* is Laurence Olivier, the champion of the English-speaking theater, the actor who so rarely has an opportunity to demonstrate that he is, in addition to everything else, a great comedian. (Olivier's stature may, ironically, have contributed to the film's failure: the critics were so happy to pounce on any possible weakness in an actor of such heroic dimensions — and Olivier's pleasant baritone, though adequate to the demands of the score, is not a *great* voice). He has never so freely entertained himself — and us — as in this role of the lecherous Captain Macheath escaping the law and the doxies. A wide range is not necessary to a screen actor (Humphrey Bogart did not have it, and was nonetheless admirable for what he *could* do) but Olivier's range is truly astonishing. The *Observer* remarked, "He is the only leading English actor of whom even the most malicious tongue has never said: 'of course, he always plays himself.'" His Macheath is a brilliant caricature of the romantic bandit; he has a glance that makes a wicked point and a gesture to counterpoint, and his exuberance — his joy in the role — leaps through the whole production.

Although Olivier, and Stanley Holloway (a magnificent Lockit), are almost the only ones who do their own singing, the others perform in such an offhand and unpretentious manner that the dubbing is inoffensive. The dubbing even comes in for a bit of parody when Dorothy Tutin, as dear Polly Peachum, sings while rowing a little boat: she obviously isn't singing as someone rowing would; she smiles like a cat who has swallowed a canary, as indeed she has. In a more flamboyant parody of movie tricks, Olivier carries on a love duet ("Oh what pain it is to part") while fighting off hordes of enemies.

Athene Seyler is a great Mrs. Trapes; George Devine is Peachum, Mary Clare is Mrs. Peachum, Daphne Anderson is Lucy Lockit. Margot Grahame, as The Actress, is less ethereal and more buxom than in *The Informer* of almost twenty years before; several of the other players have recently become much better known — Hugh Griffith (The Beggar) for his work in *Ben Hur*; Yvonne Furneaux (Jenny Diver) for *La Dolce Vita*.

Peter Brook was celebrating his tenth anniversary as the "grand old enfant terrible" of the English theater when he directed this, his first, film; he was twenty-eight. In the theater Brook is something of a one-man production crew: he has been known to do his own lighting, decor, and even music. He is the only English theatrical prodigy comparable to the American Orson Welles. Both came a cropper in the movies, but with a difference: Welles had his wounds licked by the critics, Brook had his face stepped on and it was seven years before he returned to films, and even then not in England. But, ironically, the cameraman Guy Green has since become a well-known English director (*The Angry Silence, The Mark*).

[1961]

༄༅༄༅༄༅

The Seven Samurai
(1954)

In *The Seven Samurai*, the greatest battle epic since *The Birth of a Nation* of 1915, Akira Kurosawa achieves what modern American and European epic makers vainly attempt: the excitement of the senses. Laurence Olivier had charged the screen with glorious exultation in *Henry* V; Kurosawa makes this exultation his theme. Fighting itself is the subject of *The Seven Samurai* — an epic on violence and action, a raging, sensuous work of such overpowering immediacy that it leaves you both exhilarated and exhausted.

It bears a resemblance to the Hollywood western. The beauty of the western genre is its formalization and stylization: the clarity and simplicity of the actions and motives. Although *The Seven Samurai* is brilliantly complex visually, and although it can be interpreted in terms of such complex themes as the problems of honor, the meaning of human cooperation, the interlaced responsibilities of defenders and defended, it preserves the chivalric simplicity of the western plot which is even more wonderful in the nuclear age. Seven hired knights defend a village against forty mounted bandits — their pay, a few handfuls of rice. Everybody knows what the fighting is about, who the marauders are, who the protectors are, and the particular piece of land where the battle will be joined.

An American critic attempting to describe what kind of movie *The Seven Samurai* is, and to assess its qualities as a work of art, may experience some constraint. Kurosawa has said, "I haven't read one review from abroad that hasn't read false meanings into my pictures." I might feel more uneasy about my ignorance of Japanese traditions and the "false meanings" I may read into Kurosawa's work had I not learned that Kurosawa himself was responsible for the framing device of *Rashomon*: by Yankee cunning I calculate that if he could rise above such blunders, my interpretation of his work may not be destroyed by occasional errors. For example, is the setting fifteenth or sixteenth century Japan? I can't tell the difference. And I can't really understand the Japanese code of sexual honor — the intense shame of the farmers' wives who, having been abducted by the brigands, are so dishonored that they choose death rather than rescue and reunion with their families.

As if the disadvantage of not comprehending Japanese tradition were not enough, there is another handicap. In the now standard reference volume *The Japanese Film*, Anderson and Richie point out that "The West, having seen only a much-cut print under the title *The Magnificent Seven*, has not yet seen what Kurosawa intended to show. The complete . . . film has an epic-like quality, due in part to skillful repetition of events, which in the opinion of many puts it among the best films ever made, not only in Japan but anywhere in the world." But all we can discuss is the movie we can see.* And even distorted by our point of view, and cut for our short span of attention (or was it cut so that people could get in and out of theaters faster?), it's incomparable as a modern poem of force.

There is an additional problem for this critic: *The Seven Samurai* is the kind of action-packed, thundering-hooves, death-dealing spectacle which is considered a man's picture. I propose to turn this hazard to my advantage by suggesting that the weaknesses of the film are closely linked to the limitations of this virile, masculine genre.

The Seven Samurai took over a year to photograph and cost a half million dollars; it was the biggest film made in Japan up to that time, and Toho, appalled at the time and costs, considered abandoning the project. Kurosawa employed a wide range of technical devices: an experimental use of super-powered telephoto lenses to make action and objects seem overwhelmingly close, deep focus, giant close-ups, slow motion, amazing tracking shots. The effect of these photographic methods and of the raw, fast editing is that *The Seven Samurai* doesn't seem like a historical or "period" film at all: everything is going on now, right on top of us. Kurosawa can create diversion that

* This production ran three hours twenty minutes in Japan; as shown at Venice in 1954, it ran two hours thirty-five minutes; as later circulated in the United States under the title *The Magnificent Seven* it runs two hours twenty-one minutes. An American production, also called *The Magnificent Seven*, based on the story material of the Japanese film but changing the samurai into gunmen, was released in 1960.

doesn't divert from the subject: when the farmers scan the street for hungry samurai, he presents a little scherzo of elegant figures moving through humbler humanity. The stance, the formalized carriage of the samurai, gives substance to the farmers' desperate faith in them: surely they *could* dispose of countless ordinary men. The pace and cinematic feeling, the verve, the humor are completely modern. Kurosawa is perhaps the greatest of all contemporary film craftsmen: his use of the horizon for compositional variety, the seemingly infinite camera angles, the compositions that are alive with action, the almost abstract use of trees, flowers, sky, rain, mud, and moving figures are all active. In *The Seven Samurai* your eye does not rest — you do not see any of the static, careful arrangements, the crawling, overcomposed salon photography of Hollywood's big productions.

The musical score is considered to be one of the best Japanese film scores ever written, but that really doesn't say much for it. There is no specifically Japanese tradition for film music, and the budgetary allowances for composers are minuscule. The result is what sounds to us like a parody of European music. Audiences for *Rashomon* have sometimes accused the projectionist of putting on a record of Ravel's *Bolero*; the music for *The Seven Samurai* is often absurdly anachronistic — with premature echoes of "Ol' Man River," Ravel, American movie music for westerns, and others. This, however, is a minor weakness.

There is a major weakness. When violence itself becomes the theme, when it is treated with such extraordinary range that we are caught up in what is literally an epic of action, we need protagonists commensurate with the pictorial grandeur. There is one: Kyuzo, a swordsman who has no interest in life but the perfection of his swordsmanship. His early scenes in stills and slow motion — a fable of swordplay which must then become futile sword death — are among the most beautiful in the film. But the principal characters are far more familiar — and at the creative level, familiarity should and must breed contempt. As the braggadocio link between the farmers and the samurai, Toshiro Mifune gives the movie much gusto, but he overplays: like many another great ham, he calls too much attention to himself. No actor can do more with his knees and his behind than Mifune, but he also bares his teeth almost as often as Kirk Douglas. It is not merely that his defects as an actor jeopardize his spontaneity and uninhibited energy, but that his overacting exposes the clichés of the role — which is basically a comic turn. The role of Takashi Shimura is also a series of clichés: his Kambei is the idealized father-leader figure — sage, kindly, selfless, mature, just. And there is the callow young hero who gets his sexual initiation, and so forth. When the battle is over and the village saved, one of the remaining samurai remarks, "Again we survive." Kambei corrects him: "Again we lose — the winners are those farmers, not us." To have come so far for this! Raging, stampeding violence — scenes of slaughter and devastation that, as Tony Richardson remarked, are "not unworthy of the Goya of Los Desastres" — and then this little "deep thought" which is not only highly questionable but ludicrously inadequate. It's as if the epic makers didn't realize that what we have witnessed overpowers such flabby little thoughts (which bear a dismal resemblance to the "humanistic" thinking of "message" westerns).

Here is the problem of the men's action pictures: either we get the ritual conflict of slick bad men versus strong silent heroes, i.e., evil pitted against good in a frame of reference too silly to take seriously, or we get the ritual conflict set in the commonplaces of a shopworn, socially conscious frame of reference which tries to give depth and meaning to the ritual and suceeds only in destroying its beautiful simplicity. *The Seven Samurai* triumphs over these problems by pouring all its energies into the extremities of human experience — into conflict itself — but it still looks for social "truths" beyond the action and provides an explicit content so banal that the epic beauties seem to be a virtuoso exercise. Perhaps Kurosawa, like his obsessive master swordsman, has no thoughts beyond the perfection of his craft. Action is all — the pity is that he doesn't seem to know that in *The Seven Samurai* it is enough.

[1961]

III

Broadcasts and Reviews, 1961-1963

Breathless, and the Daisy Miller Doll

Breathless, the most important New Wave film which has reached the United States, is a frightening little chase comedy with no big speeches and no pretensions. Michel, the young Parisian hood (Jean-Paul Belmondo), steals a car, kills a highway patrolman, chases after some money owed him for past thefts, so he and his young American girl friend can get away to Italy. He finances this chase after the money by various other crimes along the way. Meanwhile, the police are chasing him. But both Michel's flight and the police chase are half-hearted. Michel isn't desperate to get away — his life doesn't mean that much to him; and the police (who are reminiscent of Keystone Cops) carry on a routine bumbling manhunt. Part of the stylistic peculiarity of the work — its art — is that while you're watching it, it's light and playful, off-the-cuff, even a little silly. It seems accidental that it embodies more of the modern world than other movies.

What sneaks up on you in *Breathless* is that the engagingly coy young hood with his loose, random grace and the impervious, passively butch American girl are as shallow and empty as the shiny young faces you see in sports cars and in suburban supermarkets, and in newspapers after unmotivated, pointless crimes. And you're left with the horrible suspicion that this is a new race, bred in chaos, accepting chaos as natural, and not caring one way or another about it or anything else. The heroine, who has literary interests, quotes *Wild Palms*, "Between grief and nothing, I will take grief." But that's just an attitude she likes at that moment; at the end she demonstrates that it's false. The hero states the truth for them both: "I'd choose nothing." The characters of *Breathless* are casual, carefree moral idiots. The European critic, Louis Marcorelles, describes their world as "total immorality, lived skin-deep." And possibly because we Americans live among just such people and have come to take them for granted, the film may not, at first, seem quite so startling as it is. And that's what's frightening about *Breathless*: not only are the characters familiar in an exciting, revealing way, they are terribly *attractive*.

If you foolishly depend on the local reviewers to guide you, you may have been put off *Breathless*. To begin with, where did they get the idea that the title refers to the film's fast editing? That's about like suggesting that the title *Two-Way Stretch* refers to the wide screen. The French title, *À Bout de Souffle*, means "Out of Breath," and it refers to the hero, who keeps going until he's winded. Their confusion is, however, a tribute to the film's fast, improvisatory style, the go go go rhythm. The jazz score, the comic technique are perfectly expressive of the lives of the characters; the jump-cuts convey the tempo and quality of the activities of characters who don't work up to anything but hop from one thing to the next. And as the film seems to explain the people *in their own terms*, the style has the freshness of "objectivity." It does seem breathlessly young, newly created.

If you hold the *Chronicle's* review of *Breathless* up to the light, you may see H-E-L-P shining through it.

Certain scenes are presented with utter candor, lacking in form and impact in their frankness. A long encounter, for instance, in the small room of Jean Seberg, with whom Belmondo claims to be in love, is repetitious — but extremely lifelike. And then young Godard suddenly will present another scene in which a police inspector is tailing Miss Seberg and searching for Belmondo. This is staged so clumsily that one wonders whether parody is what the director intends. But Belmondo's peril is grave and his reaction to his predicament is sensitive. . . . Always energetic and arrogant, he still suggests both a lost quality and a tender humor. This is his facade to shield his small cynical world from all that he does not understand.

The hero of the film understands all that he wants to, but the critic isn't cynical enough to see the basic fact about these characters: they just don't give a damn. And that's what the movie is about. The *Examiner's* critic lamented that *Breathless* was a "hodge-podge" and complained that he couldn't "warm up" to the characters — which is a bit like not being able to warm up to the four Mission District kids who went out looking for homosexuals to beat up, and managed to cause the death of a young schoolteacher. For sheer not-getting-the-point, it recalls the remark recently overheard from a well-groomed, blue-rinse-on-the-hair type elderly lady: "That poor Eichmann! I don't think he's got a Chinaman's chance."

How do we connect with people who don't give a damn? Well, is it really so difficult? Even if they weren't all around us, they'd still be (to quote *Double Indemnity*) closer than that.

They are as detached as a foreign colony, as uncommitted as visitors from another planet, yet the youth of several countries seem, to one degree or another, to share the same characteristics. They're not consciously against society: they have no ideologies at all, they're not even rebels without a cause. They're not rebelling against anything — they don't pay that much attention to what doesn't please or amuse them. There is nothing they really want to do, and there's nothing they won't do. Not that they're perverse or deliberately cruel: they have charm and intelligence — but they live on impulse.

The codes of civilized living presuppose that people have an inner life and outer aims, but this new race lives for the moment, because that is all that they care about. And the standards of judgment we might bring to bear on them don't touch them and don't interest them. They have the narcissism of youth, and we are out of it, we are bores. These are the youthful representatives of mass society. They seem giddy and gauche and amusingly individualistic, until you consider that this individualism is not only a reaction to mass conformity, but, more terrifyingly, is the new form that mass society takes: indifference to human values.

Godard has used this, as it were, documentary background for a gangster story. In the traditional American gangster films, we would have been cued for the gangster's fall: he would have shown the one vanity or sentimental weakness or misjudgment that would prove fatal. But *Breathless* has removed the movie gangster from his melodramatic trappings of gangs and power: this gangster is Bogart apotheosized and he is romantic in a modern sense just because he doesn't care about anything but the pleasures of love and fast cars. There is not even the American gangster's hatred of cops and squealers. Michel likes cops because they're cops. This gangster is post-*L'Etranger* and he isn't interested in motives: it's all simple to him, "Killers kill, squealers squeal." Nobody cares if Michel lives or dies, and he doesn't worry about it much either.

Yet Godard has too much affection for Michel to make *him* a squealer: a killer yes, a squealer no. Despite the unrest and anarchy in the moral atmosphere, Michel is as romantic as Pépé Le Moko and as true to love (and his death scene is just as operatic and satisfying). A murderer and a girl with artistic pretensions. She asks him what he thinks of a reproduction she is trying on the wall, and he answers, "Not bad." This doesn't show that he's sufficiently impressed and she reprimands him with, "Renoir was a very great painter." In disgust he replies, "I said 'Not bad.'" There's no doubt which of them responds more. He's honest and likable, though socially classifiable as a psychopath; she's a psychopath, too, but the non-classifiable sort — socially acceptable but a sad, sweet, affectless doll.

There are more ironies than can be sorted out in Patricia-Jean Seberg from Iowa, selected by Otto Preminger from among thousands of American girls to play the French national heroine, Joan of Arc, and now the national heroine of France — as the representative American girl abroad. Patricia, a naive,

assured, bland and boyish creature, is like a new Daisy Miller
— but not quite as envisioned by Henry James. She has the
independence, but not the moral qualms or the Puritan conscience or the high aspirations that James saw as the special
qualities of the American girl. She is, indeed, the heiress of the
ages — but in a more sinister sense than James imagined: she is
so free that she has no sense of responsibility or guilt. She
seems to be playing at existence, at a career, at "love"; she's
"trying them on." But that's all she's capable of in the way of
experience. She doesn't want to be bothered; when her lover becomes an inconvenience, she turns him in to the police.

Shot down and dying, the young man gallantly tries to amuse
her, and then looks up at her and remarks — without judgment
or reproach, but rather, descriptively, as a grudging compliment:
"You really are a bitch." (The actual word he uses is consider-
ably stronger.) And in her flat, little-girl, cornbelt voice, she says,
"I don't know what the word means." If she does know, she
doesn't care to see how it applies to her. More likely, she really
doesn't know, and it wouldn't bother her much anyway. The
codes of love and loyalty, in which, if you betray a lover you're
a bitch, depend on stronger emotions than her idle attachment
to this lover — one among many. They depend on *emotions*,
and she is innocent of them. As she had observed earlier, "When
we look into each other's eyes, we get nowhere." An updated
version of the betraying blonde bitches who destroyed so many
movie gangsters, she is innocent even of guilt. As Jean Seberg
plays her — and that's exquisitely — Patricia is the most terrifyingly *simple* muse-goddess-bitch of modern movies. Next to
her, the scheming Stanwyck of *Double Indemnity* is as archaic
as Theda Bara in *A Fool There Was*.

Jean-Paul Belmondo, who plays the hood, is probably the
most exciting new presence on the screen since the appearance
of Brando; nobody holds the screen this way without enormous
reserves of talent. At twenty-six, he has already appeared in nine
plays and nine movies; he may be, as Peter Brook says, the best
young actor in Europe today. In minor parts, the Alfred Hitch-

cock personal-appearance bit is compounded, and Truffaut (*The 400 Blows*), Chabrol (*Le Beau Serge, The Cousins*), and Godard himself flit through. Truffaut supplied the news item on which Godard based the script; Chabrol lent his name as supervising producer. But it is Godard's picture, and he has pointed out how he works: "The cinema is not a trade. It isn't teamwork. One is always alone while shooting, as though facing a blank page." His movie is dedicated to Monogram Pictures — who were, of course, the producers of cheap American gangster-chase movies, generally shot in city locations. (*Breathless* was made for $90,000.) Another important director appears in the film — Jean-Pierre Melville — who a few years ago performed one of the most amazing feats on film: he entered into Jean Cocteau's universe and directed, with almost no funds, the brilliant film version of Cocteau's *Les Enfants Terribles*, sometimes known as *The Strange Ones*. He is regarded as a sort of spiritual father to the New Wave; he appears in the movie as a celebrity being interviewed. (The true celebrity and progenitor of the movement is, of course, Cocteau.) Asked by Patricia, "What is your ambition?" the celebrity teases her with a pseudo-profundity: "To become immortal, and then to die."

The Cousins

The Cousins was so badly received in this country that my liking it may seem merely perverse, so let me take it up in some detail. Perhaps the best introduction to this skillful, complex film is through the American critics who kept people from seeing it. The ineffable Bosley Crowther wrote in the New York *Times* that it "has about the most dismal and defeatist solution for the problem it presents — the problem of youthful disillusion — of any picture we have ever seen. . . . M. Chabrol is the gloomiest and most despairing of the new creative French di-

rectors. His attitude is ridden with a sense of defeat and ruin."
Youthful disillusion is a fact and that is how *The Cousins* treats
it. The movie doesn't offer any solution because it doesn't pose
any problem. Robert Hatch wrote in the *Nation:*

The latest of the "New Wave" French imports is *The Cousins*, a
country mouse–city mouse story that dips into the lives and affairs
of today's Paris student bohemia. The picture is written and directed
by Claude Chabrol, but I had the feeling that it was an exercise in
self-expression thrown together by the characters themselves. It is
just such a story as these bright, aimless, superficially tough and
perilously debauched boys and girls might consider profound and
moving.

Time put it down more coolly in a single-paragraph review
that distorted the plot and missed the point:

The Cousins . . . is a fairly clever, mildly depressing study of
France's I-got-it-beat generation. Made for $160,000 by a 27-year-
old film critic named Claude Chabrol, the film offers a switch on
the story of the city mouse (Jean-Claude Brialy) and the country
mouse (Gerard Blain). In this case the city mouse is really a rat.
Enrolled in law school, he seldom attends classes, spends his time
shacking up with "can't-say-no" girls, arranging for abortions,
curing one hangover and planning the next. When the country
cousin, a nice boy but not too bright in school, comes to live with
him, the rat nibbles away at the country boy's time, his girl friend
(Juliette Mayniel), and his will to work. In the end, the country
cousin fails his examinations and the city cousin casually shoots him
dead with a gun he didn't know was loaded. And that, the moral
would seem to be, is one way to keep 'em down on the farm after
they've seen Paree.

The critical term, "depressing," like "gloomiest and most despairing," almost guarantees that readers will stay away.

Time's reviewer may not have been briefed on the Catholic
background of *The Cousins*, or may have thought that its kind
of religiosity would not be inspirational enough for American
audiences. After all, it was *Time* that cautioned the public that
if they went to see *Diary of a Country Priest* — surely the one

great religious film of recent years — they "might be grateful for a resident theologian in the lobby." Yet *Time*, in its laudatory review of *The Hoodlum Priest*, indulges in a piece of upbeat theology that might confuse anyone. *Time* describes what happens when the priest tells the condemned convict about Christ's love, and, according to *Time*:

Suddenly, wonderfully, a new dimension of reality surrounds and penetrates the scene: the dimension of divine love. Like an impossible hope it flickers in his heart. In this hope the condemned man and his audience are so intensely interfused and mutually identified . . . that the spectator not only shares the victim's agony in the gas chamber but may even, at one transcendent moment in this film, feel himself dead in the dead man, feel the dead man living in himself. The experience is extraordinary — nothing less than an illusion of immortality.

The Cousins, oddly enough, is about just such an interchange — but with a complete loss of hope. The hero, who is, of course, the *city* cousin, knows that he is *dead* in the dead man. Why did American reviewers consider the honest, plodding, unimaginative, provincial cousin the hero? Possibly identification — they have certainly behaved like country innocents about *The Cousins*. What is exciting about its content is precisely the oblique view we get of the decadent, bizarre, rich young nihilist — the dissipating cynic who is the antithesis of all bourgeois virtues. It is he, not his hardworking, conscientious, romantic and idealistic cousin, who has moral force, and it is *his* character that is relevant to the actual world. The only certainties in his life are promiscuity and vice, but he recognizes them for what they are and he has established a code of behavior — it might even be construed as a code of honor.

The Cousins has the most remarkable collection of faces in recent films: in every shot there is someone to look at. And there are the remarkable principals: the suave Jean-Claude Brialy as the city cousin — we first see him made up like Toulouse-Lautrec in his Japanese-gentleman photographs; Gerard

Blain in the difficult role of the country boy; and a new young actress, Juliette Mayniel, who has the most astonishingly beautiful cat-eyes since Michele Morgan in her trenchcoat and beret came out of the fog of *Port of Shadows*.

As a production, *The Cousins* glitters as if it were terribly expensive. It contains some of the best orgies on film, and every scene is smooth and elegant. Perhaps it is Chabrol's almost extravagant command of the medium — the fluency of movement and the total subordination of the large cast to their roles and milieu — that made Americans less sympathetic than they have been toward unpolished, rough, uncontrolled work. In the film society and art-house audiences, awkwardness and pretension are often associated with film art, and there seems to be almost an appetite for filmic inadequacy — which looks like proof of sincerity and good intentions. How else can one explain the enthusiasm for that feeble refugee from a surrealist short — the union-suited devil of *Black Orpheus?* You may like or dislike *The Cousins* but you certainly won't feel that the director is an amateur to whom you should be charitable.

The sensationalism and glossy stylishness of *The Cousins* suggests commercial film making at its most proficient. As a critic, Chabrol is identified with his studies of Hitchcock. He particularly admires *Strangers on a Train*, which, as you may recall, also suggested a peculiar role transference between two men — Farley Granger and Robert Walker — and dealt with a particularly corrupt social climate of extreme wealth and extreme perversity. Chabrol is the showman of the New Wave, but he is also a moralist who uses the dissolute milieu of student life for a serious, though chic, purpose. The students are products of the post-Nazi world, and in one disturbing sequence, the city cousin interrupts a wild party he is giving to stage an extraordinary ritual: with Wagner on the hi-fi, he puts on an SS officer's hat and walks among his drunken guests with a lighted candelabrum, as he recites in German what sounds like a mawkish parody of German romantic poetry.

The older characters are, ironically, misleading or treacherous or disgusting. There is, for example, a kindly bookseller, whom, at first, one might take to be the chorus, as he counsels the country boy to stick to his studies and stay away from the nasty sophisticates. But his advice is dated and it won't work. The others — the procurer, and the Italian industrialist — are obsessed by sexual desires they can't satisfy. The students abhor the industrialist because he is an old-fashioned kind of lecher who wants to buy his way into the company of youth. The students are, within their own terms, honest in the way they take their pleasure: *The Cousins*, more than any other film I can think of, deserves to be called The Lost Generation, with all the glamour and romance, the easy sophistication and quick desperation that the title suggests.

Chabrol shows that the old concepts of romance are inadequate to a world of sexual ambiguities, and he shows that, from the point of view of the bright and gifted, and in our world — where the present, as much as the future, is uncertain — a country cousin who plods to make good and get ahead must be a little dull witted. Perhaps that country boy is not really so honest as he seems: his diligence, his sobriety, all his antique virtues may be just a self-deceiving defense against the facts of modern life. The heroine, who almost thinks she loves him, realizes that this is just an intellectual and aesthetic response; she would like to be able to believe in a pure, sweet and enduring love. It would be so much prettier than the truth about herself. The others treat him with a gentle nostalgia — as toward a figure from the past.

Canned Americana

In older films, protagonists were fighting their impulses, trying to subordinate their drives to their aspirations; they were capable of ideas and ideals. Now, Freudianized writers tell us more about their people than the people themselves know, and they are shown as smart, or as gaining insight, when they discover what we have already been posted on — their sexual desires, their fears and anxieties. The authors condescend to us, at the same time putting us in a position to feel superior to the people in the movies who know so much less than we do. The only figures in some of the recent films who could be called characters are more exactly caricatures — the father as played by Pat Hingle in *Splendor in the Grass*, the mother as played by Una Merkel in *Summer and Smoke*.

Perhaps in modern terms, character *is* a caricature. The only person who gives any sense of character to *All Fall Down*, is the mother, played by Angela Lansbury — and once again, it's a howling caricature. And yet the moments when she really moves us (and Angela Lansbury is at times extraordinarily moving, reminiscent of Bette Davis at her best) are when she steps free of the caricature and becomes a character. This makes me wonder a little if perhaps one of the reasons why character is disappearing is that audiences don't want to respond or feel. It's much easier to laugh at or feel superior to a caricature than feel with a character. For isn't the essence, the defining quality of a caricature, that it tells us how to react? It's a character with the responses built in.

All Fall Down is deep in William Inge territory — homespun and Gothic — that strange area of nostalgic Americana where the familiar is the Freudian grotesque. It's also a peculiar kind of fantasy in which hideous lecherous women (schoolteachers seem to be the worst offenders) paw handsome young men and the one girl who might seem attractive disqualifies herself by becoming pathetically pregnant. The movie turns out to be the portrait of the writer as an adolescent (Brandon de Wilde plays the part) who grows up — "matures" — when he learns that the older brother he idolizes (played by Warren Beatty) is an empty wreck. Does *anybody* really grow up the way this boy grows up? He learns the truth, squares his shoulders, and walks out into the bright sunlight as Alex North's music rises and swells in victory. How many movies have pulled this damned visual homily on us, this synthetic growing-into-a-man, as if it happened all at once and forever, this transition to self-knowledge and adulthood? Suggested party game: ask your friends to tell about the summer they grew up. The one who tells the best lie has a promising career ahead as a Hollywood screenwriter.

Inge's *Splendor in the Grass* script is based on a neo-Freudian fantasy, popular among teen-agers, that sexual repression drives you crazy. *Splendor in the Grass* is hysterically on the side of young love; it deals with a high-school pair of sweethearts — Warren Beatty and Natalie Wood — whose parents think they are too young to marry. And so, deprived of sexual love together, the boy turns to a floozy, the girl, maddened by loss of him, goes to a mental institution. The parents are the usual hypocritical monsters you expect from this sort of adolescent-slanted movie that pretends to deal with real youthful problems but actually begs the question by having the two kids tenderly and truthfully and presumably, permanently, in love. The movie does not even implicitly come out for the rights of adolescents to sexual experimentation; it just attacks the corrupted grown-ups for failure to understand that these two kids are in love, and for failure to value love above all else. In other words, it's the old corn but fermented by Kazan in a new way — with lots of screaming and a gang-bang sequence, and blood and beatings, and girls getting pawed on their twitching little school-girl behinds. This latter feature, rather than nostalgia, may explain why the movie is set in the flapper days of 1928: the girls act with their butts instead of their busts, and Miss Wood probably has the most active derrière since Clara Bow.

There's supposed to be something on fire inside Alma, the heroine of *Summer and Smoke*, but from Geraldine Page's performance and Peter Glenville's direction, t'ain't smoke that rises, just wispy little old tired ideas goin' to rejoin the Holy Ghost. There's nothing on fire in the movie. The movie looks artistic, but it's the opposite of art: it dulls the senses. There are many ways in which a performance can go wrong. Geraldine Page may have discovered a new one: she's technically so careful, so studied, so perfect in a way that she's a bore — all delicate shadings and no surprises. Who wants to see a performance that's so meticulously worked-out and worked-over, it's finished, it's dead? Besides, Miss Page's lonely, inhibited spinster, Alma, is rather an unfortunate mixture of Julie Harris and Zasu Pitts.

The subject matter of *Summer and Smoke* is a little anecdote about two people, a preacher's daughter who represents spirit and a doctor's son who represents flesh. Each influences the other and so they wind up exchanging roles: she becomes a loose woman and he becomes a dedicated, selfless man. It's a little *QED* sort of plot stretched out for two hours of overcomposed photography and decomposed characters. There's one of those hypocritical preachers who looks left over from a stock company of *Rain;* stage Mexicans flash their gleaming teeth; Thomas Gomez turns up once more, sweating and shouting; and Rita Moreno — who is always described as fiery and tigerish — comes on like a parody of Carmen Jones. Her dance of inflamed jealousy is lethally funny, but in this context of what are called poignant emotions you become too dispirited to laugh. And there's the ingenue or overgrown infant, Pamela Tiffin, with a face as soft and dimply as a baby's bottom — and just as expressive. Couldn't the stork take her back?

Sometimes Tennessee Williams seems to think with the mind of Stanley Kowalski. If Alma is being spiritual and skittish and old-maidish when she screams at a cock-fight, carry me back to old virginity.

The men who filmed *The Roman Spring of Mrs. Stone* seem to think the idea of an aging woman buying companionship and love so daring and unusual that they fumble around with it almost as much as the doctor in the screen version of *Suddenly, Last Summer,* who couldn't seem to cope with the simple facts of Sebastian's homosexuality and kept saying, "You *don't* mean *that?*" — "No, it *can't* be *that?*" — "*What* are you saying?" — "What do you *mean?*" I assumed the youngest child in the audience would get the point before he did. By trying so diligently to make Mrs. Stone sympathetic and understandable the director and writer, José Quintero and Gavin Lambert, kill all interest in her. We could accept a woman buying love, but why make her haggle over it?

The Roman Spring of Mrs. Stone is rather like *Sunset Boulevard* — without the madness and the wit. In the scene at the tailor's we can almost hear the clerk murmur — "After all, if the lady is paying . . ." In *Sunset Boulevard* there was a calculated grotesque — crazy old Norma Desmond in her macabre mansion. Mrs. Stone is more like Elsie Dinsmore on her last legs, and the camera and script persevere over it all so long that the effect is unintentionally grotesque.

Why explain so much? Anyone who has ever watched the middle-aged and elderly women going in for their Arthur Murray lessons knows that you don't even have to go to Rome to drift . . .

The Tennessee Williams novella (in the tradition of the D. H. Lawrence "Lovely Lady" stories) is about a proud cold-hearted bitch without cares or responsibilities who learns that sex is all that holds her to life, it is the only sensation that momentarily saves her from the meaningless drift of her existence. The movie is so insistent about the "shocking" mechanics of purchasing love that that's what the film seems to be about. It's too bad because the role seemed ideal for Vivien Leigh, who had been brilliant in the role of the aging woman in *The Deep Blue Sea*; but as Mrs. Stone she's parched and monotonous — though Warren Beatty somehow manages to come through. Quintero's direction is so lacking in rhythm that one might think the Roman spring had got him, that he was losing control along with Mrs. Stone.

In a variation of this theme in *Breakfast at Tiffany's*, Patricia Neal is amusing in a rather impenetrable role — she seems to be playing a lesbian and she's also keeping George Peppard. I don't think it's wise to let the mind linger too long over that.

:):):):):):

West Side Story

Sex is the great leveler, taste the great divider. I have premonitions of the beginning of the end when a man who seems charming or at least remotely possible starts talking about movies. When he says, "I saw a great picture a couple years ago — I wonder what you thought of it?" I start looking for the nearest exit. His great picture generally turns out to be *He Who Must Die* or something else that I detested — frequently a socially conscious problem picture of the Stanley Kramer variety. Boobs on the make always try to impress with their high level of seriousness (wise guys, with their contempt for *all* seriousness).

It's experiences like this that drive women into the arms of truckdrivers — and, as this is America, the truckdrivers all too often come up with the same kind of status-seeking tastes: they want to know what you thought of *Black Orpheus* or *Never on Sunday* or something else you'd much rather forget.

When a really attractive Easterner said to me, "I don't generally like musicals, but have you seen *West Side Story?* It's really great," I felt a kind of gnawing discomfort. I *love* musicals and so I couldn't help being suspicious of the greatness of a musical that would be so overwhelming to somebody who *didn't* like musicals. The gentleman's remark correlated with other expressions of taste — the various encounters in offices and on trains and planes with men who would put on solemn faces as they said, "I don't ordinarily go for poetry but have you read *This is My Beloved?*"

I had an uneasy feeling that maybe it would be better if I *didn't* go to see *West Side Story* — but, if you're driven to seek the truth, you're driven. I had to learn if this man and I were really as close as he suggested or as far apart as I feared. Well, it's a great musical for people who don't like musicals.

You will notice that nobody says *West Side Story* is a good movie; they say it's great — they accept the terms on which it is presented. It aims to be so much more than a "mere" musical like *Singin' in the Rain* (just about the best Hollywood musical of all time) that it is concerned with nothing so basic to the form as lightness, grace, proportion, diversion, comedy. It is not concerned with the musical form as a showcase for star performers in their best routines; it aspires to present the ballet of our times — our conflicts presented in music and dance. And, according to most of the critics, it succeeds. My anxiety as I entered the theater was not allayed by a huge blow-up of Bosley Crowther's review proclaiming the film a "cinematic masterpiece."

West Side Story begins with a blast of stereophonic music that had me clutching my head. Is the audience so impressed by science and technique, and by the highly advertised new developments that they accept this jolting series of distorted sounds gratefully — on the assumption, perhaps, that because it's so unlike ordinary sound, it must be *better?* Everything about *West Side Story* is supposed to stun you with its newness, its size, the wonders of its photography, editing, choreography, music. It's nothing so simple as a musical, it's a piece of cinematic technology.

Consider the feat: first you take Shakespeare's *Romeo and Juliet* and remove all that cumbersome poetry; then you make the Montagues and Capulets really important and modern by turning them into rival street gangs of native-born and Puerto Ricans. (You get rid of the parents, of course; America is a *young* country — and who wants to be bothered by the squabbles of older people?) There is Jerome Robbins to convert the street rumbles into modern ballet — though he turns out to be too slow and painstaking for high-powered moviemaking and the co-director Robert Wise takes over. (May I remind you of some of Robert Wise's previous credits — the names may be construed as symbolic. *So Big, Executive Suite, Somebody Up There Likes Me, I Want to Live.*) The writers include Arthur Laurents, Ernest Lehman, and, for the lyrics, Stephen Sondheim. The music is said to be by Leonard Bernstein. (Bernstein's father at a recent banquet honoring his seventieth birthday: "You don't expect your child to be a Moses, a Maimonides, a Leonard Bernstein." No, indeed, nor when you criticize Bernstein's music do you expect people to jump in outrage as if you were demeaning Moses or Maimonides.) Surely, only Saul Bass could provide the titles for such a production, as the credits include more consultants and assistants, production designers, sound men, editors, special effects men, and so forth than you might believe possible — until you see the result. Is it his much-vaunted ingeniousness or a hidden streak of cynicism — a neat comment on all this technology — that he turns the credits into graffiti?

The irony of this hyped-up, slam-bang production is that those involved apparently don't really believe that beauty and romance *can* be expressed in modern rhythms — for whenever their Romeo and Juliet enter the scene, the dialogue becomes painfully old-fashioned and mawkish, the dancing turns to simpering, sickly romantic ballet, and sugary old stars hover in the sky. When true love enters the film, Bernstein abandons Gershwin and begins to echo Richard Rodgers, Rudolf Friml, and Victor Herbert. There's even a heavenly choir. When the fruity, toothsome Romeo-Tony meets his Juliet-Maria, everything becomes gauzy and dreamy and he murmurs, "Have we met before?" That's my favorite piece of synthetic mysticism since the great exchange in *Black Orpheus*: "My name is Orpheus." "My name is Eurydice." "Then we must be in love." When Tony, floating on the clouds of romance (Richard Beymer unfortunately doesn't look as if he *could* walk) is asked, "What have you been taking tonight?" he answers, "A trip to the moon." Match *that* for lyric eloquence! (You'd have to go back to *Golden Boy*.)

When Tony stabs Maria's brother and your mind fills in with "O, I am fortune's fool," the expensive scriptwriters come up with a brilliant exclamation for him. "Maria!" he cries. Do not let this exquisite simplicity mislead you — for they do not call the name "Maria" lightly. She is no mere girl like Juliet — she has the wisdom of all women, she is the mother of us all. And that is why, no doubt, they depart from Shakespeare's plot at the end: suffering Maria survives. And, of course, the appeal to the Catholic audience — which might otherwise become uneasy as both gangs are probably Catholic — is thereby assured. *West Side Story* plays the game in every conceivable way: it makes a strong appeal to youth by expressing the exuberant, frustrated desires of youth in the ugly, constricted city life, but it finally betrays this youth by representing the good characters as innocent and sweet, and making the others seem rather comic and foolish. They're like Dead End kids dancing — and without much improvement in the humor of the Dead End kids.

How can so many critics have fallen for all this frenzied hokum — about as original as, say, *South Pacific* at home — and with a score so derivative that, as we left the theater, and overheard some young man exclaiming "I could listen to that music forever," my little daughter answered "We *have* been listening to it forever." (At his father's banquet, Bernstein recalled that at his debut when he was thirteen he had played variations of a song "in the manner of Chopin, Liszt and Gershwin. Now I will play it in the manner of Bernstein." How, I wonder?) Perhaps the clue is in the bigness, and in the pretensions that are part of the bigness. Arthur Knight in the *Saturday Review* called it "A triumphant work of art"; Stanley Kauffmann in the *New Republic* says:

The best film musical ever made. . . . When the film begins, and the Jets move down the streets of the West Side (studio settings faultlessly blended with location shots), as they mold swagger into ballet, we know that we are not seeing dance numbers, we are seeing street gangs for the first time *as they really are* — only we have not been able to perceive it for ourselves. . . . It is Robbins' vision — of city life expressed in stylized movement that sometimes flowers into dance and song — that lifts this picture high. If a time-

capsule is about to be buried anywhere, this film ought to be included, so that possible future generations can know how an artist
of ours made our most congenial theatrical form respond to some
of the beauty in our time and to the humanity in some of its
ugliness.

A candidate for a time-capsule is surely no ordinary multi-
million-dollar spectacle. Hasn't Kauffmann, along with a lot of
other people, fallen victim to the show of grandeur and importance? If there is anything great in the American musical tradition — and I think there is — it's in the light satire, the high
spirits, the giddy romance, the low comedy, and the unpreten-
tiously stylized dancing of men like Fred Astaire and the younger
Gene Kelly. There's more beauty there — and a lot more humanity — than in all this jet-propelled ballet. Nothing in *West
Side Story* gave me the pleasure of an honest routine like Donald
O'Connor's "Make 'Em Laugh" number in *Singin' in the Rain*
or almost any old Astaire and Rogers movie.

Despite Kauffmann's feeling that "we are seeing street gangs
for the first time *as they really are*," I wonder how the actual
street gangs feel about the racial composition of the movie's
gangs. For, of course, the Puerto Ricans are *not* Puerto Ricans
and the only real difference between these two gangs of what I
am tempted to call ballerinas — is that one group has faces and
hair darkened, and the other group has gone wild for glittering
yellow hair dye; and their stale exuberance, though magnified
by the camera to epic proportions, suggests no social tensions
more world shaking than the desperation of young dancers to
get ahead — even at the risk of physical injury. They're about
as human as the Munchkins in *The Wizard of Oz*. Maria, the
sweet virgin fresh from Puerto Rico, is the most machine-tooled
of Hollywood ingenues — clever little Natalie Wood. Like the
new Princess telephone, so ingeniously constructed that it transcends its function and makes communication superfluous (it
seems to be designed so that teen-agers can read advertising
slogans at each other), Natalie Wood is the newly-constructed
love-goddess — so perfectly banal she destroys all thoughts of

love. In his great silent film *Metropolis*, Fritz Lang had a robot woman named the false Maria: she had more spontaneity than Natalie Wood's Maria.

I had a sense of foreboding when I saw that Friar Lawrence had become a kindly old Jewish pharmacist called "Doc," but I was hardly prepared for his ultimate wisdom — "You kids make this world lousy! When will you stop?" These words Bosley Crowther tells us "should be heard by thoughtful people — sympathetic people — all over the land." Why, I wonder? What *is* there in this message that has anything to *do* with thought? These message movies dealing with Negro and white, or Puerto Rican and white, like to get a little extra increment of virtue — unearned — by tossing in a sweet, kindly, harmless old Jew full of prophetic cant. (Presumably, Jews should not be discriminated against because they are so philosophic and impotent.) The film makers wouldn't dream of having a young, pushing, aggressive Jew in the film — just as they don't dare to differentiate or characterize the racial backgrounds of the white gang. (Only sweet, reformed Tony can be identified as a Pole.) Yet this is a movie that pretends to deal with racial tensions. The lyrics keep telling us this is what it's about and the critics seem to accept the authors' word for it.

"But," counter the enthusiasts for the film, "surely you must admit the dancing is great." No, it isn't — it's trying so hard to be great it isn't even good. Those impressive, widely admired opening shots of New York from the air overload the story with values and importance — technological and sociological. The Romeo and Juliet story could, of course, be set anywhere, but *West Side Story* wrings the last drop of spurious importance out of the setting, which dominates the enfeebled love story. The dancing is also designed to be urgent and important: it is supposed to be the lyric poetry of the streets, with all the jagged rhythms of modern tensions. The bigger the leap the more, I suppose, the dancer is expressing — on the theory that America is a big, athletic country. Who would have thought that Busby Berkeley's amusing old geometric patterns and aerial views would come back *this* way? Add social ideas to geometry, and you have the new *West Side Story* concept of dance. And just as the American middle classes thought they were being daring and accepting jazz when they listened to the adaptations and arrangements of big orchestras that gave jazz themes the familiar thick, sweet sludge of bad symphonic music, and thought that jazz was being elevated and honored as an art when Louis Armstrong played with the lagging, dragging New York Philharmonic (under Leonard Bernstein), they now think that American dancing is elevated to the status of art by all this arranging and exaggerating — by being turned into the familiar "high" art of ballet. The movements are so huge and sudden, so portentously "alive" they're always near explosion point. The dancing is obviously trying to say something, to *glorify* certain kinds of movement. And looking at all those boys in blue jeans doing their calisthenic choreography, Americans say, "Why it's like ballet . . . it's art, it's really great!" What is lost is not merely the rhythm, the feel, the unpretentious movements of American dancing at its best — but its basic emotion, which, as in jazz music, is the contempt for respectability. The possibilities of dance as an expressive medium are not expanded in *West Side Story*; they're contracted. I would guess that in a few decades the dances in *West Side Story* will look as much like hilariously limited, dated period pieces as Busby Berkeley's "Remember the Forgotten Man" number in *Gold Diggers of 1933*.

After *West Side Story* was deluged with Academy Awards as the best movie of 1961, Murray Schumach reported in the *New York Times* that "there seemed to be general agreement that one reason" it won "was that its choreography, music, and direction were devoted to the serious theme of the brotherhood of man." A few weeks ago, in a talk with a Hollywood director, when I expressed surprise at the historical novel he had undertaken to film, he explained that the "idea" of the book appealed to him because it was really about "the brotherhood of man." I averted my eyes in embarrassment and hoped that my face wasn't breaking into a crooked grin. It's a great conversation closer — the "brotherhood of man." Some suggested new "serious" themes for big movies: the sisterhood of women, "no man is an island," the inevitability of death, the continuity of man and nature, "God Is All."

Sometimes, when I read film critics, I think I can do without brothers.

L'Avventura

In answer to the question, "What is the best film of 1961?"

It had begun to look as if only those with a fresh eye — working in poverty and inexperience and in underdeveloped countries, discovering the medium for themselves — could do anything new and important (like *The Apu Trilogy*). The future of movies seemed to lie with film makers who didn't know that it had all been done before. For those with great traditions behind them, the only field to explore seemed to be comedy — and "black" comedy at that — or, at least, works which suggest black comedy: *Eroica, Kagi, Breathless, The Cousins, Smiles of a Summer Night, The Seventh Seal.*

L'Avventura is, easily, the film of the year, because Antonioni, by making his movie about this very problem — depleted modern man — demonstrated that the possibilities for serious, cultivated, personal expression in the film medium were not yet exhausted. *L'Avventura* is a study of the human condition at the higher social and economic levels, a study of adjusted, compromising man — afflicted by short memory, thin remorse, easy betrayal. The characters are passive as if post-analytic, active only in trying to discharge their anxiety — sex is their sole means of contact and communication. Too shallow to be truly lonely, they are people trying to escape their boredom in each other and finding it there. They become reconciled to life only by resignation. Claudia, the only one capable of love, is defeated like the rest; her love turns to pity.

It's a barren view of life, but it's a *view*. Perhaps compassion is reserved for the lives of the poor: the corruption of innocence is tragic in *Shoeshine*; the intransigeance of defeated man is noble in *Umberto D.*; hope and gullibility are the saving grace of *Cabiria*. But modern artists cannot view themselves (or us) tragically: rightly or wrongly, we feel that we defeat ourselves — when were we innocent? when are we noble? how can we be "taken in"? Antonioni's subject, the fall (that is to say, the exposure) of rich, handsome, gifted man is treated accumulatively and analytically — an oblique, tangential view of love and society, a view not raised to the plane of despair. In its melancholy *L'Avventura* suggests Chekhov. Because it is subtle and ascetic, yet laborious in revealing its meanings, it suggests the Henry James who chewed more than he bit off. And perhaps because the characters use sex destructively as a momentary black-out, as a means of escaping self-awareness by humiliating someone else, it suggests D. H. Lawrence. Most of all, I think, it suggests the Virginia Woolf of *The Waves*: the mood of *L'Avventura* is "Disparate are we." Antonioni is an avowed Marxist — but from this film I think we can say that although he may believe in the socialist criticism of society, he has no faith in the socialist solution. When you think it over, probably more of us than would care to admit it feel the same way. A terrible calm hangs over everything in the movie; Antonioni's space is a kind of vacuum in which people are aimlessly moving — searchers and lost are all the same, disparate, without goals or joy.

For those who can take movies or leave them alone, *La Dolce Vita* is obviously the film of the year: audiences can enjoy its "vice" (the name they give their own fantasies when somebody else acts them out) and they can hold up their hands in horror (peeking through the fingers) at all that wicked decadence and all those orgies.

⁖⁖⁖⁖⁖⁖⁖

One, Two, Three

I try to reach for a simple, visual phrase that tells you what the picture is all about and evokes the essence of the story. — SAUL BASS

His design for *One, Two, Three* shows a cartoon of a girl holding up three balloon-breasts. Is he trying to tell us something about the picture? Is his come-on really a warning to stay away? Bass says, "A successful communication entices the viewer to participate. The minute you're in a position of getting him to pick up a shovel and hurl a spadeful in the pile, you're beginning to reach him."

Just about every reviewer of *One, Two, Three* has been "enticed" into shoveling it on. *One, Two, Three* has been almost universally praised: in *Show* Arthur Schlesinger, Jr., went so far as to call it an "irresistible evocation of the mood of Mark Twain. A couple of months ago, I lamented the disappearance of the uproariously funny film — the film which left one helpless, spent, and gasping for breath. My regrets were premature. *One, Two, Three* is such a film." And so forth. The critics have been picking up their shovels all right, but they're digging the grave of humor. As a member of the audience, I felt degraded and disgusted, as if the dirt were being hurled right in my face.

One, Two, Three is overwrought, tasteless, and offensive — a comedy that pulls out laughs the way a catheter draws urine. It is supposed to be a topical satire of East-West relations, and it was actually shot in Berlin and Munich (where the Brandenberg Gate was reconstructed), but the real location is the locker room where tired salesmen swap the latest variants of stale old jokes. A few examples and you can descend to the level of its rancid humor: When Arlene Francis, the wife of the Coca-Cola executive James Cagney, learns that the young Communist

Horst Buchholz doesn't wear any shorts, she says "Doesn't wear any shorts! No wonder they're winning the cold war!" Her little daughter, who has apparently inherited her mother's wit, explains that a girl is pregnant with the cute remark, "She's going to have puppies." People are described as sitting around on their "assets"; when Cagney is being bossy, Miss Francis addresses him as "My Fuehrer"; there is much humor about the SS background of various characters, and we are invited to laugh at the Russians for rejecting a shipment of Swiss cheese because it was full of holes. There is the by-now-to-be-expected female impersonation bit, with the man wearing balloons for boobies, so that the sequence can end with that weary old punch line, "I never saw one yellow one and one green one before." If you find these jokes fresh and funny, then by all means rush to see *One, Two, Three*, which will keep shouting them at you for two hours. It's like you-know-what hitting the fan.

Though I haven't seen anything but rave reviews for *One, Two, Three*, I think that, like Saul Bass, the reviewers give the show away by their tone, by the quality of the language they use in praising it. They, too, evoke "the essence of the story." Here, for example is *Time*:

> *One, Two, Three* is a yell-mell, hard-sell, Sennett-with-a-sound-track satire of iron curtains and color lines, of people's demockeracy, Coca-Colonization, peaceful noexistence, and the Deep Southern concept that all facilities are created separate but equal. What's more, Director Billy Wilder makes his attitude stick like *Schlagobers* slung in the spectator's kisser. He purposely neglects the high precision of hilarity that made *Some Like It Hot* a screwball classic and *The Apartment* a peerless comedy of officemanship. But in the rapid, brutal, whambam style of a man swatting flies with a pile driver, he has produced a sometimes beWildered, often wonderfully funny exercise in nonstop nuttiness. . . .

Surely it takes a very peculiar movie to drive *Time*'s reviewers to such a rat-tat-tatty prose. And, as examples of what is referred to as the "edge and temper" of Wilder's and I. A. L. Diamond's writing, *Time* quotes these remarks:

Cagney's wife (Arlene Francis): "But she can't stay long. Doesn't school open soon?" Cagney: "In Georgia? You never know." Cagney's ten-year-old son, hopefully, when the boss's daughter has a fainting spell: "If she dies can I have my room back?" First Communist, bitterly: "Is everybody in this world corrupt?" Second Communist, thoughtfully: "I don't know everybody."

There is a temptation to ascribe this last remark to a bit of self-awareness on the part of *Time*'s reviewer. It's almost inconceivable that he or they could write this way about a film they'd really enjoyed.

And here is Brendan Gill in the *New Yorker*:

The Messrs. Diamond and Wilder have had the gall to manufacture a hundred outrageous wisecracks about the desperate duel that Russia and the West are currently waging . . . the whole German people, as if in a trifling aside, are indicted as lickspittles or martinets, and we sit watching and roaring with delight. For this tour de force of fratricidal subversion we have to thank not only Mr. Cagney, who makes it shamefully attractive, but, again, Mr. Wilder, who produced and directed the picture, and who could no doubt wring a hearty yock from bubonic plague.

Exactly. And it's hard to believe that a man who uses a phrase about wringing "a hearty yock from bubonic plague" doesn't somehow know that that's not how one would ordinarily describe a good comedy. Brendan Gill says that it "all miraculously works" but it doesn't work — not even in his own enthusiastic description: "Mr. Wilder's not very secret formula is to keep 'em coming. Gag follows gag at breathtaking speed, and one ends by consenting to his highhanded methods as one consents to a roller coaster that is already clicking up the first fearful slope; what else is there to do?" What else is there to do! You can get sick. Gill says, "By the time the picture is over, we are exhausted, but what has caused our exhaustion is laughter, and few of us will object to paying such a price for that." I don't think it's laughter that causes our exhaustion; it's the coercive, frenzied, insulting crudity of it all, the assembly-line approach to gags. As Gill said, Diamond and Wilder "manufactured" the wisecracks. *Time* and the *New Yorker* are amazingly accurate in their descriptions; what's astonishing is that having described a very bad movie they then tell us how good it is.

In Hollywood it is now common to hear Billy Wilder called the world's greatest movie director. This judgment tells us a lot about Hollywood: Wilder hits his effects hard and sure; he's a clever, lively director whose work lacks feeling or passion or grace or beauty or elegance. His eye is on the dollar, or rather on success, on the entertainment values that bring in dollars. But he has never before, except perhaps in a different way in *Ace in the Hole*, exhibited such a brazen contempt for people. Is it possibly life in Hollywood that is so conducive to this extreme materialist position — a view of the world in which human experience is reduced to a need for sex and gadgets (with even sex turned into a gadget), a view in which people sell out their souls and their convictions for a pair of silk stockings, in which Americans, Russians, and Germans — all men — are brothers in petty corruption and lasciviousness? Hollywood may see itself as a microcosm of America, and may consider that its shoddy values are the American way of life that the rest of the world aspires to, but is this degraded view of political conflicts and human values really supposed to be funny? It would have to be relevant to something first. Surely satire must have some closer relationship to its targets than these cheap "topical" jokes which were dated decades before Berlin was divided. Is *One, Two, Three* really the irreverent political satire the critics have called it, or is it just a lot of scattershot and noise and simulated action — *Hellzapoppin'* in Berlin?

In *Eroica* in 1957 Andrzej Munk made a satire on a far more unlikely subject: the "heroic" 1944 Warsaw uprising. The black humor was in the disjunction between the humanity of the characters and the absurdity — the insane inhumanity — of the situation. Munk was tough and sardonic enough to laugh at sentimental myths about courage, about war, about prison camp life; he used comedy as a way of expressing and reacting to disillusionment, and the horror in his comedy shocks us into a new kind of clarity and vision.

Perhaps a diabolic satire *could* be written on the theme of Coca-Cola haves and have-nots, but Wilder's comedy isn't black and there are no disjunctions: his method is as mercenary as the characters. In the *New Republic*, Stanley Kauffmann, who thinks "the film has an over-all intelligent energy," says, "the picture is worth seeing just to watch Cagney . . . or to hear him say, 'the race that produced the Taj Mahal, William Shakespeare and striped toothpaste can't be all bad.' " Really? It's amazing how many critics can quote lines like that admiringly, and can sum up the movie with such boomerang compliments as "breakneck," "screwball," "hard-hitting," "relentlessly maintains the pace that refreshes." Dwight Macdonald, who picked *One, Two, Three* as one of his best films of the year, says, "The mood is established when Cagney complains that the East Germans are hijacking his shipments — 'and they don't even return the empties!' It's all like that. Wife (Arlene Francis is just right): 'Our marriage has gone flat, like a stale glass of beer!' Cagney: 'Why do you have to bring in a competing beverage?' " Yes, it's all like that. There is one nice touch — an old man singing "Yes, We Have No Bananas" in German, and there's also the dance of a behind on a table that's quite a "set piece." But even the portrait of Khrushchev slipping from its frame, revealing Stalin's picture beneath, was a reprise of a dimly remembered gag. And the three Commissars whom Wilder revived from his earlier script for *Ninotchka* have become coarsened with the years — another indication of the changing climate of Hollywood. They were grotesquely pathetic and sentimental in 1939; now they are even more grotesquely crude than the Cagney character. And buried beneath all this there is the almost unrecognizable corpse of a Molnar play.

This being the age of the big production and the big promotion, there is a tie-in with Coca-Cola which provides truck banners, supermarket ads, contests, and window displays. Who is laughing at whom? The target has been incorporated in the profits of the joke. Perhaps Wilder (who owns 90 per cent of the picture) is closer to his Coca-Colonizer than one might have expected. Is this dollar diplomacy?

I felt that we in the audience were all being manipulated in some shameful way, and that whenever this feeling might become conscious and begin to dry up the laughs, Wilder showed his manipulative skills by throwing in little sops to sentiment — even more ugly in their way than the "wisecracks." Arlene Francis has said of her role, "My character is a warm, sensible woman who has a good marriage." That's better satirical dialogue than anything I heard in *One, Two, Three* — a movie that shovels on the wit.

꩜꩜꩜꩜꩜꩜

The Mark

The advertising campaign for the Anglo-American production *The Mark* includes this statement:

SENSATIONALISM BE DAMNED . . . HERE'S THE TRUTH ABOUT "THE MARK." Because *The Mark* deals with themes that are, to say the least, touchy, we were a little reluctant to discuss it frankly. We were more than hesitant to tell the story in our advertisements for fear of being accused of "sensationalism." And so we thought in vague general terms about the picture and its high quality. Now, sensationalism be damned, we want to be truthful and fair to this very uncommon film. What's it about? In five words, it's about a victim of sexual deviation. You follow him through psychiatry, through group therapy, through his tenuous meetings with women — and finally the one woman who takes him across the threshold — into manhood. The words are blunt and dramatic. And they're words you don't have to be a psychiatrist to understand. At the expense of a blush, or even a moment's discomfort, why don't you make an appointment with *The Mark?* . .

In other words the advertising for the movie tries to do just what the movie has the good taste not to do: the advertising tries to work up prurient interest in the theme. But there is another peculiarity in the advertising — the term "a victim of sexual deviation." Now the problem of the hero of the film is that he was sexually driven to a ten-year old girl, which I think can fairly be classified as a sexual perversion. The term "deviation" suggests that it is about a homosexual — which would certainly have more box-office appeal.

This time the advertising campaign may, ironically, be more perceptive than the movie. I had the uncomfortable feeling during *The Mark* that somehow the film makers had gotten their case histories scrambled. Now it may be that the psychological background given the hero is based on the cases of those who attack little girls, but it wasn't very convincing, it didn't have the right ring. The family pattern of the suffocating, seductive monster-mother and the rejected, castrated father certainly suggested the development of a homosexual. And in that rather touchingly sweet scene in which the hero, having at last made it with a mature woman, wakes in the morning, and embraces her tenderly and in very masculine fashion, I was irresistibly reminded of a young man I once knew, a New York dancer, who talked to me late one night about how much analysis had done for him. He wasn't queer any more and he didn't need to feel humiliated and weak and afraid of people. He told me that after his first night with a woman, he'd awakened to the new day and the first thought that came to him was, "Now I don't have to be afraid to shake hands with people." Well, a week after this eulogy of heterosexuality, he was beaten up and robbed by a Negro he'd picked up.

The good taste of *The Mark* is what's pleasant about it; it's also what's the matter with it. When you're seeing it, you're carried along for the most part. It's intelligent and decent, it's generous toward the characters. It has all the virtues of a fine, sensible, humane thesis picture. Maybe it's as good as a movie is likely to be without any real imagination, or without taking any chances: it's made with intelligence rather than with art — but perhaps with not too high an order of intelligence. Could a movie that *really* dealt with a sex drive toward children be in such *un*offending good taste? In *The Mark* discretion is carried so far that there is nothing left to be discreet *about*. They have made the hero superficially plausible, and while we're watching it, it's convincing enough that he didn't actually consummate his attack on the child: he experienced a violent revulsion after abducting her, vomited and then took her safely home. But he felt he needed to be locked up: he made no defense at his trial and spent three years in prison. Yes, it's plausible, but maybe we're too ready to be convinced — because isn't it a lot more comfortable and easy to feel noble and generous and able to identify with a sex criminal who isn't really guilty of anything but confused intentions?

When you think it over, *The Mark* falls apart. You can't help wondering why the film makers have evaded the actual commission of a sex crime: would he somehow not be a suitable subject for a compassionate study if he *had actually* attacked the child? What the movie turns out to be about is a man who has expiated a crime he hasn't committed: in other words, he's morally one up on all of us, and still, he's being branded and mistreated by society. So many of these movies with what purport to be daring themes manage to dodge the issue. In a movie attack on capital punishment the man who is sentenced to death cannot be guilty; in race relations movies, the Negroes and Jews who are mistreated by sadists and bullies are men of such transcendent heroism that they are scarcely recognizable as human beings. We can only assume that if Jews or Negroes are shown as bad-tempered or nasty, or if the boy accused of homosexuality were really guilty of it, the movie would suggest that they should be in the hands of sadists and bullies. Suppose that instead of Stuart Whitman, the innocent white-collar hero of *The Mark*, we visualize Peter Lorre, the miserable, sweating, fat child-attacker of *M*, also desperate to be caught and knowing that he can't control himself — and, finally, when trapped, screaming that he can't help himself. Would the audience feel compassion if he, by some fluke, were turned over to a prison so enlightened it provided first-rate group therapy, and was then discharged — because *maybe* he could now control himself? I'd say audiences would have a hard time accepting him as a hero, and they might easily identify with that horrid, sensation-mongering newspaperman who makes a scandal when he sees the hero of *The Mark* playing with a child. Isn't it our knowledge all the way through, not only that he hasn't done anything but also that he no longer even wants to and that he certainly won't, that makes all the chit-chat about probabilities so easy to assent to? We can feel virtuous for being on his side and feel superior to the people who are suspicious of him simply because we are in on the lowdown: we know he is innocent. The movie tells us that we all have our dark impulses; but it really enables us to identify with our most progressive, commendable, enlightened social consciousness because it has taken the danger out of the dark side.

I must admit also that I got the uncomfortable feeling at times that we were supposed to feel sympathetic toward Whitman because he was such a pained, unhappy, dull man — dull despite his indicated intelligence and business skill. (That was quite a business, incidentally — I've never worked for one like that. "A public-relations firm" one reviewer called it — I couldn't tell what it was: I decided it was just a moviemaker's dream of the creative life in business.) But about Whitman's anxious expression — I had the feeling that had he showed a frivolous side, had he ever forgotten his problem or showed a desire for drink, or even a hobby, the concept of the film would have collapsed. Weren't we being asked to be sympathetic because of his desperate, single-minded anxiety rather than for his humanity (which might include some other traits of character, some irrelevancies that would give him *human* relevance)? One difference between *The Mark* and Dostoyevsky, between thesis and art, is that Dostoyevsky would have given the man so many other dimensions. This hero never forgets the crime he almost committed — it is the *only* focus of interest in him. He has no life as a character; he is a walking anxiety.

It's interesting to note that in *The Hustler*, the movie had tension and excitement at the billiard table and was diffuse and rhetorical away from it — in the love affair and other relationships. Here, in *The Mark*, the emotions that one would expect to go into the love affair go into the *analytic* sessions. The audience transfers all its affection to Rod Steiger's Brendan Behanlike analyst; in the only personally characterized of the roles, he is warm and lovable, and it is suggested that such human generosity is rather eccentric — he's a droll fellow.

I suspect the irony is unconscious that in this ever so discreetly Freudian view of things, the only person allowed any eccentricity, or behavior not directly concerned with the hero's problem, is the analyst. Are people only free to show some human feeling and spirit when they're post-analytic themselves — when they've been through the scientific fire and been tested? Is it only then that you can act like an old-fashioned human being — i.e., in the screenwriters' terms, a "character"? Or is it perhaps that the film makers have such a dogged devotion to analysis that they transfer all charm to the analyst? He can afford to have weaknesses and still be lovable. Unfortunately in their plot concept, he alone can afford to be human.

Even simple, intelligent films are becoming rare, and I enjoyed *The Mark*. But I wish that it hadn't so carefully plotted the human soul and then handed us the blueprint; I wish it had used insight to explore a character, instead of using the data of psychiatry to sketch one; I wish Stuart Whitman's head, particularly from the side and back, weren't so remarkably thick and ugly; I wish the director, Guy Green, had an eye for more than the obvious; I also wish the scriptwriters had not indulged in such symbolic touches as the broken dish, with the hero bending down to pick up the pieces of his shattered life. I wish, I wish it were a *really* good movie instead of just a commendable one.

Kagi

Among the good films ignored or ludicrously misinterpreted by the critics is, currently, the Japanese film *Kagi*, or *Odd Obsession*, a beautifully stylized and highly original piece of film making — perverse in the best sense of the word, and worked out with such finesse that each turn of the screw tightens the whole comic structure. As a treatment of sexual opportunism, it's a bit reminiscent of *Double Indemnity*, but it's infinitely more complex. The opening plunges us into the seat of the material. A young doctor, sensual and handsome, smug with sexual prowess, tells us that his patient, an aging man, is losing his virility. And the old man bends over and bares his buttocks — to take an injection. But the old man doesn't get enough charge from the injection, so he induces the young doctor, who is his daughter's suitor, to make love to his wife. By observing them, by artificially making himself jealous, the old man is able to raise his spirits a bit.

The comedy, of course, and a peculiar kind of black human comedy it is, is that the wife, superbly played by Machiko Kyo, is the traditional, obedient Japanese wife — and she cooperates in her husband's plan. She is so obedient and cooperative that, once aroused by the young doctor, she literally kills her old husband with kindness — she excites him to death. The ambiguities are malicious and ironic: the old man's death is both a perfect suicide and a perfect murder. And all four characters are observed so coldly, so dispassionately that each new evidence of corruption thickens the cream of the jest.

The title *Kagi* — the key — fits the Tanizaki novel, but does not fit the film, which might better be called the keyhole. Everybody is spying on everybody else, and although each conceals his motives and actions, nobody is fooled. The screen is *our* keyhole, and we are the voyeurs who can see them all peeking at each other. When the old man takes obscene pictures of his wife, he gives them to the young man to develop. The young man shows them to his fiancée, the daughter, whose reaction is that she can do anything her mother can do.

But a further layer of irony is that she *can't*. For the film is also a withering satire on the Westernized modern Japanese girl. The mother — mysterious, soft, subtle — uses her traditional obedience for her own purposes. She never says what she thinks about anything — when she starts a diary she puts down romantic hypocrisy worthy of a schoolgirl — and she is infinitely desirable. The daughter, a college student who explains what is going on quite explicitly, is just as corrupt as her mother, but has no interest or appeal to her parents or even to her fiancé. In her sweaters and skirts, and with her forthright speech, she is sexually available but completely unattractive. When she tells her father that nothing so simple as adultery is being practised by her mother and the young doctor, she seems simply ludicrous; her mother can lower her eyes and murmur distractedly about the terrible things she is asked to do — and excite any man to want to try out a few.

The director, Kon Ichikawa, is probably the most important new young Japanese director. His study of obsessive expiation, *The Burmese Harp*, was subjected to a brutal, hack editing job, and has reached only a small audience in this country; *Enjo* (1958), based on Mishima's novel about a great crime, the young Zen Buddhist burning the Golden Pavilion, has not yet played here. (An earlier film of Ichikawa's — a puppet version of a Kabuki dance — was destroyed by MacArthur's aides because, according to Japanese film historian Donald Richie, they regarded Kabuki as feudalistic. What did they think MacArthur was?)

Kagi, made in 1959, took a special prize at the Cannes Festival in 1960 (the other special prize went to *L'Avventura*). *Kagi* was given "Special commendation for 'audacity of its subject and its plastic qualities.' " I've indicated the audacity of the subject; let me say something about the film's plastic qualities. It is photographed in color, with dark blue tones predominating, and with an especially pale soft pinkish white for flesh tones. I don't think I've ever seen a movie that gave such a feeling of flesh. Machiko Kyo, with her soft, sloping shoulders, her rhythmic little paddling walk, is like some ancient erotic fantasy that is more suggestive than anything Hollywood has ever thought up. In what other movie does one see the delicate little hairs on a woman's legs? In what other movie is flesh itself not merely the surface of desire but totally erotic? By contrast, the daughter, like the exposed, sun-tanned healthy American girl, is an erotic joke — she is aware, liberated, passionate, and, as in our Hollywood movies, the man's only sexual objective is to get *into* her and have done with it. With Machiko Kyo the *outside* is also erotic substance.

Ichikawa's cold, objective camera observes the calculations and designs, the careful maneuvers in lives that are fundamentally driven and obsessive; and there's deadly humor in the contrast between what the characters pretend they're interested in and what they actually care about.

Kagi is conceived at a level of sophistication that accepts pornography as a fact of life which, like other facts of life, can be treated in art. The subject matter is pornography, but the movie is not pornographic. It's a polite, almost clinical comedy about moral and sexual corruption. It even satirizes the clinical aspects of sex. Modern medicine, with its injections, its pills, its rejuvenating drugs, adds to the macabre side of the comedy. For *Kagi* has nothing to do with love: the characters are concerned with erotic pleasure, and medicine is viewed as the means of prolonging the possibilities of this pleasure. So there is particular humor in having the doctors who have been hastening the old man's death with their hypodermics try to place the blame for his death on the chiropractor who has been working on his muscles. They have all known what they were doing, just as the four principals all know, and even the servant and the nurse. The film has an absurd ending that seems almost tacked on (it isn't in the book); if it ended with the three survivors sitting together, and with Machiko Kyo reading her diary aloud, it could be a perfect no-exit situation, and the movie would have no major defects or even weaknesses.

Reading the reviews, you'd think that no American movie critic had even so much as heard of that combination of increasing lust and diminishing potency which destroys the dignity of old age for almost all men; you'd think they never behaved like silly, dirty old men. Japanese films in modern settings have a hard time with the art-house audience: perhaps the Americans who make up the foreign-film audience are still too bomb-scarred to accept the fact that business goes on as usual in Japan. In *Kagi* the beds — where a good part of the action takes place — are Western-style beds, and when the people ply each other with liquor, it's not saki, it's Hennessy. *Kagi* is the first Japanese comedy that has even had a chance in the art houses: if the judgments of incompetent critics keep people from seeing it, when will we get another? Crowther finds the husband of *Kagi* "a strictly unwholesome type." Let's put it this way: if you've never gotten a bit weary of the classical Western sex position, and if you've never wanted to keep the light on during intercourse, then you probably won't enjoy *Kagi*. But if you caught your breath at the Lady Wakasa sequences in *Ugetsu*, if you gasped when Masayuki Mori looked at Machiko Kyo and cried out, "I never dreamed such pleasures existed!" then make haste for *Kagi*.

The Innocents

When you see *The Innocents*, you think how amazing that this crew of film makers could take such familiar material and make it so fresh. Then you read the reviews and discover that this material, far from being familiar to movie critics, is incom-

prehensible to them. They don't even *get* it. From Paine Knick-
erbocker in the San Francisco *Chronicle* you will discover that
The Innocents "is dominated by the idea that two children — a
brother and his sister — may be developing very unhealthy attitudes toward one another" and that it deals with "their incestu-
ous love for one another." (As a friend remarked, "Now we
know why Miles was sent down from school: that sinister business is all solved — he'd snuck his sister into the dormitory.")
If you read Bosley Crowther in the New York *Times*, you will
find a new enigma: the children ". . . are played with glibness
and social precocity, but it is difficult to grasp whether their man-
ners are actually adult or the figments of the governess' mind."
If you look at *Show Business Illustrated,* you may have this illu-
mination: "What unnatural, hypnotic hold have Quint and
Miss Jessel over the children? What was their relationship with
these otherworldly tots? Homosexuality has been one of the
favorite guesses among those who have had a go at the James
riddle." (Maybe . . . but not in relation to *The Turn of the
Screw!*) In the *Observer,* you will find Penelope Gilliatt, the
most erratically brilliant of modern film critics, at low ebb: "In
the book, the governess is vaguely attracted to the uncle who
hires her; Jack Clayton, born after Freud, shows that she's really
in love with one of the children. . . ." And in the *New Statesman,* John Coleman, stuffily rationalistic, says: "Perhaps the
children . . . are possessed; and, on these perhapses, intelligent
interest dissipates."

Don't let these new developments in Jamesian scholarship
keep you away from the movie — which is closer to Henry James
than you might think from the reviews. It's a movie with the
pleasures of elegance and literacy. The little girl's song by Paul
Dehn before the titles and then the hands with the titles are
marvelous; from the very first scene, we know these people
know what they're doing and we can relax. It's going to be all
right: there may be mistakes, but they won't be vulgar or stupid
mistakes. The presence of Michael Redgrave and Deborah Kerr
is wonderfully reassuring: when they speak, the nuances are all

there, and just the right note of suppressed hysteria in the voices. The house and the park are magnificent — so magnificent they're rather unreal (unreal in a way that's right for *The Turn of the Screw*). I don't know where this photographer Freddie Francis sprang from. You may recall that in the last year just about every time a British movie is something to look at, it turns out to be his (*Room at the Top, Sons and Lovers, Saturday Night and Sunday Morning* — in each case with a different director), and what he has done for *The Innocents* seems at times almost more inspired than the work of Jack Clayton, the director; Georges Auric, the composer; and William Archibald, Truman Capote, and John Mortimer, the scenarists. It's always difficult in a movie to judge who should get the credit, who the blame. In this case, it is simply a matter of trying to judge who should get the *most* credit.

Who, for example, thought of using those curiously frozen, indistinct long shots of Miss Jessel's ghost? We peer at these images with the governess's eyes, and we are transfixed by their beauty. They're like the memory of an old photograph; we retain a definite impression even though it's impossible to describe what was in it. And did we even see it or did we just hear about it and think we saw it? Or did we only see something like it?

And who thought of the marvelous shot of Deborah Kerr with her long hair floating as she kisses the boy, so that as her frightened lips draw back in confusion, we see the hairs hanging below her chin like the sparse beard of an old Chinese?

The Innocents is not a great movie, but it's a very good one, and maybe Deborah Kerr's performance should really be called great. The story isn't told quite clearly enough: the elegant setting and our story sense lead us to expect a stately plot line, but instead of moving in a clear developmental rhythm, the plot advances through sudden leaps, as if the film makers have concentrated on the virtuoso possibilities of the material. There is a beautiful montage sequence, exquisite in itself, but too long and elaborate to advance the story; what is even worse, the sequence comes too fast upon us; and the abrupt developments and some noisy, easy effects tend to disturb the pleasures of analyzing what is going on. Perhaps the problem is simply that, reading the novel, we can set the book down, smile and enjoy thinking it over, and then take it up again. Here we are rushed along without time for reflection.

It's probably the combination of a rather jerky rhythm in the film with our missing reader's pauses for reflection that slightly (but only slightly) interferes with our enjoyment of the possible interpretive levels of the material — the game the film makers and the original author play, of suggesting that the apparitions the governess sees may have some horribly unspecified kind of control over the children, or may be evidence of the intensifying monomania of the governess who has terrifyingly absolute power over them. The fun of it all is the deliberate mystification — represented in the film by the tear that the ghost of Miss Jessel drops. All else can be more or less comprised within the system of the repressed governess's madness; but not that little wet tear, that little pearl of ambiguity.

People love to be scared by ghost stories; James intensifies this pleasure by allowing us to scare ourselves — we perceive the ghosts in terms of what most frightens us. What is really beautiful about *The Innocents* is that almost everything is at the right *distance*. The children are so impersonal that we are not anxious about them: their fates are never quite real. It is all a game of a ghost story: we know that in this cultivated domain the ghosts wouldn't dream of doing anything so vulgar as themselves impinging on the action. James was a man of taste, and the film makers, even when they fail as artists, remain gentlemen: the movie may not be up to James, but it doesn't violate his code. Whatever happens in *The Innocents* happens because of fear. And the fascination in this kind of ghost story is that the horrors cannot be resolved.

It is the unreality of *The Innocents* — the distance — which makes the whole concept work. The further away the ghosts are, the more truly ghostly. Close scenes, like the dialogues between the governess and the housekeeper (which have the all-too-care-

fully-placed middle-class sounds of radio — they go at each other
with all the conspiratorial finesse of veterans of *John's Other
Wife*), even the close scenes between the governess and the
children — are too familiar. We listen attentively to the arch
patterns in the speech, the loaded remarks, and we assent: yes,
they're really getting it — the overtones, the suggestions are
good, they're excitingly well done. But the *mystery* — that comes
when the camera pulls away and we half-see something in the
distance, or it comes when Miles recites a poem that seems so
remote and strange for a child to recite that our perspectives on
age and understanding become blurred and confused. The landscape with the ghost of Miss Jessel — was it perhaps after all not
a photograph we remember, but the work of some painter
whose name we can't recall, though we seem to remember something else by him so much like this landscape, or is it all just a
mirage from the summer heat? This Miss Jessel is not merely
the best ghost I've ever seen, she is the only one who has the
qualities I associate with ghostliness — that is to say, not only
the governess but *we, the audience*, think we have seen her before. (Quint is less successful: it's understandable that he should
be conceived more physically as a sexual, almost animal force,
but he looms up as the familiar bestial menacing type out of horror films. His first appearance on the bell tower is by far the
best: there, dim and indistinct, he puzzles us. We're sure we saw
something but we can't describe what.)

The dialogue has, at times, the same beauty and ambiguity as
the images. I assume that Truman Capote, who is one of the
finest prose stylists — as distinguished from writers — this country has ever produced, is responsible for some of these phrases.
And the boy who plays Miles, a child named Martin Stephens,
is superb, not only visually, but in his poised and delicate enun-
ciation of lines that are so beautiful they communicate a sense
of the terror latent in such beauty. He is a true creature of
Henry James — the writer with his children who are too beautiful to live. This beauty is what makes *The Innocents* the best
ghost movie I've ever seen: the beauty raises our terror to a

higher plane than the simple fears of most ghost stories. It is the great virtue of the men who made this movie that they perceive the qualities of the Jamesian method: we are not simply being tricked, we are carried to a level where trickery — that is to say, master craftsmanship — is art.

I don't know why so many of the critics have been so remarkably unenthusiastic about *The Innocents*. Stanley Kauffmann wrote in the *New Republic*, "In his famous essay *The Ambiguity of Henry James*, Edmund Wilson advanced the possibility that the story is a sexual allegory, the ghosts being figments imagined by the repressed governess. If this is the case, it is doubly Freudian because James created the allegory unconsciously." Henry James, the most *conscious* craftsman in American literature, writing an *unconscious allegory!* "Now we are engaged in a small civil war, testing whether that notion can long endure. . . . The film will not settle this controversy, but it does settle that there is only one way in which James' story can be well dramatized: not for stage or television or screen but as a radio play. This is for two reasons. The ghosts are much less effective when seen than when described; and a radio play can confine itself to the highlights, as James does."

I don't think that anybody who tries to put a great work of literature on the screen stands much of a chance of reproducing its *greatness* in another medium and probably much of its richness will be lost, but there is an irresistible and certainly not-to-be-condemned desire to visualize works we love. It is perhaps testimony to the love of literature that we want to cast a beautiful actress as Eustacia Vye or Dorothea Brooke, that we can't help conceiving a film version of *The Confidence Man*. We may squirm when we see the work we love on the screen but surely we must recognize that someone else has been carried away by *his* love. And in the case of *The Innocents*, we don't have to squirm: *The Turn of the Screw* was not *that* great, and this is no simplification or vulgarization. It is an interpretation of a literary work that honors its sources, just as Olivier in taking

Shakespeare from the stage to the screen shows his love for both Shakespeare and for the new medium.

One can understand, if not be very sympathetic toward, the purist monotony that Shakespeare is for the stage, Henry James for the printed page. (Suggested parlor game: try to think of five good movies *not* adapted or derived from any other medium.) But Kauffmann's suggestion that radio is the only possible medium is positively freakish.

Brendan Gill dismisses the movie for the *New Yorker* audience with a paragraph — "the story," he informs us, "isn't intrinsically pictorial." Well, I'm not sure just what story *is* intrinsically pictorial; nor am I convinced that the motion picture is just a pictorial medium. The story is a suspense story; and there is a fairly solid tradition by now that the movies are pretty good at handling suspense. And if we think of a story that seems to be pictorial, like say, *The Return of the Native*, does that necessarily mean its pictorial qualities would be easy to transfer to the screen? Possibly a film version, by substituting its own pictorial qualities, would wreck Hardy far more than it can endanger a melodramatist like James, whose dialogue and method are so highly dramatic. Surely it all depends on who does it, and how.

Time magazine, in a semi-complimentary review of the film, raises what I guess can fairly be called theological objections. If I were religious I think I would cry blasphemy and sacrilege at the way *Time* rams God and Satan into its movie reviews.

Henry James once deplored *The Turn of the Screw* as a shameless potboiler. There is irony in the confession. For in this little novel the creative flame that boils the pot rushed up from black abysses of religion seldom plumbed in this author's insuperably civil art. Though the book is known to schoolboys [what schoolboys?] merely as a grand ghost story, it is experienced by mature readers as a demonological document of shuddery profundity. [Mature readers are evidently those who can make hell-fire with only *Time* to burn.] Some of that profundity is sacrificed to saleability in this film . . .

and so forth. I am afraid these "black abysses of religion" are just a big hole *Time* is digging, filling it in with every important picture no matter what its culture or tradition — thus the Japanese film *Ikiru* becomes "the Calvary of a common man" and *The Five-Day Lover* becomes, of all things, a study of religious "desperation."

Time, having discovered these black abysses, next suggests that the film makers don't understand the nature of evil and horror in Henry James:

The film is seriously flawed by a fundamental misconception that arises from a fundamental disagreement among students of the novel. Some say the ghosts are irreally real; others say they are hysterical fantasies developed by the governess, who has repressed a passion for her employer. . . . But the men who wrote this picture, Truman Capote and Playwright Archibald, unhappily press hard, much harder than James did, for the psychiatric interpretation. They have obviously failed to perceive that in suggesting a normal, everyday basis for the ghastly phenomena, they must inevitably relieve the spectator of his nameless horror of what happens.

The movie (and James) do not suggest a "normal everyday basis" for the ghastly phenomena: they suggest that ghastly phenomena may be hidden in the normal everyday — for there is nothing *more* frightening than evil and horror *there*. And it is this level, this possibility in the novel that makes it, like other James works, so fascinating to the modern reader. It is the evil in the governess's singlemindedness, her insistence, her determination; it is the destructive power of *her* innocence that makes the story great. I don't see why *Time* and so many of the other reviews call this a "psychiatric interpretation" as if it were a new-fangled modern way to read James — invented presumably by Edmund Wilson. Pick up almost any story by James — *Portrait of a Lady* or *Madame de Mauves* — and you find yourself caught up in the destructive elements in virtue, and you are frequently told the story by a narrator whose interpretation of the material is, precisely, an exposure of himself. You read

James because of the intellectual pleasure of speculating about what is really going on. *The Turn of the Screw* is not any different in method: what made it a "potboiler" in James's terms was simply the use of spooks rather than the more conventional "influences" of his other work — the heiresses and villains and social climbers who try to possess your soul, marry you for money, or drain your energy. However you interpret either *The Turn of the Screw* or *The Innocents*, the theme is the abiding Jamesian theme: the corruption of innocence. And the trickery is Jamesian — not letting you be sure whether the children are innocents who are corrupted by the servants who once had control over them, or whether they are destroyed by the innocent who now controls them (in her idealism, she may expect children to be so innocent that she regards actual children as corrupt).

The evidence that the screenwriters *haven't* slanted it is that the critics who complain of slanting are all complaining of different slants. Some of the reviewers have made a good deal of fuss about the supposedly "Freudian" perspective or slant imposed on the material by having the child Miles kiss the governess on the mouth — I don't see how this slants the material in any direction. I once worked as a governess for six weeks and I've never been so mauled in my life: the ten-year old would trap me in corners demanding kisses. Does this prove that the child was corrupt or possessed by an adult spirit, or that I, who got almost as nervous about it as the governess in *The Innocents*, was hysterical? Both interpretations are possible.

Unless *Time* is suggesting that every housewife keeps a set of hallucinations next to the mixmaster, I don't see how the spectator is relieved of his horror by the possibility that the source of evil is in the governess's tortured Puritan mind. That kind of evil is not what is usually meant by "normal everyday." For whether the children see the ghosts or not, the governess certainly *does* see them, and her forcing Miles to confront the ghost kills him. Is there really more horror in this confrontation if Miles actually sees a ghost than if he dies from fear of *her*?

A good strong, determined woman, so tortured by fears and visions that all her passion goes into making others look her fear in the face, is about as complexly dreadful a demon as any horror story can encompass.

Deborah Kerr's performance is in the grand manner — as modulated and controlled, and yet as flamboyant, as almost anything you'll see on the stage. And it's a tribute to Miss Kerr's beauty and dramatic powers that, after twenty years in the movies — years of constant overexposure — she is more exciting than ever. Perhaps she *is* a demon.

As for the reviewers who have kept people away from the movie — perhaps the title includes them?

A View from the Bridge, and a Note on *The Children's Hour*

I wouldn't have thought A *View from the Bridge* was worth much discussion, but it has gotten such very-important-picture treatment from the press (including Dwight Macdonald!) that I think maybe I should say a few unkind words. A *View from the Bridge* is an attempt to make a neo-realist Greek tragedy about a longshoreman in Brooklyn. Eddie Carbone (Raf Vallone) neglects his wife (Maureen Stapleton) because he's in love — although he doesn't know it — with his wife's eighteen-year-old niece. He helps two of his wife's cousins enter the country illegally, but when one of them (Jean Sorel) makes love to the niece, he accuses him of being homosexual, and then betrays both men to the immigration department.

The audience — what there is of it — often brings a special cachet of good will toward these slum-set or — to judge by appearances — proletarian dramas. It is supposed to be a more important effort than, say, a story of incest in a middle-class family, and the audience — which, for a film like this, tends to be a liberal, educated audience — respects the *good will* of the author and those involved in the project. The converse is that the critic who says "But it isn't any good!" is regarded as a snob who doesn't care about the best interests of the proletarians — and certainly a snob toward the honest, hardworking movie-makers who *do* care.

Miller's intention is to create tragedy: but what we see is a man behaving so insanely and stupidly that we keep wondering why he isn't put away or treated. We keep wondering why his wife doesn't have him locked up or why the lawyer — played by Morris Carnovsky in his full rich tones of pear-shaped passion (he seems to be playing Arthur Miller as an old man) — doesn't send him to a doctor? They all just wait for the disaster; we can only assume they don't want to disturb the tragic inevitability.

We get the feeling of inevitability simply because we see the mechanics of what Miller is trying to do, and we get the feeling of tragedy simply because the atmosphere is so obviously ominous we know it's all going to end badly. We all know what Miller is trying to do: he seems incapable of keeping a secret. It's not so much a drama unfolding as a sentence that's been passed on the audience. What looks like and, for some people, passes for tragic inevitability is just poor playwriting.

We begin to wonder why we're being put through all this when nothing good can come of it — no poetry, no deepening awareness. The problem is right at the center of Miller's concep-tion: in some peculiarly muddled democratic way he is trying to make a tragic hero out of a common man. But a hero cannot be a common man: he must have greater aspirations, ambitions, drives, or dreams than other men. What does Eddie Carbone *want*? He wants his wife's niece. According to the press sheets on the film, he is "a man blindly obsessed with an unnatural passion for his wife's niece." Well, what's so unnatural about it? You'll note that even the incest theme is fake — the girl is his *wife's* niece. When you think of the number of uncles who make passes at their own nieces, you begin to see how absurd this "unnatural passion" theme is. Presumably the norm for

Eddie — what would be "natural" — would be that after twenty years he should still be physically attracted only to his wife. Well, the wife we see is Maureen Stapleton in a wrapper, biting her lips like a rabbit working on a carrot — carrying naturalism to those extremes of Actor's Studio perfection in which the people on stage and screen seem not only like the people next door but like the people next door when they're discussing crabgrass or the lack of rainfall. A man would have to be blindly obsessed to want her at all. When, behaving like Arthur Miller's official view of a good normal wife, she asks her husband why he doesn't want to go to bed with her, you fairly want to cry out for him — "Because you're so damned unattractive." You will notice that dramatists who write about proletarian characters often have this view of a good normal healthy marriage in which a man is supposed to have a good normal healthy desire for even his fat dull wife. There's something peculiarly condescending and sanctimonious about this view of the common man: he's supposed to be happy and settled and content with so much less than a more complex or uncommon man asks of life. The play is written in the old sentimental proletarian tradition in which the working man is good and monogamous and the rich are corrupt and lascivious; Miller has much in common with Wilde's Algernon Moncrieff: "Really, if the lower orders don't set us a good example, what on earth is the use of them?"

A *View from the Bridge* has a couple of good performances — Raf Vallone is a powerful, commanding presence, and he's a marvelous image (a sort of urban man with a hoe) and Raymond Pellegrin is very good. The movie, despite the little preview trailer with Lumet and Miller, which suggested almost a documentary approach to Brooklyn, was made in France in two versions — French and English. As Stanley Kauffmann pointed out, Vallone's English, enunciated with difficulty, is completely wrong for the role of Eddie: Arthur Miller specializes in a kind of colloquial speech which sounds ridiculous on the tongue of a man who is obviously struggling to pronounce a foreign language. Perhaps the idioms are so familiar, Miller thinks they're universal.

There is, in the structure of the work, an even more serious error. Eddie, in order to discredit the niece's suitor, accuses him of being homosexual, and at one point, in order to degrade the boy in the niece's eyes, kisses him. The accusation is supposed to be without foundation: the boy is supposed to be completely straight. Why, then, this particular accusation? The charge is specious and irrelevant unless Eddie has some suppressed homosexual drive which makes him accuse others. Where does the charge come from if not from the character of one or the other? (As Eddie keeps saying, "something isn't right.") In having both accused and accuser innocent, Miller is left with a loose motive that has no relationship to anybody's character: it doesn't belong in the play at all. And the kiss — which would have a kind of dramatic horror if Eddie was attempting to degrade the boy by revealing what he himself experienced as degradation — *has* no meaning: it's just embarrassing. It has its irony, however: after all these years of tabus, we finally get two men kissing on the screen and neither of them is even supposed to be enjoying it. You'd think there were no homosexuals in America, only heterosexuals falsely accused. (If I may indulge in a little game of psychologizing, I would say that, given the character of Eddie as a man unconsciously in love with his niece, he would probably be delighted if he thought the boy was homosexual, because he would then have no real competition for the girl.)

Those are my unkind words on A *View from the Bridge,* except to add that Sidney Lumet doesn't do a very good job of direction, and that, in particular, his handling of the crowd in the street toward the end of the film is oppressively clumsy.

Miller seems to want to love his worker stereotypes; Lillian Hellman hates her upperclass stereotypes. William Wyler's production of *The Children's Hour* is such a portentous, lugubrious dirge (that seems to be part of the funeral of Hollywood moviemaking) that I developed a rather perverse sympathy for the rich old lady villainess — I thought the schoolteachers treated her abominably. Where I come from, if somebody, particularly an older person, says, "I've been wrong, I'm sorry, what can I do to make amends?" you take the hand they hold out to you. I've never understood Lillian Hellmanland, where rich people are never forgiven for their errors. But then, has Miss Hellman even recognized hers? I can't help thinking she wouldn't waste any sympathy on sexual deviation among the rich. Aren't we supposed to feel sorry for these girls because they're so hard-working, and because, after all, they don't *do* anything — the lesbianism is all in the mind (I always thought this was why lesbians needed sympathy — that there isn't much they *can* do).

There has been some commiseration with Wyler about the studio hacking out the center of the film: that's a bit like complaining that a corpse has had a vital organ removed. Who cares? I'm not sure the material of *The Children's Hour* would work even if you camped it up and played it for laughs; I don't know what else you could do with it.

ꙮꙮꙮ

The Day the Earth Caught Fire

I mentioned on the last broadcast that I had been disappointed in *The Day the Earth Caught Fire*, and that I would discuss it on this broadcast, and I received an extraordinary communication from a man who says he would "like to dissuade me" from an unfavorable review. He cautions me that I should not apply the same standards to science fiction that I would to *The Seventh Seal* or *L'Avventura* — and I can only assure him that I had not *intended* to. I have read his communication carefully and I cannot disagree that *The Day the Earth Caught Fire* attempts to accomplish a worthy purpose. I hope that he — and you — will not think I am anxious for nuclear war or avid to see the world go off its axis if I say that, worthy purpose or no, *The Day the Earth Caught Fire* is not a very good movie. And perhaps I can make this a little stronger by saying that precisely because its avowed aims are so high, it should be a better movie: artists who want to save the world should not make the world seem so banal. It rather takes the gloss off things, don't you think?

In bookstores you can buy a paperback of *The Day the Earth Caught Fire* and on the jacket you'll see the blurb: "The book of the movie that the *Saturday Review* calls even greater than *On the Beach*." This is the kind of greatness, isn't it, that dwarfs our poor powers of speech or analysis? It is the greatness not of art but of calamity. The film is, I suppose, better than *On the Beach*, but I shall always be grateful to Stanley Kramer for either intentionally or unintentionally including that beautiful moment when Gregory Peck, after spurning Ava Gardner's advances, returns to find her in a wheat field, and asks, "Is your invitation to spread a little fertilizer still open?"

After seeing *The Day the Earth Caught Fire* I was so puzzled by the ecstatic reviews that I did a bit of research. There had to be some reason why Arthur Schlesinger, Jr., wrote a think piece with such glowing embers as, "Life today is filled with tragic choices" (one of them was his decision to become a film reviewer), and why this film was being treated so seriously. As science fiction it isn't nearly so amusing as, say, *The Time Machine*, and as drama it doesn't exist. I think I found a partial answer in *Variety*:

PITCH TO INTELLECTUALS & WORRYERS FOR
U'S USA-USSR EXPLOSION PIC

A sort of nuclear question hangs over Universal — how to sell the public (domestic market) on a downbeat picture dealing with the No. 1 issue of the day?

Film is the British "Day the Earth Caught Fire," which cost U $350,000 for western hemisphere rights. Yarn depicts Soviet-U.S. simultaneous test explosions at either pole which get the planet off its axis and out of its orbit, headed for the sun and extinction. The horror is left unresolved at fadeout.

Anxiety in the U echelons is not whether the pic can turn a nice profit — they're convinced it can, obviously — but the shrewdest policy for tapping revenue. As a first step toward solution, but as part of the total effort in any case, the distrib is wooing the so-called opinion-makers per one of the most intensive pre-release screening schedules ever to engage a major company. Slated over a nine-week period, the showings are being aimed almost exclusively for the intelligentsia — scientists, diplomats, religionists, labor leaders, and such.

Pic has already been screened for such groups as the National Press Club, Committee for a Sane Nuclear Policy, National Conference of Christians and Jews, National Lawyers' Guild, United World Federalists, Synagogue Council of America, and American Assn. for the United Nations.

Variety subsequently reported that Universal had spent more than twice the purchase price of the film on the promotion, and that the schedule of preview screenings had set a new high record for the company. I think the intellectuals — the opinion makers — were wooed and flattered and won. And I guess Universal is getting more than its money back. As science fiction the film is really a bit of a cheat, for it employs stock disaster footage — subtly but completely wrong for the final catastrophe: we expect something more mind shattering than familiar newsreel horrors of fire and flood and famine.

I don't think there's really too much more to say about this film, though at least it disposes of the myth of city-room wit. We view the disasters through the eyes and imaginations of the newspapermen of the London *Daily Express*, and what should be black graveyard humor among the newspapermen is just tattletale gray. So many newspaper critics have applauded the veracity of this picture of newspaper life that I suppose they couldn't rise any higher to the occasion. One trouble with the film is that the film makers, who want to do good, portray average men because they think that will help us identify with them. But as protagonists, average — which comes to mean stereotyped — men are so limited and unimaginative that when

we react on their commonplace level, even the end of the world
is a dud.

The Come-Dressed-As-the-Sick-Soul-of-Europe Parties

La Notte, Last Year at Marienbad, La Dolce Vita

La Notte and *Marienbad* are moving in a new filmic direction: they are so introverted, so interior that I think the question
must be asked, is there something new and deep in them, or
are they simply empty? When they are called abstract, is that
just a fancy term for empty? *La Notte* is supposed to be a study
in the failure of communication, but what new perceptions of
this problem do we get by watching people on the screen who
can't communicate if we are never given any insight into what
they would have to say if they *could* talk to each other?

For the past year on the radio I had tried to persuade, goad,
and even shame people into seeing *L'Avventura*, which I think
is a great film. Then *La Notte* opened in San Francisco and people were phoning and writing to tell me how marvelous it was
and to thank me for opening the world of Antonioni to them.
They hadn't much liked *L'Avventura*, but they loved *La Notte*
and felt that *now* they understood why I had been so excited
about Antonioni. And I dislike *La Notte*. Perhaps detest is the
better word.

Antonioni is a master of the medium — but in a highly individualistic and peculiar way. He has none of the conventional
director's tricks of the trade, perhaps not even the ordinary
syntax, and he is painfully inept and obvious when he has to fall
back on a simple action sequence (like the street fight in *La
Notte*). But he doesn't often need this kind of simple expertise

because he doesn't tell conventional stories. He uses a seemingly random, peripheral course of development, apparently merely following the characters through inconsistencies and inadvertences; and without all the usual plot cues and paraphernalia, we can be far more interested in following him. We go into byways, we don't stay on the U.S. 40 of most American plots. In *L'Avventura*, and in *La Notte*, Antonioni's camerawork is an extraordinarily evocative mixture of asceticism, lyricism and a sense of desolation. He is a master of space; he can take bleak landscapes and compose or transform them into visions of elegance and beauty. The people are rich but the atmosphere is cold: it is upper-class neorealism — the poetry of moral and spiritual poverty. But in *La Notte*, the architectural sense, integral to the theme and characters of *L'Avventura*, begins to dominate the characters, and as the abstract elements take over, the spacial becomes glacial: drama and character and even narrative sense are frozen.

During *La Notte*, a woman sitting in back of me kept explaining the movie to her husband. She had obviously come to the wrong sort of "art" film, and she was trying to give a conventional narrative interpretation of the story. Determined not to admit that she had led him to the theater by mistake, she was soon reduced to a desperate admiration of the scenery and clothes. But then something came on the screen that she could exclaim over with delight and full approval — it was the performance of the Negro girl contortionist in the nightclub scene, which, like the bitch-elegant Negro performers in Fellini's films, was, of course, introduced to show the decadence and boredom of the beholders. There was nothing else in the movie the female Babbitt in back of me could enjoy and she gave up.

Most of the audience seemed to accept Antonioni's terms. But I wonder if perhaps Americans don't accept the all-passion-is-spent bit in a special way that relates to the failure of his method and something distasteful and offensive in his whole conception. There is a glamour that his characters seem to find in their own desolation and emptiness, and I think to an American art-house audience this glamorous world-weariness looks very elegant indeed. How exquisitely bored and decadent are the Antonioni figures, moving through their spiritual wasteland, how fashionable is their despair.

The images are emptied of meaning. Marcello Mastroianni is used as a handsome, mindless mask, the actor as mature juvenile, the experienced, tired, fortyish man of all these films (he is also the hero of *La Dolce Vita*, and the hero of *Marienbad* is just like him). The intellectual gifts attributed to Mastroianni in *La Notte* are not so much unconvincing, unproved, as totally alien. His face fails to show the ravages of an artist's mind.

And there is the repeated view of Jeanne Moreau walking away from the camera. Jeanne Moreau is a brilliant film actress and her face is a marvel of sullen boredom that can suddenly be brought to life by a smile, even a forced, meaningless reflex of a smile; but what are we to make of this camera fixation on her rear? In *Marienbad* I had laughed at the views of Delphine Seyrig's elegant backside, with its delicate Swiss-watch movements, the walk that was so absurdly high-toned that I took it, rightly or wrongly, for parody, but in *La Notte*, obviously we are supposed to be interested in Jeanne Moreau's thoughts and feelings while we look at her from the back, walking around the city. What kind of moviemaking, what kind of drama is this? Is the delicate movement of the derrière supposed to reveal her Angst, or merely her ennui? Are we to try to interpret the movement of her rear, or are we to try to interpret the spacial and atmospheric qualities of the city streets — and the only kind of interpretation we can draw from the settings is, for example, that the impersonal modern glass city reflects the impersonal life of modern man, that city people have lost their roots in the earth and all that sort of thing. It isn't much, is it?

In *La Notte* we see people for whom life has lost all meaning, but we are given no insight into why. They're so damned inert about their situation that I wind up wanting to throw stones at people who live in glass houses. At a performance of Chekhov's *Three Sisters*, only a boob asks, "Well, why don't they go to

Moscow?" We can *see* why they don't. Chekhov showed us why these particular women didn't do what they said they longed to do. But in movies like *La Notte* or *Marienbad*, or, to some degree, *La Dolce Vita* the men and women are not illuminated or ridiculed — they are set in an atmosphere from which the possibilities of joy, satisfaction, and even simple pleasures are eliminated. The mood of the protagonists, if we can call them that, is lassitude; there is almost no conflict, only a bit of struggling — perhaps squirming is more accurate — amid the unvoiced acceptance of defeat. They are the post-analytic set — they have done everything, they have *been* to Moscow and everywhere else, and it's all dust and ashes: they are beyond hope or conviction or dedication. It's easy enough to say "They are alienated; therefore, they exist," but unless we know what they are alienated from, their alienation is meaningless — an empty pose. And that is just what alienation is in these films — an empty pose; the figures are cardboard intellectuals — the middle-class view of sterile artists. Steiner's party from *La Dolce Vita* is still going on in *La Notte*, just as the gathering of bored aristocrats in *La Dolce Vita* is still going on in *Marienbad*.

The characters in this group of films seem pawns or puppets rather than characters (this, of course, is carried to the extreme in *Marienbad* of deliberately treating them as pawns). They have very little personality or individuality; they have no convincing existence. Mastroianni in *La Notte* is supposed to be a talented and famous writer, but would he behave any differently in the course of the film if he were a hairdresser, or the advertising manager of an airline, or a movie star? But then how can we accept him as a writer? A writer, we assume, is involved in the life around him; he interprets and helps to transform his experience; he has needed will as well as talent to develop his individuality and to fight conformity and insensitivity. When we are told that the hero of *La Notte* is a writer, he automatically acquires an importance, an almost symbolic status that his character in no way justifies.

And here, perhaps, we begin to get at something centrally

wrong in this group of films. *La Dolce Vita, La Notte,* and *Marienbad* are all about people who are bored, successful and rich — international café society — but in at least two of them we are told they are *artists,* and because we know that artists embody and express their age, its soul and its temper, we are led to believe that these silly manikins represent the soul-sickness, the failure of communication, the moral isolation of modern man.

Fellini and Antonioni ask us to share their moral disgust at the life they show us — as if they were illuminating *our* lives, but are they? Nothing seems more self-indulgent and shallow than the dissatisfaction of the enervated rich; nothing is easier to attack or expose. The decadence of aristocracy and its attraction to and for Bohemia, are nothing new, not especially characteristic of our age, nor even much of a social problem. Unless we can recognize this barren way of life in ourselves, then all we are being asked to do is stare in horror at the decadent upper classes — a pastime as shallow as their own. They show us people walking in a dream, dead without even putting up a fight for life; it's as if there were nothing to fight for, as if no *new* experiences were possible. In *La Notte* the wife goes back to where she and her husband *used* to go, reads him a letter to remind him how he *used* to *feel.* Like the nagging hypochondriacs who enjoy poor health, she has nothing to do but savor the dregs of old experiences as she wanders aimlessly in her melancholy. Well, what has defeated them all? I don't want to sound like a Doris Day character — the All-American middle-aged girl — but when I put the coffee on in the morning and let the dogs out, I don't think I feel more alienated than people who did the same things a hundred years ago.

I have heard that at the graduate-school level Antonioni's endings are said to be very beautiful, even inspiring, that the "shared hopelessness" indicates that modern human experience need not be altogether downhill, that you must make the best of a bad world, and that there is nobility and beauty in resigning yourself to the futility of life. Surely this is the last gasp of de-

pleted academia. In *La Notte* Antonioni has intentionally created a ghastly spectacle: two people sharing an empty life. The
problem of interpretation is simply whether we can accept the
meanings and overtones with which he surrounds this dead marriage; is it so central and so symbolic that all these ornaments
and icicles can be hung from it?

I reject the terms of the film on commonplace grounds: why
the devil do they stay together, why doesn't she leave him if this
is how she feels? What has made this a world in which there are
no alternatives, no hope? And what is so shocking about a married couple, after ten years or so, no longer being in love or having anything to say to each other? What is so dreadful about
their looking for other people to whom they can feel some response? Why are they shown as so withered away, destroyed,
dead because they are weary of each other? And if they have no
other interests, why should we care about them?

And isn't it rather adolescent to treat the failure of love with
such solemnity? For whom does love last? Why try to make so
much spiritual desolation out of the transient nature of what we
all know to be transient, as if this transiency somehow defined
our time and place? If it is the sickness of our time that married
people get fed-up with each other, when was the world healthy?
I thought it was the health of our culture that when married
people have had it, they are free and sufficiently independent to
separate. (Perhaps the marriage in *La Notte* just lasted too long:
I don't know anybody who has stayed married for ten years —
nobody except relatives.) Surely there are some institutions, like
magazines, to which we must apply criteria other than dura-
bility: we do not, for example, call Dwight Macdonald's *politics*
a failure because it ceased publication or the *Saturday Review of
Literature* a success because it is interminable.

The symbol of the end of the world and the failure of human
relations is a big dull party in both *La Notte* and *La Dolce Vita*.
But I don't understand how these film artists can think they are
analyzing or demonstrating their own — that is to say, *our* own,
emptiness by showing the rich failing to enjoy a big party.

Whose experience are they expressing — or is the party just an easy photogenic symbol of modern life that is being loaded with meanings it can't carry?

I suspect many Americans are attracted by this view of fabulous parties, jaded people, baroque palaces; to an American who works damned hard, old-world decadence doesn't look so bad — all those desperately unhappy beautiful people, surrounded by champagne, lobster, dance orchestras, and a wide selection of gorgeously dressed sex partners to be had for the lifting of an eyebrow. Forgive me if I sound plaintive: I've never been to one of these dreadfully decadent big parties (the people I know are more likely to give bring-your-own-bottle parties). And isn't it likely that these directors, disgusted though they may be, also love the spectacle of wealth and idleness, or why do they concentrate on these so empty and desiccated rich types? If the malaise is general, why single out the rich for condemnation? If the malaise affects only the rich, is it so very important? As usual, there is a false note in the moralist's voice.

These movies are said to be "true" and "important" because this kind of high life has been observed (gossip columnists assure us that they have been eyewitnesses); do the people who read the gossip columns get so much vicarious pleasure that they think they're living it? Here we are in an age of increasing mechanization and dehumanization — with the trends horribly the same under both capitalism or socialism, with no relief in sight, and people go to Fellini's and Antonioni's Marxist-Catholic-Hollywood glamour parades and come away carrying the banner that *fornication* is the evil of our times! And whom do these directors pick to symbolize the victims of materialism: the artists — just the ones who escape into freedom. I'll admit that I once knew an apparently bored artist, a famous composer, born wealthy, who said to me, "The days are always two hours too long for me." I wanted to hit him with a poker because the days are always too short for me and I am always trying to prolong them by staying up half the night. But I decided that he was using his boredom as a come-on — a lure so that people would want to fascinate him, to awaken him from his sleeping beauty trance.

The term "sleeping beauty" provides, I think, a fairly good transition to *Last Year at Marienbad* — or Sleeping Beauty of the International Set, the high-fashion experimental film, the snow job in the ice palace. Here we are, back at the no-fun party with non-people, in what is described to us as an "enormous, luxurious, baroque, lugubrious hotel — where corridors succeed endless corridors." I can scarcely quote even that much of the thick malted prose without wanting to interject — "Oh, come off it." The mood is set by climaxes of organ music and this distended narration; it's all solemn and expectant — like High Mass. But then you hear the heroine's thin little voice, and the reiterated questions and answers, and you feel you shouldn't giggle at High Mass, even if it's turning into a game of Idiot's Delight. Surely conversation about whether people met before at Frederiksbad or Marienbad or Baden-Salsa can only be a parody of wealthy indolence — but is the film supposed to be comic? Probably not, but it's always on the edge — so the effect is ludicrous. The settings and costumes seem to be waiting for a high romantic theme or a fantasy; the people, pawns who are manipulated into shifting positions, seem to be placed for wit, or for irony. But all we get are games, and tricks that look like parodies of old movies and decorators' versions of film art. Once again the sick souls are damned well dressed — from the look of all these movies, you might begin to suspect that soul-sickness is a product of the couturier.

The author Robbe-Grillet says: "This movie is no more than the story of a persuasion, and one must remember that the man is not telling the truth. The couple did not meet the year before." The director Resnais says: "I could never have shot this film if I had not been convinced that their meeting had actually taken place." But who cares if they met before and who cares what happens to them? Enthusiasts for the film start arguing about whether something happened last year at Marienbad, and this becomes rather more important than what happens on the screen in front of them — which isn't much. The people we see have no warmth, no humor or pain, no backgrounds or past, no point of contact with living creatures, so who cares about their past or future, or their present? Does it matter if it's a chess game or a recurring dream game? Resnais dissolves time all right — by destroying any sense of relationship to events or characters. He says he has cut out the "explanatory scenes" and the dialogue whose sole purpose is "to keep the action going" — I think this is exactly what he is giving us: all the mechanics of drama without any drama. We know nothing about these people except that they move up and down corridors, open and close doors, change clothes, so it seems a mere idle game, as idle as the match game the men play, to speculate about what has happened or is going to happen to them. (About the only question I came out asking was: how many changes of costume did the girl actually have?) It is one thing to cut out the unnecessary mechanical transitions of film (as Godard did in *Breathless*), but Resnais cuts away something that *is* basic to drama — our caring about the characters and what they are doing. (I don't mean this in the naive sense that we must *like* the characters; there are many ways of *caring*.)

Resnais: "Perhaps it may seem pointless to some people to train a camera on the inner minds of the characters rather than on their external behavior, but it is fascinating once in a while." But that is exactly what we get — their external behavior; we get no sense of what he calls their "inner minds" at all. (I wonder what he thinks their *outer* minds are like.) He says that in order to "bring the art of film-making to this abstract plane," he "has eliminated the 'non-essentials' — plot, action and rational explanations. . . . My films are an attempt, still very crude and tentative, to visualize the complexity of the mechanism of thought." But without those "non-essentials" of plot and action and rational explanations we are left with figures going through unmotivated movements. If changing clothes and going in to dinner is all that is in their heads, he doesn't have much to visualize. And if the crisis of all this thought is whether to change partners, going from one dummy to another, how are we to find the girl's vacillations and visions anything but faintly comic? If she sees herself as a femme fatale in feathers, posturing like an early movie siren — Evelyn Brent or Marlene Dietrich in a Von Sternberg setting — if this is all that is in her head, then hasn't Resnais selected a singularly vacuous specimen of woman, and of man, to suggest the complexity of the mechanism of thought? (The international playgirl figure in *La Notte*, Monica Vitti, can be seen, rather like Delphine Seyrig, as a parody derived from Hollywood's glamour periods, but is the parody intentional in her case either?)

I don't know the source of this notion that film making should be brought to an "abstract plane" (is this plane, by some analogy with mathematics, supposed to be *higher* than the level on which directors like D. W. Griffith and Jean Renoir have worked?) and I don't know what battles will be fought on that plane stripped of plot and action and rational explanations, but there seem to be a few skeletons from old movies lying about. The characters of *Marienbad*, it is indicated, do what they *must* do: it's all supposed to be preordained, simple and irrevocable, in a world without choice or responsibility. And in this not so very intellectually-respectable aspect *Marienbad* is a "classier" version of those forties you-can-call-it-supernatural-if-you-want-to movies like *Flesh and Fantasy* — only now it's called "Jungian."

Resnais: "Make of it what you will . . . whatever you decide is right." This is like making a mess and asking others to clean it up; it's also a cheap way of inviting audiences and critics to make fools of themselves. And they do: they come up with "solutions" like "*Marienbad* is supposed to be interpreted like a Rorschach test — you are supposed to give it whatever meanings you wish." But, but — a Rorschach test is a blot, an accident onto which you project your own problems and visions; it is the opposite of a work of art, which brings the artist's vision to *you*. And *Marienbad*, though it's silly, albeit at times amusing and pretty, is in no way an *accidental* blot. And whatever is there to

decide *about?* A riddle that has no answer may seem deep if
that's your turn of mind or it may just seem silly and pointless.
Did they meet before or didn't they? It's rather like Which
Twin Has the Toni. You have to work hard to pretend it's a
complicated metaphysical question. If you compose a riddle and
then say all solutions are right, then obviously there is no solution, and the interest must be in the complexity or charm or
entertainment of the riddle and the ideas or meanings it suggests to you — in its *artfulness*. And at this level, *Marienbad* is a
mess — or, rather, it's a neat mess, and it's too heavy to be so
lightweight.

No wonder nobody remembers anything — if the days of the
intervening year were all alike and all chopped into pieces like
this hour and a half. The fragmentation of conventional chro-
nology doesn't do more, in this case, than break up in bits and
then arbitrarily repeat the externals of behavior. (It has, however, the advantage of disguising the banality of the material by
making it confusing — and as an extraordinary number of people
take confusion for depth, even the embarrassingly paranoid
Guns of the Trees may acquire a following now that Jonas
Mekas has re-edited — and fragmented — it.)

Mustn't the movie be seen — if it is to be enjoyed — as an
exercise in decor and romantic mystification? I was intrigued by
the palaces and parks and wanted to know where they were,
who had built them, and for what purposes (I was interested in
the specific material that Resnais was attempting to make
unspecific). I enjoyed some of the images: an over-exposed moment when the screen is flooded with light; dancers and game-
players who might be evocative of something or other if glimpsed
just briefly or in the distance. But when this exercise goes on for
an hour and a half, the figures abstracted from all living detail
become as tiresome as shadow dancers. Lousy story, but great
sets. The trouble with sets like this is, what possible story could
be told in them? Robbe-Grillet and Resnais tell the audience to
do the artists' work and inhabit the empty movie with life and
meaning. This peculiar presumption, all too common in "avant-

garde" film circles, can pass for new and daring and experimental in art houses. And those familiar with "avant-garde" film program notes with their barmy premise that what can't be seen in the film is what makes the film important, will recognize Robbe-Grillet as the definitive, classical practitioner of the genre.*

Let's leave the ice palace and go down to Fellini's hotel in hell, his gilded apocalypse. If Fellini meant it when he said his aim was "to put a thermometer to a sick world," his method and subject matter make no sense. It's a waste of effort to stick a thermometer into a pesthole. It's like poking your head into a sack of fertilizer and then becoming indignant because you're covered with excrement. The aim, the scale, the pretensions, the message are too big for the subject matter: tabloid sensationalism and upper-class apathy and corruption. Fellini is shocked and horrified — like the indignant housewives who can't get enough details on Elizabeth Taylor's newest outrage, and think she should be banned from the screen. I don't think he's simply exploiting the incidents and crimes and orgies of modern Rome in the manner of a Hollywood biblical spectacle, but *La Dolce Vita* is a sort of a *Ben Hur* for the more, but not *very* much more, sophisticated. And in attempting a modern parallel with the revelations of the apocalypse, he's very close to the preachers who describe the orgies of high life and the punishments of eternal hell fire.

* "In *Marienbad*, the important phenomenon is always the basic lack of substance at the heart of this reality. In *Marienbad*, what is chimerical is 'last year.' What happened — if something did happen once upon a time — constantly produces sort of a gap in the story. . . . In *Marienbad*, at first we believe that there was no last year and then we notice that last year has crept in everywhere: there you have it, entirely. In the same way we believe that there was no Marienbad (the place, that is), and then we realize we're at home there from the beginning. The event refused by the young woman has, at the end, contaminated everything. So much so that she hasn't stopped struggling and believing she won the game, since she always refused all of it; and, at the end, she realizes that it's too late, that in the final analysis she has accepted everything. As if all that *were* true, although it well might not be. But *true* and *false* no longer have any meaning." How's that again?

It doesn't make very much difference in the world if people who have a lot of money or people who want publicity are bored or drunk or autoerotic or queer. They may be disgusting (and they may also be highly entertaining) but they don't do much harm, and their casual promiscuity which doesn't hurt anyone except possibly themselves is not so shocking or immoral as, for example, the cruelties that can be found at any social level — like the way middle-class and laboring people can feel virtuous and righteous while taking out their frustrations on their children. Is Fellini really so appalled by the rich girl and the hero making love in the prostitute's room, by the transvestites, by the striptease which gives the woman gratification? Is he at heart a country boy who can never take for granted the customs and follies of the big city? Perhaps, and perhaps also a showman who knows that these episodes will be juicy fodder for the mass audience — middle-class and working people always hungry to learn the worst about the terrible dirty rich.

The movie is so moral in its emphasis that all vice (all non-innocent fun?) seems to be punished by boredom and defeat. But why are people looking so eagerly at the movie, hoping for ever more horrifying views of that unrestrained high life? The sweet, soft life is just what hardworking, moralistic people envy; maybe they don't think it's so dull and awful as Fellini tells them it is. And Fellini presents more and more and more of it — until the audience is more tired than the characters at the all-night parties. (Perhaps you don't decide it's dull until after you've had a lot of it? Morality becomes a function of exhaustion.) Surely to audiences the drinking and bodies and striptease parties are more interesting than the message of condemnation, which is like a moral consolation prize for the opportunities they don't have. He uses the swarming photographers as a chorus of Furies, a remarkable piece of sophomoric self-indulgence: they are as eager as he to "expose" vice, i.e. — to catch the rich in the act. (Perhaps the artists who capture the popular imagination are those who retain the fervor and grandiloquence of a high-school orator: people all over the world were moved by the spiritual message of *La Strada* that everyone has a purpose in the universe.)

La Dolce Vita wants to be a great film — it cries out its intentions — and it's frequently clever, as in the statue hanging from the helicopter, and it's sometimes effective, as, near the end, when Marcello throws the feathers. And that is all it is. Perhaps what it needs to be more than that is some more serious examination of human folly: perhaps we need to see some intelligent, hardworking or creative people who nevertheless have the same outlets — or vices, if you will — as these shallow people. There are plenty of serious artists, as well as plenty of business and professional men, who are lecherous, promiscuous, homosexual; there are plenty of narcotics addicts on Wall Street (maybe it helps, if you've got to wear one of those hats). Why use the silly publicity-seekers or aimless rich as scapegoats for all our follies? Does no Communist or working-class girl ever fantasize taking off her clothes in public? Does no American college girl ever fantasize changing places with a whore? The rich are in a position to act out our fantasies, but surely an artist like Fellini, knowing that these fantasies are general, should not allow the middle class to cluck with glee and horror at seeing the rich do just what the middle class secretly wants to do. The world wouldn't end if they did, nor would capitalism or Communism rise or fall. Fellini's desire for a great theme notwithstanding, even if the subject of "vice" were treated more seriously, it still wouldn't make an apocalypse.

La Dolce Vita is very different in directorial style from the semi-abstract kind of movement in *La Notte*, and the fooling around in the intellectual sports arena of *Marienbad*. I'd better say that very clearly, because as I dislike all three, there is a temptation to lump them together. And they *are* lumpy. Structurally, all three are disasters, and perhaps that's why it's so easy to confuse them. If you remember a scene at a party — was it in *La Dolce Vita* or *La Notte*, or *Marienbad*, or was it in the big hotel of *L'Avventura?* The Morandi paintings link the Steiner episode of *La Dolce Vita* with *La Notte*; and both have the same dull writer-hero played by the same actor. Who can remember who did what to whom in which movie? The rich hostess of *La Notte*, who greets her guests in the garden, and points to the house, saying, "They're all dead in there," might just as well be pointing at the hotel in *Marienbad*. Are the people who play the *Marienbad* game any different from those who play games on the floor in *La Notte*? Did they meet last year in *La Dolce Vita*?

The episodes in these films don't build, they are all on the same level. The view is panoramic, and there's even a rather peculiar concept of documentary — many people playing themselves, some using their own names, or names like their own, or no names (names, like definite characterization, seem to be regarded as unimportant). Despite the length of the films, so much is vague and unspecified, and the characters are inexplicable. We sometimes get the impression that Fellini thinks that the lives and fates of the people in *La Dolce Vita* are very important, but we can't tell if Emma, the hero's mistress, is supposed to be some kind of life-force the hero should cling to in order to be saved, or just a jealous nagging ninny. People say the girl in *Marienbad* is an anima or perhaps they say she is the eternal feminine. But what clue do we have for her? You could say of Garbo that she was all women, but this girl is *no* woman, she's just a nameless puzzle for those who want to create artificial problems for themselves. And who can say what the wife in *La Notte* is — is she weak or strong, does she stay with her husband out of inertia or pity or indifference? The directors show us people playing pointless games in order to reveal the pointlessness of their lives; like the fairground in recent English movies, it's an oddly simple-minded device (and a maladroit symbol — as some of the most active and energetic people relax with games of chance and skill). And, depressingly, it's a boomerang: the latest intellectual game is devising interpretations of these movies. If it is all a dream, it is a bad dream.

All these films have their source, I think, in Renoir's great *The Rules of the Game* [1939] — but how different *his* party was: it was a surreal fantasy, the culmination of the pursuit of love, a great chase, a great satirical comedy, a dance of death. The servants were as corrupt as the masters. And how different were the games — the shooting party in which almost all living creatures were the targets, and then the unplanned shooting party. But the themes were set — the old castle that seems to symbolize the remains of European civilization, and the guests with their weekend activities — sex and theatricals and games. Renoir's film was a dazzling, complex entertainment, brilliantly structured, building its themes toward a climax. These new party films are incoherent message movies — at least *La Dolce Vita* and *La Notte* are. Who can say what *Marienbad* is? (*Marienbad* has at least one definite relationship to *The Rules of the Game*: Chanel dressed the ladies in both.) They are important, not because they are great movies (they are not) but because of the way people are responding to them. Their audience may be enormous (as for *La Dolce Vita*) or small, but Fellini, Antonioni, Resnais have caught its pulse: they are telling people what they want to hear, which, I think, means they are obscuring problems in a way that people like to see them obscured. The message of *La Dolce Vita* or *La Notte* isn't very different from what they might hear in any church, but it looks different, and so they are being struck and moved by all sorts of "profound" ideas (our lives are a living death, we have lost the capacity to act, we are losing the "life force," and all that).

At the end of *La Notte* (conceptually, the ugliest sequence in modern films), the writer and his wife leave the party, and dawn's early light finds them walking across the golf course and coupling — if we can call it that — near a sandtrap. I couldn't resist subversive thoughts: why can't he wait until they get home? And finally I whispered to my companion, a professor of English, "How can he do it with his clothes on?" and my friend answered, "Maybe that's why those Italian suits are becoming so popular." The sleepwalking husband and wife do a turn worthy of the contortionist.

These reactions will no doubt infuriate *La Notte* lovers —

I know very well that we are supposed to be so involved in the interior problems of the characters that we shouldn't think in such terms. But how far can we go in following a director who has refined narrative and character out of his drama, who is attempting to turn the peripheral elements of drama into its center, who is so preoccupied with boredom and isolation and drifting and the failure of communication and the impermanence of desire, that he has lost the sense that people share other interests and pleasures not so impermanent? (The only parent in these movies is Steiner, who murders his children! Don't these people even have any pets?) If there are people this bored and vacuous, how did they get this way, and what makes the directors think these people are so central to the modern world that they symbolize our experience? (I admit that when I talk with people who find *La Notte* "beautiful," they sound as weak and empty as the people in the movie. Surely this must be the power of suggestion? They also accept Antonioni's self-serious, literary dialogue as art.)*

Is Antonioni so different from his contortionist? Doesn't he experience a sense of accomplishment after completing this ugly, pointless, but difficult-to-do act, this film with its titillations for the blasé (the nymphomaniac in the hospital) and its arty-intellectual appeal for the naive (the tape-recorded poetry)? But, more dishonest than the contortionist, he condemns the act while performing it: he builds in the *morality* for the audience so that they can feel the desolation of their own emptiness — oh, the pity of it all. And if they have ever experienced despair, they can imagine that it was like this, part of the universal sickness of the rich and gifted, and that they, too, were elegantly above it all.

Antonioni's dawn is not merely the dawn of people who have been up all night; it is dawn as the fag end of the night before;

---

* Even while I was saying these words on the radio, I was aware that they weren't adequate, that I was somehow dodging the issue. Though I believe that whatever moves people is important, I am, perhaps by temperament, unable to understand or sympathize with those who are drawn to the *La Notte* view of life.

it is the cold light in which you see yourself and know that there is no new day — just more sleepwalking and self-disgust.

In film after film, the contortionist and the sleepwalkers. The symbols are artistically arranged, beautifully composed, but they are not really under control. The directors are not saying what they think they are saying. All we need to undermine and ridicule this aimless, high-style moral turpitude passing itself off as the universal human condition is one character at the parties — like, say, Martha Raye in *Monsieur Verdoux* — who enjoys every minute of it, who really has a ball, and we have the innocent American exploding this European mythology of depleted modern man who can no longer love because he has lost contact with life.

A Taste of Honey

The audiences at popular American movies seem to want heroes they can look up to; the audiences at art houses seem to want heroes they can look down on. Does this mean that as we become more educated, we no longer believe in the possibilities of heroism? The "realistic," "adult" movie often means the movie in which the hero is a little man like, presumably, the little men in the audience.

A year or so ago art-house audiences were carried away by *Ballad of a Soldier* and its "refreshing" look of purity and innocence. The new refresher may be *A Taste of Honey*. The inexperienced young hero of *Ballad of a Soldier* was too shy and idealistic to make any direct overtures to the heroine; the hero of *A Taste of Honey* goes beyond inexperience, he's inadequate — and audiences love him all the more for it. I didn't much like the material of *Ballad of a Soldier*, but it was well handled to achieve its effects; I *do* like Shelagh Delaney's material, but the movie treatment is rather coarse. Tony Richardson is beginning to gain assurance of the wrong kind: in A *Taste of Honey* his direction is more *controlled* than in *Look Back in Anger* or *The Entertainer*, but it is at the expense of some of the best material in the modern theater. His treatment of A *Taste of Honey* is both more pretentious and less exciting than the slender material of the play. He has learned how to package the material and build in the responses like an American director. He doesn't take a chance on our reaching out to the characters or feelings; everything is pushed at us. What should be a lyric sketch is all filled in and spelled out until it becomes almost a comic melodrama.

The play, written by an eighteen-year-old working-class Lancashire girl, has fresh dialogue and feeling and warmth. The story is simple: Jo (Rita Tushingham), a schoolgirl, temporarily abandoned by her fun-loving mother who goes off with a new husband, has an affair with a Negro seaman, and then meets a lonely fellow-spirit, a homosexual, Geoff (Murray Melvin), who moves in with her and looks after her during her pregnancy. I use the novelettish term "fellow-spirit" intentionally, because I think it helps to establish the idyllic frame of reference. The story is about a little mock paradise that is lost: the mother comes back and throws Geoff out, but Jo has had her taste of the honey of sweet companionship. A *Taste of Honey* is a fairy tale set in modern industrial ugliness. Little, sad, shy, dignified Geoff in this story is a combination Peter Pan and homemaking Wendy who had to have a pretend baby, and he's a fairy godmother as well. The girl Jo is herself a Peter Pan figure: stubborn, independent, capering and whimsical, ignoring most of the world, moved only by what interests her. The background music — children's songs — further aligns Jo and Geoff with the world and the charm of children. Their pleasures are innocent and carefree; by contrast, the grown-ups are almost all horrible objects, sexual in a nasty, grotesque way.

The dialogue has lovely turns of humor — and rather old-fashioned but sweet pathos. The film kept reminding me of Janet Gaynor and Charles Farrell in *Seventh Heaven*, of scenes in *A Man's Castle* and other old Frank Borzage films. They, too, were set in poverty, and the characters found humor and poetry in it. The sweet man is now a motherly little queen who looks after the heroine, but the basic emotion is the same as it was in the gentle sentimental love stories of the twenties and thirties — the hero and heroine, friendless babes in the woods who need each other. Geoff's last scenes — suddenly fascinated by the children in the street, then moving off alone — take us right back to a Chaplin finale, but now "the little fellow" is carried to its psychosexual extreme.

Perhaps the greatest charm of *A Taste of Honey*, and this is a distinctively modern charm, is in the poetry of role confusion. The mother and daughter don't have a parent-child relationship; they are more like bickering siblings. And Jo and Geoff are not like woman and man but like *non*-bickering siblings, Geoff the older sister looking after Jo, the disorderly younger sister, in what is a bit of a parody of the maternal relationship Jo has not previously experienced. These role confusions are presented by Shelagh Delaney with simple directness and without any moralizing.

What's the matter with the film? Perhaps I can get at this indirectly. Have you ever, after an exhausting all-night party or conversation, taken a walk at dawn? It's cleansing and beautiful and you decide that you'll change your way of life, get up early, breathe the fresh air. But by nightfall, your drinking companions are good and who wants to go to *bed* in order to get up early? If you think at all about the clear air of dawn, it's with a shudder. How awful it would be to have to *get* up to go out into it, and you laugh at yourself for having thought it was *your* air. Well, the movie is about the way the morning air feels for those who naturally get up in it, but it appears to be made by people who stayed up all night and then, tired and hung over, *discovered* the morning air and thought it was a great thing and more people should know about it.

It's not as if it were done in Hollywood — you may have

heard about the Hollywood producer who wanted to make the film with Audrey Hepburn as Jo and give it a typical American upbeat ending by having the child born dead. You have to be familiar with Hollywood's curious codes to understand that killing off the little bastard squares everything; and the heroine, having suffered, would then be redeemed. This film doesn't attempt to lick the material at the Hollywood level, but the director simply can't find the innocence or the imagination or the style that the boisterous, contagious material deserves and *needs*; he makes too much of every good thing. The performers are good, but the camera emphasizes their qualities until even their best work seems overdone. If only we could discover the lyric qualities in Rita Tushingham's Jo — but Richardson doesn't give us credit for enough vision (perhaps because his own eye isn't very good); he keeps shoving close-ups at us until we've had too much of her homely gamin beauty. And the mother (Dora Bryan), in particular, is handled with low comic crudity. It's enough to see her singing and on a dance floor; do we also need the easy laugh of seeing her in a room alone bending over, with the camera glued to her corseted backside? Do we need to see her aging flesh in the bathtub? Do we need to have her behaving like a crude villainess, turning the hapless, unwanted little Geoff out of the house? (You may want to quip "odd girl out" but the director treats it like the most heartrending eviction since *Way Down East*.)

As a director, Richardson *does* moralize. He's always looking for points he can drive home, for larger social nuances — for the obvious that he finds so meaningful. (The working-class author couldn't be expected to have the social consciousness that an educated liberal can supply.) He isn't content with the material; he wants to make a *statement*. And what can make a statement so *visually* as the grimy working-class wastelands of industrial England? Richardson uses actual locations, but he uses them like sets; the backgrounds are cleverly selected, but merely cleverly selected. The documentary backgrounds are *additional* visual material: they don't so much help to tell Jo and Geoff's story as to reveal the director's story.

There *is* an attempt to tell the story by images in the contrast of the fairground scenes. In the first, a remarkable and upsetting sequence, Jo is miserable with her mother's raucous and ugly friends and she uncontrollably, but consciously and deliberately, makes a pest of herself and makes *everyone* miserable. In the second, Jo is with Geoff: they are orphans in the storm who have found each other, and the fairground is an enchanted, innocent background for their delight. Unfortunately, the fairground, the setpiece of so many recent English movies, has become overloaded with social comment: all too obvious as a symbolic playground for impoverished lives it has now become an actual playground for impoverished directorial imaginations. It is but one example of Richardson's strong and I think lamentable tendency to use backgrounds for too facile a social comment (he's very keen on the poetry in naturalism) — which is not so very different from the way Hollywood composers use soaring passages of romantic music to swell up emotional response to the plot.

With all these reservations, the film is one to see: Shelagh Delaney's dialogue *is* as clear and surprising as dawn. What a movie this and the Osborne adaptations might have been! The English have so many good actors, so much good material, and so many unimaginative directors. It's like gathering together all the ingredients for an exquisite soufflé and putting a scullion in charge.

A *Taste of Honey* doesn't do anything for the art of the film, but it has, nevertheless, altered our environment. The sad-eyed queen is the new hero. Audiences longing for a hero to lavish their sympathies on have a new unfortunate they can clasp to their social-worker hearts: the ideal "little man," the homemaker, the pure-in-heart, childlike, non-threatening male, the man a girl can feel safe with — and who could be more "deprived"? They can feel tender and tolerant, and they can feel contemptuous, and in-the-know at the same time: the man a girl can feel safe with is a joke, he's not a man at all. The role confusion of the story becomes the source of gratification for the audience: Geoff is poetic because he's inadequate, and you're not just having a dirty laugh, you're accepting life. Romance and comedy are one: the hero is the butt. And the audience, having had him both ways, feels worldly and satisfied.

Victim

It was a bit startling to pick up an English newspaper and see that the review of *Victim* was entitled "Ten-letter word" — but as it turned out, the *Observer* was referring not to Lenny Bruce's much publicized hyphenated word but to the simple term "homosexual," which it appears is startling enough in a movie to make the Johnston office refuse to give *Victim* a seal of approval.

I suppose it's too crude simply to say that *Victim* is *The Mark* in drag but that's not so far from the truth. Like the man who wanted to rape a child but didn't, the hero of *Victim* wants to but doesn't make it with another guy. The lesser characters make out; they don't have the hero's steel will, and they are very pathetic indeed, given to such self-illuminating expressions as "Nature played me a dirty trick." I'm beginning to long for one of those old-fashioned movie stereotypes — the vicious, bitchy old queen who said mean, funny things. We may never again have those Franklin Pangborn roles, now that homosexuals are going to be treated seriously, with sympathy and respect, like Jews and Negroes. It's difficult to judge how far sensitivities will go: *Remembrance of Things Past* may soon be frowned upon like *Huckleberry Finn* and *The Merchant of Venice*. Social progress makes strange bedfellows.

Victim manages to get past other censorial bodies by being basically a thriller, a fairly slick suspense story about a blackmailing ring. But it's a cleverly conceived *moralistic* thriller: as the victims of the ring are homosexuals, various characters are able to point out the viciousness of the English laws, which, by making homosexuality a crime, make homosexuals the victims of ninety per cent of the blackmail cases. Just about everyone in the movie has attitudes designed to illuminate the legal problems of homosexuality; without the thriller structure, the moralizing message could get awfully sticky. As it is, the film is moderately amusing.

A number of the reviewers were uneasy about the thesis that consenting adults should be free from legal prosecution for their sex habits; they felt that if homosexuality were not a crime it would spread. (The assumption seems to be that heterosexuality couldn't hold its own in a free market.) *Time*'s attitude to the film is a classic example of *Time*'s capacity for worrying:

But what seems at first an attack on extortion seems at last a coyly sensational exploitation of homosexuality as a theme — and, what's more offensive, an implicit approval of homosexuality as a practice. Almost all the deviates in the film are fine fellows — well dressed, well spoken, sensitive, kind . . . Nowhere does the film suggest that homosexuality is a serious (but often curable) neurosis that attacks the biological basis of life itself.

On one page *Time* is worried about the population explosion, and on the next it's upset because homosexuals aren't reproducing. (An unwarranted assumption, by the way.)

Time should really be very happy with the movie, because the hero of the film is a man who has never given way to his homosexual impulses; he has fought them — that's part of his heroism. Maybe that's why he seems such a stuffy stock figure of a hero. Oedipus didn't merely want to sleep with Jocasta; he slept with her.

There is, incidentally, a terribly self-conscious and unconvincing attempt to distinguish between the "love" the barrister feels for his wife and the physical desire — presumably some lower order of emotion — that he felt for a boy who is more interesting in every way than his wife. And I find it difficult to accept all the upper-class paraphernalia of stage melodrama; it's hard to believe in people who live at the level on which if you feel insulted by someone's conversation, you show him the door. Generally when I tell someone to leave, that's when he most wants to stay, and I'm stuck for eighteen hours of sordid explanations of how he got so repulsive and how much he hates himself. A minor problem in trying to take *Victim* seriously even as a thriller is that the suspense involves a series of "revelations" that several of the highly-placed characters have been concealing their homosexuality; but actors, and especially English actors, generally look so queer anyway, that it's hard to be surprised at what we've always taken for granted — in fact, in this suspense context of who is and who isn't, it's hard to believe in the actors who are supposed to be straight.

Some months ago, reviewing *The Mark*, I discussed the uncomfortable feeling I got that we were supposed to feel sympathetic toward the hero because he was such a pained, unhappy, dull man, and that his sexual problem was the only focus of interest in him. In *Victim* there is so much effort to make us feel sympathetic toward the homosexuals that they are never even allowed to be *gay*. The dreadful irony involved is that Dirk Bogarde looks so pained, so anguished from the self-sacrifice of repressing his homosexuality, that the film seems to give rather a black eye to the heterosexual life.

꙰꙰꙰꙰꙰꙰

Lolita

The ads asked "How did they ever make a movie of *Lolita* for persons over 18 years of age?" A few days later the question mark was moved, and the ads asked "How did they ever make a movie of *Lolita?*" and after that, the caution: "for persons over 18 years of age." Either way, the suggestion was planted that the movie had "licked" the book, and that *Lolita* had been turned into the usual kind of sexy movie. The advertising has been slanted to the mass audience, so the art-house audience isn't going. A sizable part of the mass audience doesn't like the movie (their rejection is being interpreted as a vote for "wholesomeness," which according to *Variety* is about to stage a comeback) and the art-house audience is missing out on one of the few American films it might enjoy.

Recommend the film to friends and they reply, "Oh I've *had* it with *Lolita*." It turns out (now that *Lolita* can be purchased for fifty cents and so is in the category of ordinary popular books) that they never thought much of it; but even though they didn't really like the book, they don't want to see the movie because of all the changes that have been made in the book. (One person informed me that he wouldn't go to see the movie because he'd heard they'd turned it into a comedy.) Others had heard so much about the book, they thought reading it superfluous (they had as *good* as read it — they were *tired* of it); and if the book was too much talked about to necessitate a reading, surely going to the film was really *de trop*?

Besides, wasn't the girl who played Lolita practically a *matron*? The New York *Times* had said, "She looks to be a good seventeen," and the rest of the press seemed to concur in this peculiarly inexpert judgment. *Time* opened its review with "Wind up the Lolita doll and it goes to Hollywood and commits nymphanticide" and closed with "*Lolita* is the saddest and most important victim of the current reckless adaptation fad . . ." In the *Observer* the premiere of the film was described under the heading "Lolita fiasco" and the writer concluded that the novel had been "turned into a film about this poor English guy who is being given the runaround by this sly young broad." In the *New Republic* Stanley Kauffmann wrote, "It is clear that Nabokov respects the novel. It is equally clear that he does not respect the film — at least as it is used in America . . . He has given to films the *Lolita* that, presumably, he thinks the medium deserves . . ." After all this, who would expect anything from the film?

The surprise of *Lolita* is how enjoyable it is: it's the first *new* American comedy since those great days in the forties when Preston Sturges recreated comedy with verbal slapstick. *Lolita* is black slapstick and at times it's so far out that you gasp as you laugh. An inspired Peter Sellers creates a new comic pattern — a crazy quilt of psychological, sociological commentary so "hip" it's surrealist. It doesn't cover everything: there are structural weaknesses, the film falls apart, and there's even a forced and humiliating attempt to "explain" the plot. But when the wit is galloping who's going to look a gift horse in the mouth? Critics, who feel decay in their bones.

The reviews are a comedy of gray matter. Doubts may have remained after Arthur Schlesinger, Jr.'s, ex cathedra judgment that *Lolita* is "willful, cynical and repellent . . . It is not only inhuman; it is anti-human. I am reluctantly glad that it was made, but I trust it will have no imitators." Then, "for a learned and independent point of view, *Show* invited Dr. Reinhold Niebuhr, the renowned theologian, to a screening in New York and asked him for an appraisal." The higher primate discovered that "the theme of this triangular relationship exposes the unwholesome attitudes of mother, daughter, and lover to a mature observer." (Ripeness is all . . . but is it enough?) This mature observer does however find some "few saving moral insights" — though he thinks the film "obscures" them — such as "the lesson of Lolita's essential redemption in a happy marriage." (Had any *peripheral* redemptions lately?) If you're still hot on the trail of insights, don't overlook the *New Republic*'s steamy revelation that "the temper of the original might . . . have been tastefully preserved" if Humbert had narrated the film. "The general tone could have been: 'Yes, this is what I did then and thought lovely. Dreadful, wasn't it? Still . . . it has its funny side, no?'" It has its funny side, oui oui.

The movie adaptation tries something so far beyond the simple "narrator" that a number of the reviewers have complained: Bosley Crowther, who can always be counted on to miss the point, writes that "Mr. Kubrick inclines to dwell too long over scenes that have slight purpose, such as scenes in which Mr. Sellers does various comical impersonations as the sneaky villain who dogs Mr. Mason's trail." These scenes "that have slight purpose" are, of course, just what make *Lolita* new, these are the scenes that make it, for all its slackness of pace and clumsy editing, a more exciting comedy than the last American comedy, *Some Like It Hot*. Quilty, the success, the writer of scenarios and school plays, the policeman, the psychologist; Quilty the genius, the man whom Lolita loves, Humbert's brother and tormenter and parodist; Quilty the man of the world is a conception to talk about alongside Melville's *The Confidence Man*. "Are you with someone?" Humbert asks the policeman. And Quilty the policeman replies, "I'm not with someone. I'm with you."

The Quilty monologues are worked out almost like the routines of silent comedy — they not only carry the action forward, they comment on it, and this comment is the *new* action of the film. There has been much critical condescension toward Sellers, who's alleged to be an impersonator rather than an actor, a man with many masks but no character. Now Sellers does a turn with the critics' terms: his Quilty is a character employing masks, an actor with a merciless talent for impersonation. He is indeed "the sneaky villain who dogs Mr. Mason's trail" — and he digs up every bone that "Mr. Mason" ineptly tries to bury, and presents them to him. Humbert can conceal nothing. It is a little like the scene in Victor Sjostrom's magnificent *The Wind*, in which Lillian Gish digs a grave for the man she has murdered and then, from her window, watches in horror as the windstorm uncovers the body. But in *Lolita* our horror is split by laughter: Humbert has it coming — *not* because he's having "relations" with a minor, but because, in order to conceal his sexual predilections, he has put on the most obsequious and mealy-minded of masks. Like the homosexual professors who are rising fast in American academia because they are so cautious about protecting their unconventional sex lives that they can be trusted not to be troublesome to the college administrations on any important issues (a convoluted form of blackmail), Humbert is a worm and Quilty knows it.

Peter Sellers works with miserable physical equipment, yet he has somehow managed to turn his lumbering, wide-hipped body into an advantage by *acting* to perfection the man without physical assets. The soft, slow-moving, paper-pushing middle-class man is his special self-effacing type; and though only in his mid-thirties he all too easily incarnates sly, smug middle-aged man. Even his facial muscles are kept flaccid, so that he always looks weary, too tired and cynical for much of a response. The rather frightening strength of his Quilty (who has enormous — almost sinister — reserves of energy) is peculiarly effective just because of his ordinary, "normal" look. He does something that seems impossible: he makes unattractiveness magnetic.

Quilty — rightly, in terms of the film as distinguished from the novel — dominates *Lolita* (which could use much more of him) and James Mason's Humbert, who makes attractiveness tired and exhausted and impotent, is a remarkable counterpart. Quilty who doesn't care, who wins Lolita and throws her out, Quilty the homewrecker is a winner; Humbert, slavishly, painfully in love, absurdly suffering, the lover of the ages who degrades himself, who cares about nothing but Lolita, is the classic loser. Mason is better than (and different from) what almost anyone could have expected. Mason's career has been so mottled: a beautiful *Odd Man Out*, a dull Brutus, an uneven, often brilliant Norman Maine in *A Star Is Born*, a good Captain Nemo, and then in 1960 the beginnings of comic style as the English naval commander who pretends to have gone over to the Russians in *A Touch of Larceny*. And now, in *Lolita* he's really in command of a comic style: the handsome face gloats in a rotting smile. Mason seems to need someone strong to play against. He's very good in the scenes with Charlotte and with her friends, and especially good in the bathtub scene (which Niebuhr thinks "may arouse both the laughter and the distaste of the audi⌐

ence" — imagine being so drained of reactions that you have to be *aroused* to distaste!) but his scenes with Lolita, when he must dominate the action, fall rather flat.

Perhaps the reviewers have been finding so many faults with *Lolita* because this is such an easy way to show off some fake kind of erudition: even newspaper reviewers can demonstrate that they've read a book by complaining about how different the movie is from the novel. The movie *is* different but not *that* different, and if you can get over the reviewers' preoccupation with the sacredness of the novel (they don't complain this much about Hollywood's changes in biblical stories) you'll probably find that even the characters that *are* different (Charlotte Haze, especially, who has become the culture-vulture rampant) are successful in terms of the film. Shelley Winters's Charlotte is a triumphant caricature, so overdone it recalls Blake's "You never know what is enough until you know what is more than enough."

Sue Lyon is perhaps a little less than enough — but not because she looks seventeen. (Have the reviewers looked at the schoolgirls of America lately? The classmates of my fourteen-year-old daughter are not merely nubile: some of them look badly used.) Rather it is because her role is insufficiently written. Sue Lyon herself is good (at times her face is amusingly suggestive of a miniature Elvis Presley) though physically too *young* to be convincing in her last scenes. (I don't mean that to sound paradoxical but merely descriptive.) Kubrick and company have been attacked most for the area in which they have been simply accurate: they could have done up Sue Lyon in childish schoolgirl clothes, but the facts of American life are that adolescents and even pre-adolescents wear nylons and make-up and two-piece strapless bathing suits and have *figures*.

Lolita isn't a consistently good movie but that's almost beside the point: excitement is sustained by a brilliant idea, a new variant on the classic chase theme — Quilty as Humbert's walking paranoia, the madness that chases Humbert and is chased by him, over what should be the delusionary landscape of the actual United States. This panoramic confusion of normal and mad that can be experienced traveling around the country is, unfortunately, lost: the film badly needs the towns and motels and highways of the U.S. It suffers not only from the genteel English landscapes, but possibly also from the photographic style of Oswald Morris — perhaps justly famous, but subtly wrong (and too tasteful) for *Lolita*. It may seem like a dreadfully "un-cinematic" idea, but I rather wish that Kubrick, when he realized that he couldn't shoot in the U.S. (the reasons must have been economic) had experimented with stylized sets.

There *is* a paradox involved in the film *Lolita*. Stanley Kubrick shows talents in new areas (theme and dialogue and comedy), and is at his worst at what he's famous for. *The Killing* was a simple-minded suspense film about a racetrack robbery, but he structured it brilliantly with each facet shining in place; *Paths of Glory* was a simple-minded pacifist film, but he gave it nerv-ous rhythm and a sense of urgency. *Lolita* is so clumsily struc-tured that you begin to wonder what was shot and then cut out, why other pieces were left in, and whether the beginning was intended to be the end; and it is edited in so dilatory a fashion that after the first hour, almost every scene seems to go on too long. It's as if Kubrick lost his nerve. If he did, it's no wonder; the wonder is, that with all the pressures on American movie-makers — the pressures to evade, to conceal, to compromise, and to explain everything for the literal-minded — he had the nerve to transform this satire on the myths of love into the medium that has become consecrated to the myths. *Lolita* is a wilder comedy for being, now, family entertainment. Movie theaters belong to the same world as the highways and motels: in first-run theaters, "for persons over 18 years of age" does not mean that children are prohibited but simply that there are no reduced prices for children. In second-run neighborhood theaters, "for persons over 18 years of age" is amended by "unless accom-panied by a member of the family." That befits the story of Humbert Humbert.

꙳꙳꙳꙳꙳꙳

Shoot the Piano Player

The cover of David Goodis's novel *Down There*, now issued by Grove Press under the title of the film adapted from it, *Shoot the Piano Player*, carries a statement from Henry Miller — "Truffaut's film was so good I had doubts the book could equal it. I have just read the novel and I think it is even better than the film." I don't agree with Miller's judgment. I like the David Goodis book, but it's strictly a work in a limited genre, well-done and consistent; Truffaut's film busts out all over — and that's what's wonderful about it. The film is comedy, pathos, tragedy all scrambled up — much I think as most of us really experience them (surely all our lives are filled with comic horrors) but not as we have been led to expect them in films.

Shoot the Piano Player is about a man who has withdrawn from human experience; he wants not to care any more, not to get involved, not to *feel*. He has reduced life to a level on which he can cope with it — a revery between him and the piano. Everything that happens outside his solitary life seems erratic, accidental, unpredictable — but he can predict the pain. In a flashback we see why: when he *did* care, he failed the wife who needed him and caused her death. In the course of the film he is once more brought back into the arena of human contacts; another girl is destroyed, and he withdraws again into solitude.

Truffaut is a free and inventive director — and he fills the piano player's encounters with the world with good and bad jokes, bits from old Sacha Guitry films, clowns and thugs, tough kids, songs and fantasy and snow scenes, and homage to the American gangster films — not the classics, the socially conscious big-studio gangster films of the thirties, but the grade-B gangster films of the forties and fifties. Like Godard, who dedicated *Breathless* to Monogram Pictures, Truffaut is young, and he loves the cheap American gangster films of his childhood and youth. And like them, *Shoot the Piano Player* was made on a small budget. It was also made outside of studios with a crew that, according to witnesses, sometimes consisted of Truffaut, the actors, and a cameraman. Part of his love of cheap American movies with their dream imagery of the American gangster — the modern fairy tales for European children who go to movies — is no doubt reflected in his taking an American underworld novel and transferring its setting from Philadelphia to France.

Charles Aznavour who plays the hero is a popular singer turned actor — rather like Frank Sinatra in this country, and like Sinatra, he is an instinctive actor and a great camera subject. Aznavour's piano player is like a tragic embodiment of Robert Hutchins's Zukerkandl philosophy (whatever it is, stay out of it): he is the thinnest-skinned of modern heroes. It is his own capacity to feel that makes him cut himself off: he experiences so sensitively and so acutely that he can't bear the suffering of it — he thinks that if he doesn't do anything he won't feel and he won't cause suffering to others. The girl, Marie Dubois — later the smoky-steam-engine girl of *Jules and Jim* — is like a Hollywood forties movie type; she would have played well with Humphrey Bogart — a big, clear-eyed, crude, loyal, honest girl. The film is closely related to Godard's *Breathless*; and both seem to be haunted by the shade of Bogart.

Shoot the Piano Player is both nihilistic in attitude and, at the same time, in its wit and good spirits, totally involved in life and fun. Whatever Truffaut touches seems to leap to life — even a gangster thriller is transformed into the human comedy. A *comedy* about melancholia, about the hopelessness of life can only give the lie to the theme; for as long as we can joke, life is not hopeless, we can enjoy it. In Truffaut's style there is so much pleasure in life that the wry, lonely little piano player, the sardonic little man who shrugs off experience, is himself a beautiful character. This beauty is a tribute to human experience, even if the man is so hurt and defeated that he can only negate experience. The nihilism of the character — and the anarchic nihilism of the director's style — have led reviewers to call the film a surrealist farce; it isn't that strange.

When I refer to Truffaut's style as anarchic and nihilistic, I am referring to a *style*, not an absence of it. I disagree with the critics around the country who find the film disorganized; they seem to cling to the critical apparatus of their grammar-school teachers. They want unity of theme, easy-to-follow-transitions in mood, a good, coherent, old-fashioned plot, and heroes they can identify with and villains they can reject. Stanley Kauffmann in the *New Republic* compares *Shoot the Piano Player* with the sweepings of cutting room floors; *Time* decides that "the moral, if any, seems to be that shooting the piano player might, at least, put the poor devil out of his misery." But who but *Time* is looking for a moral? What's exciting about movies like *Shoot the Piano Player*, *Breathless* (and also the superb *Jules and Jim*, though it's very different from the other two) is that they, quite literally, move with the times. They are full of unresolved, inexplicable, disharmonious elements, irony and slapstick and defeat all compounded — *not* arbitrarily as the reviewers claim — but in terms of the film maker's efforts to find some expression for his own anarchic experience, instead of making more of those tiresome well-made movies that no longer mean much to us.

The subject matter of *Shoot the Piano Player*, as of *Breathless*, seems small and unimportant compared to the big themes of so many films, but it only *seems* small: it is an effort to deal with contemporary experience in terms drawn out of that experience. For both Godard and Truffaut a good part of this experience has been moviegoing, but this is just as much a part of their lives as reading is for a writer. And what writer does not draw upon what he has read?

A number of reviewers have complained that in his improvisatory method, Truffaut includes irrelevancies, and they use as chief illustration the opening scene — a gangster who is running away from pursuers bangs into a telephone pole, and then is helped to his feet by a man who proceeds to walk along with him, while discussing his marital life. Is it really so irrelevant? Only if you grew up in that tradition of the well-made play in which this bystander would have to reappear as some vital link in the plot. But he's relevant in a different way here: he helps to set us in a world in which his semi-normal existence seems just as much a matter of chance and fringe behavior and simplicity as the gangster's existence — which begins to seem semi-normal also. The bystander talks; we get an impression of his way of life and his need to talk about it, and he goes out of the film, and that is that: Truffaut would have to be as stodgy and dull witted as the reviewers to bring him back and link him into the story. For the meaning of these films is that these fortuitous encounters illuminate something about our lives in a way that the old neat plots don't.

There is a tension in the method; we never quite know where we are, how we are supposed to react — and this tension, as the moods change and we are pulled in different ways, gives us the excitement of drama, of art, of *our* life. Nothing is clear-cut, the ironies crisscross and bounce. The loyal, courageous heroine is so determined to live by her code that when it's violated, she comes on too strong, and the piano player is repelled by her inability to respect the weaknesses of others. Thugs kidnaping a little boy discuss their possessions with him — a conversation worthy of a footnote in Veblen's passages on conspicuous expenditure.

Only a really carefree, sophisticated film maker could bring it off — and satisfy our desire for the unexpected that is also *right*. Truffaut is a director of incredible taste; he never carries a scene *too* far. It seems extraordinarily simple to complain that a virtuoso who can combine many moods, has not stuck to one familiar old mood — but this is what the reviews seem to amount to. The modern novel has abandoned the old conception that each piece must be in place — abandoned it so thoroughly that when we read something like Angus Wilson's *Anglo-Saxon Attitudes* in which each piece does finally fit in place, we are astonished and amused at the dexterity of the accomplishment. That is the way Wilson works and it's wonderfully satisfying, but few

modern novelists work that way; and it would be as irrelevant
to the meaning and quality of, say, *Tropic of Capricorn* to complain that the plot isn't neatly tied together like *Great Expectations*, as to complain of the film *Shoot the Piano Player*
that it isn't neatly tied together like *The Bicycle Thief*. Dwight
Macdonald wrote that *Shoot the Piano Player* deliberately
mixed up "three genres which are usually kept apart; crime
melodrama, romance, and slapstick comedy." And, he says, "I
thought the mixture didn't jell, but it was an exhilarating try."
What I think is exhilarating in *Shoot the Piano Player* is that it
doesn't "jell" and that the different elements keep *us* in a state
of suspension — we react far more than we do to works that
"jell." Incidentally, it's not completely accurate to say that these
genres are usually kept apart: although *slapstick* rarely enters
the mixture except in a far-out film like *Beat the Devil* or *Lovers
and Thieves* or the new *The Manchurian Candidate*, there are
numerous examples of crime melodrama–romance–comedy
among well-known American films — particularly of the forties
— for example *The Maltese Falcon, Casablanca, The Big Sleep,
To Have and Have Not*. (Not all of Truffaut's models are cheap
B pictures.)

Perhaps one of the problems that American critics and audiences may have with *Shoot the Piano Player* is a peculiarly
American element in it — the romantic treatment of the man
who walks alone. For decades our films were full of these gangsters, outcasts, detectives, cynics; Bogart epitomized them all
— all the men who had been hurt by a woman or betrayed by
their friends and who no longer trusted anybody. And although
I think most of us enjoyed this romantic treatment of the man
beyond the law, we rejected it intellectually. It was part of hack
moviemaking — we might love it but it wasn't really intellectually respectable. And now here it is, inspired by our movies,
and coming back to us via France. The heroine of *Shoot the
Piano Player* says of the hero, "Even when he's with somebody,
he walks alone." But this French hero carries his isolation much
farther than the earlier American hero: when his girl is having a

fight on his behalf and he is impelled to intervene, he says to himself, "You're out of it. Let them fight it out." He is brought into it; but where the American hero, once impelled to move, is a changed man and, redeemed by love or patriotism or a sense of fair play, he would take the initiative, save his girl, and conquer everything, this French hero simply moves into the situation when he must, when he can no longer stay out of it, and takes the consequences. He finds that the contact with people is once again defeating. He really doesn't believe in anything; the American hero only *pretended* he didn't.

Breathless was about active, thoughtless young people; *Shoot the Piano Player* is about a passive, melancholic character who is acted upon. Yet the world that surrounds the principal figures in these two movies is similar: the clowns in one are police, in the other gangsters, but this hardly matters. What we react to in both is the world of absurdities that is so much like our own world in which people suddenly and unexpectedly turn into clowns. But at the center is the sentimentalist — Belmondo in *Breathless*, Aznavour here — and I think there can be no doubt that both Godard and Truffaut love their heroes.

There are incidentally a number of little in-group jokes included in the film; a few of these are of sufficiently general interest to be worth mentioning, and, according to Andrew Sarris, they have been verified by Truffaut. The piano player is given the name of Saroyan as a tribute to William Saroyan, particularly for his volume of stories *The Man on the Flying Trapeze*, and also because Charles Aznavour, like Saroyan, is Armenian (and, I would surmise, for the playful irony of giving a life-evading hero the name of one of the most rambunctious of life-embracing writers). One of the hero's brothers in the film is named Chico, as a tribute to the Marx Brothers. And the impresario in the film, the major villain of the work, is called Lars Schmeel, as a disapproving gesture toward someone Truffaut does *not* admire — the impresario Lars Schmidt, known to us simply as Ingrid Bergman's current husband, but apparently known to others — and disliked by Truffaut — for his theatrical activities in Paris.

If a more pretentious vocabulary or a philosophic explanation will help: the piano player is intensely human and sympathetic, a character who empathizes with others, and with whom we, as audience, empathize; but he does not want to accept the responsibilities of his humanity — he asks only to be left alone. And because he refuses voluntary involvement, he is at the mercy of accidental forces. He is, finally, man trying to preserve his little bit of humanity in a chaotic world — it is not merely a world he never made but a world he would much rather forget about. But schizophrenia cannot be willed and so long as he is sane, he is only partly successful: crazy accidents happen — and sometimes he must deal with them. That is to say, no matter how far he retreats from life, he is not completely safe. And Truffaut himself is so completely engaged in life that he pleads for the piano player's right to be left alone, to live in his withdrawn state, *to be out of it*. Truffaut's plea is, of course, "Don't shoot the piano player."

⅃⅃⅃⅃⅃⅃⅃

Jules and Jim

When the Legion of Decency condemned *Jules and Jim*, the statement read: the story has been developed "in a context alien to Christian and traditional natural morality." It certainly has. The Legion went on to say: "If the director has a definite moral viewpoint to express, it is so obscure that the visual amorality and immorality of the film are predominant and consequently pose a serious problem for a mass medium of entertainment." It would be possible to make a fraudulent case for the film's morality by pointing out that the adulterous individuals suffer and die, but this is so specious and so irrelevant to the meanings and qualities of the work that surely the Legion, expert in these matters, would recognize that it was casuistry. The Legion isn't wrong about the visual amorality either, and yet, *Jules and Jim* is not only one of the most beautiful films ever made, and the greatest motion picture of recent years, it is also, viewed as a work of art, exquisitely and impeccably *moral*. Truffaut does not have "a definite moral viewpoint to express" and he does not use the screen for messages or special pleading or to sell sex for money; he uses the film medium to express his love and knowledge of life as completely as he can.

The film is adapted from Henri-Pierre Roché's autobiographical novel, written when he was seventy-four, with some additional material from his even later work, *Deux Anglaises et le Continent*. If some of us have heard of Roché, it's probably just the scrap of information that he was the man who introduced Gertrude Stein to Picasso — but this scrap shouldn't be discarded, because both Stein and Picasso are relevant to the characters and period of *Jules and Jim*. Roché is now dead, but the model for Catherine, the Jeanne Moreau role, is a German literary woman who is still alive; it was she who translated *Lolita* into German. Truffaut has indicated, also, that some of the material which he improvised on location was suggested by Apollinaire's letters to Madeleine — a girl whom he had met for a half-hour on a train.

The film begins in Paris before the First World War. Jules the Austrian (Oskar Werner) and Jim the Frenchman (Henri Serre) are Mutt and Jeff, Sancho Panza and Don Quixote, devoted friends, contentedly arguing about life and letters. Catherine enters their lives, and Jules and Jim try to have both the calm of their friendship and the excitement of her imperious, magical presence. She marries Jules who can't hold her, and in despair he encourages Jim's interest in her — "That way she'll still be *ours*." But Catherine can't subjugate Jim: he is too independent to be dominated by her whims. Not completely captivated, Jim fails to believe in her love when she most desperately offers it. She kills herself and him.

The music, the camera and editing movement, the rhythm of

the film carry us along without pauses for reflection. Truffaut doesn't linger; nothing is held too long, nothing is overstated or even *stated*. Perhaps that's why others besides the Legion of Decency have complained: Stanley Kauffmann in the *New Republic* says that *Jules and Jim* "loses sight of purposes . . . It is a confusion of the sheer happiness of being in the studio . . . with the reason for being there." Truffaut, the most youthfully alive and abundant of all the major film directors, needs a *reason* for making movies about as much as Picasso needs a reason for picking up a brush or a lump of clay. And of what film maker could a reference to a *studio* be less apt? He works everywhere and with anything at hand. Kauffmann says of *Jules and Jim*, "There is a lot less here than meets the eye," and Dwight Macdonald, who considers Kauffmann his only peer, is reassured: "one doesn't want to be the only square," he writes. If it gives him comfort to know there are two of them . . .

What is the film about? It's a celebration of life in a great historical period, a period of ferment and extraordinary achievement in painting and music and literature. Together Jules and Jim have a peaceful friendship (and Jim has a quiet love affair with Gilberte) but when Jules and Jim are with Catherine they feel alive. Anything may happen — she's the catalyst, the troublemaker, the source of despair as well as the source of joy. She is the enchantress who makes art out of life.

At the end, Jules, who has always given in to everything in order to keep Catherine, experiences relief at her death, although he has always delighted in the splendor she conferred on his existence. (Don't we all experience this sort of relief when we say goodbye to a particularly brilliant houseguest?) The dullness in Jules, the bourgeois under the Bohemian, the passivity is made clear from the outset: it is why the girls don't fall in love with him. At the end, the excitements and the humiliations are over. He will have peace, and after a lifetime with Catherine he has earned it.

Catherine is, of course, a little crazy, but that's not too surprising. Pioneers can easily become fanatics, maniacs. And

Catherine is part of a new breed — the independent, intellectual modern woman, so determined to live as freely as a man that while claiming equality she uses every feminine wile to gain extra advantages, to demonstrate her superiority, and to increase her power position. She is the emerging twentieth-century woman satirized by Strindberg, who also adored her; she is the woman with rights and responsibilities who entered Western literature after the turn of the century and has almost always been seen by the male authors as demanding the rights but refusing the responsibilities. This is the traditional male view of the feminist, and the film's view is not different. Don't we now hear complaints that Negroes are so sensitive about their rights that you can't treat them casually and equally as you would anybody else, you can't disagree on a job or question their judgment, you have to defer to their sensitivities and treat them as if they were super-whites — always in the right? So it is with Catherine.

Catherine, in her way, compensates for the homage she demands. She has, despite her need to intrude and to dominate, the gift for life. She holds nothing in reserve; she lives out her desires; when she can't control the situation, she destroys it. Catherine may be wrong-headed, as those who aspire to be free spirits often are (and they make this wrongness more visible than pliable, amiable people do), but she is devoid of hypocrisy and she doesn't lie. In one of the most upsetting and odd little scenes in the film she takes out a bottle which she says is "vitriol for lying eyes" — and Jim doesn't react any more than if it were aspirin. Catherine the free spirit has the insanity of many free spirits — she believes that she knows truth from lies, right from wrong. Her absolutism is fascinating, but it is also rather clearly *morally insane*. She punishes Jim because he has not broken with Gilberte, though she has not broken with Jules. Only the relationships *she* sets and dominates are *right*. Catherine suffers from the fatal ambivalence of the "free and equal" woman toward sex: she can leave men, but if they leave her, she is as abandoned and desolate, as destroyed and helpless as any clinging vine (perhaps *more* destroyed — she cannot even ask for sympathy). *Jules and Jim* is about the impossibility of freedom, as it is about the many losses of innocence.

All these elements are elliptical in the film — you catch them out of the corner of your eye and mind. So much happens in the span of an hour and three quarters that even if you don't take more than a fraction of the possible meanings from the material, you still get far more than if you examined almost any other current film, frame by frame, under a microscope. *Jules and Jim* is as full of character and wit and radiance as *Marienbad* is empty, and the performance by Jeanne Moreau is so vivid that the bored, alienated wife of *La Notte* is a faded monochrome. In *Jules and Jim* alienation is just one aspect of her character and we see how Catherine got there: she *becomes* alienated when she can't get her own way, when she is blocked. It is not a universal condition as in *La Notte* (neither Jules nor Jim shares in it): it is her developing insanity as she is cut off from what she wants and no longer takes pleasure in life.

Jules and Jim are portraits of artists as young men, but they are the kind of artists who grow up into something else — they become specialists in some field, or journalists; and the dedication to art of their youth becomes the *civilizing* influence in their lives. The war blasts the images of Bohemian life; both Jules and Jim are changed, but not Catherine. She is the unreconstructed Bohemian who does *not* settle down. She needed more strength, more will than they to live the artist's life — and this determination is the *un*civilizing factor. Bohemianism has made her, underneath all the graces, a moral barbarian: freedom has come to mean whatever she says it is. And when she loses what she believes to be freedom — when she can no longer dictate the terms on which Jim will live — she is lost, isolated. She no longer makes art out of life: she makes life hell.

She chooses death, and she calls on Jules to observe her choice, the last demonstration of her power over life and death, because Jules by a lifetime of yielding his own freedom to her has become, to her, a witness. He can only observe grand gestures; he cannot *make* them. In the last moment in the car, when self-destruction is completely determined, she smiles the smile of the statue: this was the mystery that drew them to her — the smile that looks so easy and natural but which is self-contained and impenetrable.

Jules and Jim ends after the burning of the books in Germany, the end of an epoch, as Truffaut has said, for intellectual Bohemians like Jules and Jim. The film is, in a way, a tribute to the books that were burned; I can't think of another movie so full of books, and of references to books and of writing and translating books. Books were the blood of these characters: they took their ideas of life from books, and writing books was their idea of living.

Jules and Jim is, among other things, the best movie ever made about what I guess most of us think of as the Scott Fitzgerald period (though it begins much earlier). Catherine jumping into the waters of the Seine to demonstrate her supremacy over Jules and Jim, who are discussing the weaknesses of women, is not unlike Zelda jumping over that balustrade. This film treatment of the period is a work of lyric poetry and a fable of the world as playground, a work of art as complex and suggestive in its way as the paintings and poetry and novels and music of the period that it is based on. It is a tribute to the school of Paris when art and Paris were synonymous; filmically it is a new school of Paris — and the new school of Paris is cinema. You go to movies, you talk movies, and you make movies. The young French painters don't compare with the Americans, and French literature is in a fancy trance, but oh, how the young French artists can make movies!

Several of the critics, among them Kauffmann, have complained that the song Jeanne Moreau sings is irrelevant to the action of the film. It's embarrassing to have to point out the obvious, that the song is the theme and spirit of the film: Jules and Jim and Catherine are the ones who "make their way in life's whirlpool of days — round and round together bound." And, in the film, the song is an epiphany: when Catherine sings, the story is crystallized, and the song, like Jim and the child rolling on the hill, seems to belong to memory almost before it is over. In the same way, the still shots catch for us, as for the characters, the distillation, the beauty of the moment. Throughout the film, Georges Delerue's exquisite music — simple and fragrant, popular without being banal — is part of the atmosphere; it is so evocative that if you put the music on the phonograph, like the little phrase from Vinteuil's sonata, it brings back the images, the emotions, the experience. Though emotionally in the tradition of Jean Renoir, as a work of film craftsmanship *Jules and Jim* is an homage to D. W. Griffith. Truffaut explores the medium, plays with it, overlaps scenes, uses fast cutting in the manner of *Breathless* and leaping continuity in the manner of *Zero for Conduct,* changes the size and shape of the images as Griffith did, and in one glorious act of homage he recreates a frame out of *Intolerance,* the greatest movie ever made. *Jules and Jim* is the most exciting movie made in the West since *L'Avventura* and *Breathless* and Truffaut's earlier *Shoot the Piano Player;* because of the beauty and warmth of its images, it is a richer, a more satisfying film than any of them. I think it will rank among the great lyric achievements of the screen, right up there with the work of Griffith and Renoir.

ꙮꙮꙮ

Hemingway's
Adventures of a Young Man

I don't want to waste space discussing this film, which is rather like a Portrait of the Artist as a Young Man as Norman Rockwell might have conceived it for a *Saturday Evening Post* cover — the dreariest kind of Americana, with all the full-bodied flavor of a can of Campbell's cream of chicken soup served cold, right from the tin. It's the moviemakers' mixture as before of

Freudianism and anti-Momism in which the young man is torn between the castrating mother and the castrated father, and must free himself in order to become a man. *Adventures of a Young Man*, one of the thickest servings of this formula, fails to take into consideration what makes the young man in the film an artist: I suggest it didn't come out of that All-American manly hunting and fishing with Papa — it probably had something to do with the cultural aspirations of that nagging castrating mom, the villainness of the story. But the film is hardly worth talking about — heavy and dull and clearly marked with moral signposts, each episode a lesson in growing up. Even the high spots — the sequences with Dan Dailey and Paul Newman and the romantic cynicism of the Ricardo Montalban scenes — lack rhythm and structure. I want to discuss a basic moral issue that the film raises.

I think it is a disgrace and a moral offense to take short stories by Hemingway and a piece of a novel and combine them with incidents from his life in a sentimental pastiche which is then presented as some sort of biographical film about Ernest Hemingway. It's a violation of his life as well as of his work — the integrity of neither is respected in this kind of treatment. And I fear that this kind of opportunistic screenwriting will soon leave only obscure writers with lives they can call their own. It's so easy to do — and it has the superficial justification that most writers' early work *is* partly autobiographical. But, in destroying the boundaries between a man's life and his art, the meanings are all homogenized. The problem is not merely that the writer has drawn *all* of his characters out of himself, and the film reduces him to the one that most resembles him, but that his particular qualities as a writer — the shape and form he gave to his experiences — are destroyed. His art is turned back into an imitation of the raw material out of which he made his art. And it's part of the personality cult of modern life that the movies are more interested in exploiting Hemingway himself than in trying to find some way of making a movie that would do anything like justice to his style and method. There has rarely been even an approximation of the particular qualities of Hemingway's work in the films based on his novels — the closest was perhaps the first ten minutes of Robert Siodmak's *The Killers*, and the next closest, the first two-thirds of *The Macomber Affair*. *Adventures of a Young Man* follows the direction set in *The Snows of Kilimanjaro* — in which the hero, played by Gregory Peck, seemed already to be drawn more from Hemingway's life and legend than from the story on which the film was based. From a film like *Adventures of a Young Man* you would never be able to guess what kind of a writer Hemingway was trying to be, nor anything of the qualities of his style. He cleaned out the stuffy upholstery of "fine" writing; this movie brings it right back again, padding out the clean lines. Even when his dialogue is retained, it is set in a context of Cinema-Scope and De Luxe-colored calendar art — and paced in such an old-fashioned way that you may want to cry out that this is the film equivalent of everything Hemingway was trying to eliminate from his writing.

The movie is neither about his life nor is it truly drawn from his work. *Time* says, "Time has given Hemingway's life an aura of the magical. Hence this is an enchanted movie in the same way that forests and sleeping beauties and Prince Charmings in children's storybooks are enchanted." But Hemingway was a true writer, not a false magician, and in order to turn him into the Prince Charming of a movie, the film violates what he was as a man also. He has been turned into the most commonplace and generalized public idea of a struggling artist, and I suppose we can look forward to the same kind of sugar-coated sanctification of D. H. Lawrence, James Joyce, Thomas Wolfe, and just about anybody else you can think of — all turned into the same figure of the artist — all endowed "with an aura of the magical" (I wonder where *Time* gets all its nimbuses?). Movies have been doing it to painters and singers and actors and dancers — I suppose writers are next. Thus everyone who pulled himself out of the mediocrity of his surroundings is brought back to it, and glorified for having been just like everyone else. The moviemakers who claim to be watering the flowers on the graves of the great seem to use their own water.

Fires on the Plain (Nobi)

Cautious as I am about superlatives, I think the term "masterpiece" must be applied to *Fires on the Plain*. It has the disturbing power of great art: it doesn't leave you quite the same. A few hours after seeing it, or a few days or weeks, it rushes up and overwhelms you.

If Dostoyevsky had been a film maker telling his Grand Inquisitor story with a camera, it might have been much like this great visual demonstration that men are not brothers. *Fires on the Plain* is an obsessive, relentless cry of passion and disgust. The subject is modern man as a cannibal, and after a few minutes of *Fires on the Plain*, this subject does not seem at all strange or bizarre: it seems, rather, to be basic. When violence is carried to the extremes of modern war, cannibalism may appear to be the ultimate truth.

The setting is Leyte. Tamura, the hero, is one of the stragglers of the disintegrating retreating Japanese army — terrified of the Americans, the Filipinos, and each other. Tamura walks across the plain unharmed because he is already a dead man; he is tubercular, no one wants his flesh. In the middle of this desolation, there are bonfires — ambiguous flames in the distance that kindle hope. (Perhaps they are signal fires? Perhaps Filipino farmers are burning corn husks? Perhaps there is still some normal life going on?) At the end Tamura approaches the flames and the last illusion is dispelled.

What can be said of a work so powerfully felt and so intensely expressed that it turns rage into beauty? *Fires on the Plain* is an appalling picture; it is also a work of epic poetry. The director, Kon Ichikawa, and the writer, his wife Natto Wada, are among the foremost screen artists of Japan; their other collaborations include *The Burmese Harp, Enjo,* and *Kagi. Fires on the Plain* is based on the book by Shohei Ooka, the greatest Japanese novel to come out of the war, which, as the translator Ivan Morris says, draws a shocking analogy "between the cannibalism of the starving soldiers . . . and the Christian doctrine of the Mass."

Fires on the Plain is a passion film — and a new vision of hell. The passion that informs the character of Tamura is so intense, so desperate and overwhelming, that he seems both painfully close to us and at the same time remote, detached from what is ordinarily thought of as emotion. The atmosphere of the film is also remote from our normal world: there is nothing banal, nothing extraneous to the single-minded view of man *in extremis.* And what is both shocking and, in some terrible sense, beautiful is the revelation of man's extraordinary passion for life even in an inferno. The soldiers will commit any crime, will kill each other, devour each other, to go on living a few more minutes, a few more hours. Even though there is no future, they are trying to sustain life as if there were; it becomes the new variant of *La Grande Illusion* — that if they can just make it to this forest or that port, they will be saved. Historically, in terms of World War II, some *were* saved; but Ichikawa's film is not, at this level, realistic. It is not merely about World War II, or the experiences on Leyte; it is not an anti-war film in the usual sense. We see no causes, no cures, no enemy; it goes beyond nationalism or patriotism. All men are enemies. It is a post-nuclear-war film — a vision of the end, the final inferno. And oddly, when survival is the only driving force, when men live only to live, survival comes to seem irrelevant.

There is a fiendish irony involved in the physical condition of the hero: he alone can be a hero — act human — because he can't save his own life anyway. He can be human because he is beyond self-interest; he becomes a Japanese Christ-figure. Tamura, so close to death, is passionately — instinctively and intellectually — committed to the amenities of humanity and civilization. He shares his potatoes with another man because this is how *men* behave; he refuses to eat human flesh because this practice is a destruction of human behavior. It is the only place left to draw the line: Tamura has been degraded in every other way; he has murdered a helpless, terrified girl, but cannibalism is the final degradation. It is the line he will not cross: it becomes the only remaining dividing line, not between man and beast but between beast and beast who clings to the memory, the *idea* of man. Tamura's rejection of cannibalism is the only morality left. Yet, in the circumstances, his behavior — obsessed with the image of man — is what is called "unrealistic"; that is to say, in total war, man preserves himself (if he is lucky) only by destroying his humanity. *Nothing* is left.

Just as Ivan Karamazov is obsessed with the evil in the world that stands in the way of believing in God because he *wants* to believe, Ichikawa's revulsion is the negative image of aspiration and hope. In this film, so harshly realistic, so apparently inevitable that it becomes surrealistic, man is defined as man who cannot forget he is man. As in Céline's novels, there is the poetry of disgust, of catharsis. There is even a black form of humor in a weird Mack Sennett-like sequence — the sudden astonishment of comedy as a succession of soldiers discard their shoes and put on the ones discarded by others.

The film follows the novel very closely except that in the novel Tamura does cross the line: he eats human flesh, or "monkey meat" as the soldiers call it (a term that's like a hideous self-inflicted use of the wartime American expression of contempt for the Japanese). And there is an epilogue to the novel which has not been filmed. At the end of the novel, several years have passed, and Tamura, who has been telling the story, is revealed to be a madman in a mental hospital near Tokyo. Guiltily, he believes that in rejecting the proffered flesh of a dying soldier who had raised his emaciated arm and said, "When I'm dead, you may eat this," he rejected God's flesh. His new formulation is that "all men are cannibals, all women are whores. Each of us must act according to his nature." In his madness, he concludes, ". . . if as a result of hunger human beings were constrained to eat each other, then this world of ours was no more than the result of God's wrath. And if I at this moment, could vomit forth anger, then I, who was no longer human, must be an angel of God, an instrument of God's wrath." Ichikawa (wisely, I think) has infused the whole story with this obsessive angelic wrath, rather than attempting to film the epilogue.

As an ironic aside to the subject of mankind devouring its humanity, man becoming "monkey meat," here is John Coleman's description in the *New Statesman* of an English audience's reaction to the film:

Fires on the Plain is showing to an audience of turnip-headed morons . . . screams of laughter welcoming such acts as the impaling of a mad dog on a bayonet (the spray of blood that hit the ground really rolled them in the aisles), titters as the Japanese hero declines the invitation to cannibalism, bellows of fun as machine guns stuttered and gaunt men ran away.

I have seen just one review in a San Francisco paper: it seems to have been written by one of those turnip-headed morons. I don't know how American audiences — if there are any — will react. If it's anything like the English reaction, perhaps the mad Tamura is right and all men are cannibals.

Replying to Listeners

I am resolved to start the New Year right; I don't want to carry over any unnecessary rancor from 1962. So let me discharge a few debts. I want to say a few words about a communication from a woman listener. She begins with, "Miss Kael, I assume you aren't married — one loses that nasty, sharp bite in one's voice when one learns to care about others." Isn't it remarkable that women, who used to pride themselves on their chastity, are now just as complacently proud of their married status? They've read Freud and they've not only got the idea that being married is healthier, more "mature," they've also got the illusion that it improves their character. This lady is so concerned that I won't appreciate her full acceptance of femininity that she signs herself with her husband's name preceded by a Mrs. Why, if this Mrs. John Doe just signed herself Jane Doe, I might confuse her with one of those nasty virgins, I might not understand the warmth and depth of connubial experience out of which she writes.

I wonder, Mrs. John Doe, in your reassuring, protected marital state, if you have considered that perhaps caring about others may bring a bite to the voice? And I wonder if you have considered how difficult it is for a woman in this Freudianized age, which turns out to be a new Victorian age in its attitude to women who *do* anything, to show any intelligence without being accused of unnatural aggressivity, hateful vindictiveness, or lesbianism. The latter accusation is generally made by men who have had a rough time in an argument; they like to console themselves with the notion that the woman is semi-masculine. The new Freudianism goes beyond Victorianism in its placid assumption that a woman who uses her mind is trying to compete with men. It was bad enough for women who had brains to be considered freaks like talking dogs; now it's leeringly assumed that they're trying to grow a penis — which any man will tell you is an accomplishment that puts canine conversation in the shadows.

Mrs. John Doe and her sisters who write to me seem to interpret Freud to mean that intelligence, like a penis, is a male attribute. The true woman is supposed to be sweet and passive — she shouldn't argue or emphasize an opinion or get excited about a judgment. Sex — or at least regulated marital sex — is supposed to act as a tranquilizer. In other words, the Freudianized female accepts that whole complex of passivity that the feminists battled against.

Mrs. Doe, you know something, I don't mind sounding sharp — and I'll take my stand with those pre-Freudian feminists; and you know something else, I think you're probably so worried about competing with male egos and those brilliant masculine intellects that you probably bore men to death.

This lady who attacks me for being nasty and sharp goes on to write, "I was extremely disappointed to hear your costic speech on and about the radio station, KPFA. It is unfortunate you were unable to get a liberal education, because that would have enabled you to know that a great many people have many fields of interest, and would have saved you from displaying your ignorance on the matter." She, incidentally, displays her liberal education by spelling caustic c-o-s-t-i-c, and it is with some expense of spirit that I read this kind of communication. Should I try to counter my education — liberal and sexual — against hers, should I explain that Pauline Kael is the name I was given at birth, and that it does not reflect my marital vicissitudes which might over-complicate nomenclature?

It is not really that I prefer to call myself by my own name and hence Miss that bothers her or the other Mrs. Does, it is that I express ideas she doesn't like. If I called myself by three names like those poetesses in the *Saturday Review of Literature*, Mrs. Doe would still hate my guts. But significantly she attacks me for being a Miss. Having become a Mrs., she has gained moral superiority: for the modern woman, officially losing her virginity is a victory comparable to the Victorian woman's officially keeping hers. I'm happy for Mrs. Doe that she's got a husband, but in her defense of KPFA she writes like a virgin mind. And is that really something to be happy about?

Mrs. Doe, the happily, emotionally-secure-mature-liberally-educated-womanly-woman has her opposite number in the mail-bag. Here is a letter from a manly man. This is the letter in its entirety: "Dear Miss Kael, Since you know so much about the art of the film, why don't you spend your time making it? But first, you will need a pair of balls." Mr. Dodo (I use the repetition in honor of your two attributes), movies are made and criticism is written by the use of intelligence, talent, taste, emotion, education, imagination and discrimination. I suggest it is time you and your cohorts stop thinking with your genital jewels. There is a standard answer to this old idiocy of if-you-know-so-much-about-the-art-of-the-film-why-don't-you-make-movies. You don't have to lay an egg to know if it tastes good. If it makes you feel better, I have worked making movies, and I wasn't hampered by any biological deficiencies.

Others may wonder why I take the time to answer letters of this sort: the reason is that these two examples, although cruder than most of the mail, simply carry to extremes the kind of thing so many of you write. There are, of course, some letter writers who take a more "constructive" approach. I'd like to read you part of a long letter I received yesterday:

I haven't been listening to your programs for very long and haven't heard all of them since I began listening . . . But I must say that while I have been listening, I have not heard one favorable statement made of any "name" movie made in the last several years. . . . I have heard no movie which received any kind of favorable mention which was not hard to find playing, either because of its lack of popularity or because of its age. In your remarks the other evening about De Sica's earlier movies you praised them all without reservation until you mentioned his "most famous film — The Bicycle Thief, a great work, no doubt, though I personally find it too carefully and classically structured." You make me think that the charge that the favorability of your comments on any given movie varies inversely with its popularity, is indeed true even down to the last nuance.

But even as I write this, I can almost feel you begin to tighten up, to start thinking of something to say to show that I am wrong. I really wish you wouldn't feel that way. I would much rather you leaned back in your chair, looked up at the ceiling and asked yourself, "Well, how about it? Is it true or not? Am I really biased against movies other people like, because they like them? When I see a popular movie, do I see it as it is or do I really just try to pick it apart?" You see, I'm not like those other people that have been haranguing you. I may be presumptuous, but I am trying sincerely to be of help to you. I think you have a great deal of potential as a reviewer. . . . But I am convinced that great a potential as you have, you will never realize any more of that potential than you have now until you face those questions mentioned before, honestly, seriously, and courageously, no matter how painful it may be. I want you to think of these questions, I don't want you to think of how to convince me of their answers. I don't want you to look around to find some popular movie to which you can give a good review and thus "prove me wrong." That would be evading the issue of whether the questions were really true or not. Furthermore, I am not "attacking" you and you have no need to defend yourself to me.

May I interrupt? *Please, attack* me instead — it's this kind of "constructive criticism" that misses the point of everything I'm trying to say that drives me mad. It's enough to make one howl with despair, this concern for my potential — as if I were a cow giving thin milk. But back to the letter —

In fact, I would prefer that you make no reply to me at all about the answers to these questions, since I have no need of the answers and because almost any answer given now, without long and thoughtful consideration, would almost surely be an attempt to justify yourself, and that's just what you don't have to do, and shouldn't do. No one needs to know the answers to these questions except you, and you are the only person who must answer. In short, I would not for the world have you silence any voices in you . . . and most certainly not a concerned little voice saying, "Am I really being fair? Do I see the whole movie or just the part I like — or just the part I don't like?"

And so on he goes for another few paragraphs. Halfway through, I thought this man was pulling my leg; as I got further and read "how you missed the child-like charm and innocence of *The Parent Trap* . . . is quite beyond me," I decided it's mass culture that's pulling both legs out from under us all. Dear man, the only real question your letter made me ask myself is, "What's the use?" and I didn't lean back in my chair and look up at the ceiling, I went to the liquor cabinet and poured myself a good stiff drink.

How completely has mass culture subverted even the role of the critic when listeners suggest that because the movies a critic reviews favorably are unpopular and hard to find, that the critic must be playing some snobbish game with himself and the public? Why are you listening to a minority radio station like KPFA? Isn't it because you want something you don't get on commercial radio? I try to direct you to films that, if you search them out, will give you something you won't get from *The Parent Trap*. You consider it rather "suspect" that I don't praise more "name" movies. Well, what makes a "name" movie is simply a saturation advertising campaign, the same kind of campaign that puts samples of liquid detergents at your door. The "name" pictures of Hollywood are made the same way they are sold: by pretesting the various ingredients, removing all possible elements that might affront the mass audience, adding all possible elements that will titillate the largest number of people. As the CBS television advertising slogan put it — "Titillate — and dominate." *South Pacific* is seventh in *Variety*'s list of all-time top grossers. Do you know anybody who thought it was a good movie? Was it popular in any meaningful sense or do we just call it popular because it was sold? The tie-in campaign for Doris Day in *Lover Come Back* included a Doris Day album to be sold for a dollar with a purchase of Imperial margarine. With a schedule of 23 million direct mail pieces, newspaper, radio, TV and store ads, *Lover Come Back* became a "name" picture.

I try not to waste air time discussing obviously bad movies — popular though they may be; and I don't discuss unpopular bad movies because you're not going to see them anyway; and there wouldn't be much point or sport in hitting people who are already down. I do think it's important to take time on movies which are inflated by critical acclaim and which some of you might assume to be the films to see.

There were some extraordinarily unpleasant anonymous letters after the last broadcast on "The New American Cinema." Some were obscene; the wittiest called me a snail eating the tender leaves off young artists. I recognize your assumptions: the critic is supposed to be rational, clever, heartless and empty, envious of the creative fire of the artist, and if the critic is a woman, she is supposed to be cold and castrating. The artist is supposed to be delicate and sensitive and in need of tender care and nourishment. Well, this nineteenth-century romanticism is pretty silly in twentieth-century Bohemia.

I regard criticism as an art, and if in this country and in this age it is practiced with honesty, it is no more remunerative than the work of an avant-garde film artist. My dear anonymous letter writers, if you think it so easy to be a critic, so difficult to be a poet or a painter or film experimenter, may I suggest you try both? You may discover why there are so few critics, so many poets.

Some of you write me flattering letters and I'm grateful, but one last request: if you write me, please don't say, "This is the first time I've ever written a fan letter." Don't say it, even if it's true. You make me feel as if I were taking your virginity — and it's just too sordid.

Billy Budd

Billy Budd is not a great motion picture, but it is a very good one — a clean, honest work of intelligence and craftsmanship. It ranks as one of the best films of 1962, and by contrast, it exposes what a slovenly, incoherent production *Mutiny on the Bounty* is. *Billy Budd* not only has a strong story line; it has a core of meaning that charges the story, gives it tension and intellectual excitement.

In the film version of *Billy Budd*, Melville's story has been stripped for action; and I think this was probably the right method — the ambiguities of the story probably come through more clearly than if the film were not so straightforward in its narrative line. The very cleanness of the narrative method, Peter Ustinov's efficient direction, Robert Krasker's stylized, controlled photography, help to release the meanings. The film could easily have been clogged by metaphysical speculation and homo-erotic overtones. Instead, it is a good, tense movie that doesn't try to tell us too much — and so gives us a very great deal.

Terence Stamp is a remarkably intelligent casting selection for Billy. If he were a more feminine type — as the role is often filled on the stage — all the overtones would be cheapened and limited. Stamp, fortunately, can wear white pants and suggest angelic splendor without falling into the narcissistic poses that juveniles so often mistake for grace. Robert Ryan gives a fine performance in the difficult role of Claggart. Ryan has had so few chances at anything like characterization in his movie career that each time he comes across, it seems amazing that he could have retained such power and technique. I don't know how many dozens of times I've seen him, but the roles that I remember are his prizefighter in *The Set-Up*, the anti-Semite in *Cross-fire*, the vicious millionaire in Max Ophuls's *Caught*, the projectionist in *Clash by Night*, the central figure in *God's Little Acre*. Considering that he is a very specialized physical type — the tall, rangy American of Western mythology — his variety of characterizations is rather extraordinary. Perhaps just because he is the type who looks at home in cowboy movies, critics rarely single out his performances for commendation. The American reviewers of *Billy Budd* seem more concerned to complain that his Claggart doesn't have an English accent than to judge his performance. But it is not at all necessary that Claggart speak with an English accent: his antecedents are deliberately vague in Melville as in the film, and the men on board are drawn from all over. It may even be better that Claggart's accent does not define his background for us.

Ryan's Claggart has the requisite Satanic dignity: he makes

evil comprehensible. The evil he defines is the way the world works, but it is also the self-hatred that makes it necessary for him to destroy the image of goodness. In the film Claggart is drawn to Billy but overcomes his momentary weakness. Melville, with all his circumlocutions, makes it overwhelmingly clear that Claggart's "depravity according to nature" is, among other things, homosexual, or as he coyly puts it, "a nut not to be cracked by the tap of a lady's fan." Billy's innocence and goodness are intolerable to Claggart because Billy is so beautiful.

Neither Stamp nor Ryan can be faulted. Unfortunately, the role of Captain Vere as played by Ustinov is a serious misconception that weakens the film, particularly in the last section. Ustinov gives a fine performance but it doesn't belong in the story of *Billy Budd*: it reduces the meanings to something clearcut and banal. Ustinov's physical presence is all wrong; his warm, humane, sensual face turns Melville's Starry Vere into something like a cliché of the man who wants to do the right thing, the liberal. We *believe* him when he presents his arguments about justice and law.

Perhaps it is Ustinov's principles that have prevented him from seeing farther into Melville's equivocations. Ustinov has explained that he was concerned "with a most horrible situation where people are compelled by the letter of the law, which is archaic, to carry out sentences which they don't wish to do. That obviously produces a paradox which is tragic." This is, no doubt, an important subject for Ustinov, but it is not the kind of paradox that interested Melville. Melville, so plagued by *Billy Budd* that he couldn't get it in final form (he was still revising it when he died), had far more unsettling notions of its content. As Ustinov presents the film, the conflict is between the almost abstract forces of good (Billy) and evil (Claggart) with the Captain a human figure tragically torn by the rules and demands of authority. Obviously. But what gives the story its fascination, its greatness, is the ambivalent Captain; and there is nothing in Ustinov's performance, or in his conception of the story, to suggest the unseemly haste with which Vere tries to hang Billy. In Melville's account the other officers can't understand why Vere doesn't simply put Billy in confinement "in a way dictated by usage and postpone further action in so extraordinary a case to such time as they should again join the squadron, and then transfer it to the admiral." The surgeon thinks the Captain must be "suddenly affected in his mind." Melville's Vere, who looks at the dead Claggart and exclaims, "Struck dead by an angel of God. Yet the angel must hang!" is not so much a tragic victim of the law as he is Claggart's master and a distant relative perhaps of the Grand Inquisitor. Sweet Starry Vere is the evil we *can't* detect: the man whose motives and conflicts we can't fathom. Claggart we can spot, but he is merely the underling doing the Captain's work: it is the Captain, Billy's friend, who continues the logic by which saints must be destroyed.

Though it is short, *Billy Budd* is one of the most convoluted, one of the strangest works Melville wrote (in some ways even stranger than *Pierre*). Among its peculiarities is a chapter entitled "A Digression," which is given over to a discussion between the ship's purser and the ship's surgeon after Billy's death. Their subject is why Billy's body during the hanging did not go through the movements which are supposed to be invariable in such cases. The absence of spasm — which is a euphemism for ejaculation — is rather like a variation or a reversal of the famous death stink of Father Zossima in *The Brothers Karamazov*. I don't want to stretch the comparison too far, but it's interesting that Melville and Dostoyevsky, so closely contemporary — Melville born in 1819, Dostoyevsky in 1821 — should both have been concerned in works written just before their own deaths with the physical phenomena of death. Billy Budd, by the absence of normal human reactions at the moment of death, turns into a saint, a holy innocent, both more and less than a man. Father Zossima, by the presence of all-too-mortal stench after death, is robbed of his saintliness. Melville's lingering on this singularity about Billy Budd's death didn't strike me so forcibly the first time I read the story, but reading it again recently, and, as it happened, reading it just after William Burroughs's *The Naked Lunch*, with all its elaborate fantasies of violent deaths and gaudy ejaculations, Melville's treatment seems odder than ever. Billy Budd's goodness is linked with presexuality or nonsexuality; his failure to comprehend evil in the universe is linked with his not being really quite a man. He is, in Melville's view, too pure and beautiful to be subject to the spasms of common musculature.

Before this rereading I had associated the story only with that other work of Dostoyevsky's to which it bears more obvious relationships — *The Idiot*. It is, of course, as a *concept* rather than as a character that Billy resembles Prince Myshkin. It may be worth pointing out that in creating a figure of abnormal goodness and simplicity, both authors found it important for their hero to have an infirmity — Myshkin is epileptic, Billy stammers. In both stories the figure is also both naturally noble and also of aristocratic birth: Myshkin a prince, Billy a bastard found in a silk-lined basket. And in the structure of both, the heroes have their opposite numbers — Myshkin and Rogozhin, Billy and Claggart. For both authors, a good man is not a whole man; there is the other side of the human coin, the dark side. Even with his last words, "God bless Captain Vere," Billy demonstrates that he is not a man: he is unable to comprehend the meaning of Vere's experience, unable to comprehend that he will die just because he is innocent.

What's surprising about the film is how much of all this *is* suggested and comes through. What is missing in the film — the reason it is a very good film but not a great one — is that passion which gives Melville's work its extraordinary beauty and power. I wonder if perhaps the key to this failure is in that warm, humane face of Peter Ustinov, who perhaps, not just as an actor, but also as adaptor and director, is too much the relaxed worldly European to share Melville's American rage — the emotionality that is blocked and held back and still pours through in his work. Melville is not a civilized, European writer; he is our greatest writer because he is the American primitive struggling to say more than he knows how to say, struggling to say more than he knows. He is perhaps the most confused of all great writers; he wrestles with words and feelings. It is probably no accident that Billy's speech is blocked. Dostoyevsky is believed to have shared Myshkin's epilepsy, and when Melville can't articulate, he flails in all directions. Even when we can't understand clearly what he is trying to say, we respond to his Promethean torment, to the unresolved complexities.

The movie does not struggle; it moves carefully and rhythmically through the action to the conclusion. Its precision — which is its greatest virtue — is, when compared with the oblique, disturbing novella, evidence of its limitations. Much of what makes the story great is in Melville's effort to achieve new meanings (and some of the meanings we can only guess at from his retreats and disguises) and it is asking rather too much of the moviemakers to say what he wasn't sure about himself. But as Ustinov interprets Vere, Billy is just a victim of unfortunate circumstances, and the film is no more than a tragedy of *justice*. There's a good deal in the film, but the grandeur of Melville is not there.

Yojimbo

Kurosawa has made the first great shaggy-man movie. *Yojimbo* (The Bodyguard) is a glorious comedy-satire of force: the story of the bodyguard who kills the bodies he is hired to guard. Our Westerner, the freelance professional gunman, the fastest draw in the West, has become the unemployed samurai; the gun for hire has become the sword for hire. But when our Westerner came into town, although his own past was often shady, he picked the *right* side, the farmers against the gamblers and cattle thieves, the side of advancing law and order and decency and schools and churches. Toshiro Mifune, the samurai without a master, the professional killer looking for employment, walks into a town divided by two rival merchants quarreling over a gambling concession, each supporting a gang of killers. The hero is the Westerner all right, the stranger in town, the disinterested outsider with his special skills and the remnants of a code of behavior, but to whom can he give his allegiance? Nobody represents any principle, the scattered weak are simply weak.

The Westerner has walked into the gangster movie: both sides are treacherous and ruthless (trigger-happy, they would be called in American pictures). He hires out to each and systematically eliminates both. He is the agent of their destruction because they offend his sense of how things should be: he destroys them because they disgust him. This black Robin Hood with his bemused contempt is more treacherous than the gangsters; he can defend his code only by a masterly use of the doublecross, and he enjoys himself with an occasional spree of demolition ("Destruction's our delight"). The excruciating humor of his last line, as he surveys the carnage — "Now there'll be a little quiet in this town" — is that we've heard it so many times before, but not amidst total devastation. His clean-up has been so thorough and so outrageously bloody that it has achieved a hilarious kind of style.

We would expect violence carried to extremity to be sickening; Kurosawa, in a triumph of bravura technique, makes it explosively comic and exhilarating. By taking the soft romantic focus off the Westerner as played by Gary Cooper or Alan Ladd or John Wayne, Kurosawa has made him a comic hero — just because of what he does, which was always incredible. Without his nimbus, he is unbelievably, absurdly larger-than-life. In *Shane*, the rather ponderously "classic" version of the Western, good and evil were white and black. The settlers, morally strong but physically weak, naive and good but not very bright or glamorous, had to be represented in their fight against the rustling-gambling-murderous prince of darkness by a disinterested prince of light. Shane was Galahad. The Western dog, who howled at his master's grave in *Shane,* who crossed the road to frame the action at the beginning and end of *The Ox-Bow Incident,* has a new dimension in *Yojimbo* — he appears with a human hand for a bone. This dog signals us that in this movie the conventions of the form are going to be turned inside out, we'll have to shift expectations, abandon sentiments: in this terrain dog eats man. And if we think that man, having lost his best friend, can still count on his mother, Kurosawa has another shock for us. A boy from one gang, held prisoner by the other, is released; he rushes to his mother, crying "Oka" (ma or mother). She responds by slapping him. Mother isn't sentimental: first things first, and what she cares about is that gambling concession. This Eastern Western isn't merely a confusion in the points of the compass; Kurosawa's control and his sense of film rhythm are so sure that each new dislocation of values produces both surprise and delight, so that when the hero tries to free an old man who has been trussed-up and suspended in air, and the old man protests that he's safer where he is, we giggle in agreement.

Other directors attempt to recreate the pastness of a story, to provide distance, perspective. For Kurosawa, the setting may be feudal or, as in this case, mid-nineteenth century, but we react (as we are supposed to react) as modern men. His time is now, his action so immediate, sensuous, raging, that we are forced to disbelieve, to react with incredulity, to admire. (This is partly the result of using telephoto lenses that put us right into the fighting, into the confusion of bared teeth and gasps and howls.) He shakes spears in our faces. This is more alive than any living we know; this, all our senses tell us, is art, not life. Ironic detachment is our saving grace.

Of all art forms, movies are most in need of having their concepts of heroism undermined. The greatest action pictures have often been satirical: even before Douglas Fairbanks, Sr., mocked the American dreams, our two-reelers used the new techniques of the screen to parody the vacuous heroics of stage melodrama. George Stevens' *Gunga Din,* a model of the action genre, was so exuberant and high-spirited that it both exalted and mocked a schoolboy's version of heroism. But in recent years John Ford, particularly, has turned the Western into an almost static pictorial genre, a devitalized, dehydrated form which is "enriched" with pastoral beauty and evocative nostalgia for a simple, heroic way of life. The clichés we retained from childhood pirate, buccaneer, gangster, and Western movies have been awarded the status of myths, and writers and directors have been making infatuated tributes to the myths of our old movies. If, by now, we dread going to see a "great" Western, it's because "great" has come to mean slow and pictorially composed. We'll be lulled to sleep in the "affectionate," "pure," "authentic" scenery of the West (in "epics" like *My Darling Clementine, She Wore a Yellow Ribbon, Fort Apache*) or, for a change, we'll be clobbered by messages in "mature" Westerns like *The Gunfighter* and *High Noon* (the message is that the myths we never believed in anyway were false). Kurosawa slashes the screen with action, and liberates us from the pretensions of our "serious" Westerns. After all those long, lean-hipped walks across the screen with Cooper or Fonda (the man who knows how to use a gun is, by movie convention, the man without an ass), we are restored to sanity by Mifune's heroic personal characteristic — a titanic shoulder twitch.

The Western has always been a rather hypocritical form. The hero represents a way of life that is becoming antiquated. The solitary defender of justice is the last of the line; the era of lawlessness is over, courts are coming in. But the climax is the demonstration that the old way is the only way that works — though we are told that it is the last triumph of violence. The Westerner, the loner, must take the law into his hands for one last time in order to wipe out the enemies of the new system of justice. *Yojimbo* employs an extraordinary number of the conventions of the form, but takes the hypocrisy for a ride. The samurai is a killer with a code of honor and all that, but no system of justice is supplanting him. He's the last of the line not because law and order will prevail, but because his sword for hire is already anachronistic. Guns are coming in. One of his enemies is a gun-slinger, who looks and acts a parody of American Method actors. That ridiculous little gun means the end of the warrior caste: killing is going to become so easy that it will be democratically available to all. In *Yojimbo* goodness triumphs satirically: the foil at the point of the sword is a huge joke. The samurai is not a man with a poker face, and he's not an executioner who hates his job. He's a man of passion who takes savage satisfaction in his special talents. Violence triumphs whoever wins, and our ideas of courage, chivalry, strength, and honor bite the dust along with the "bad" men. The dogs will have their human fodder.

Yojimbo is not a film that needs much critical analysis; its boisterous power and good spirits are right there on the surface. Lechery, avarice, cowardice, coarseness, animality, are rendered by fire; they become joy in life, in even the lowest forms of human life. (Kurosawa's grotesque variants of the John Ford stock company include a giant — a bit mentally retarded, perhaps.) The whimpering, maimed and cringing are so vivid they seem joyful; what in life might be pathetic, loathsome, offensive is made comic and beautiful. Kurosawa makes us accept even the most brutish of his creatures as more alive than the man who doesn't yield to temptation. There is so much displacement that we don't have time or inclination to ask why we are enjoying the action; we respond kinesthetically. It's hard to believe that others don't share this response. Still, I should remember Bosley Crowther with his "the dramatic penetration is not deep, and the plot complications are many and hard to follow in Japanese." And Dwight Macdonald, who writes, "It is a dark, neurotic, claustrophobic film . . ." and, "The Japanese have long been noted for their clever mimicry of the West. *Yojimbo* is the cinematic equivalent of their ten-cent ball-point pens and their ninety-eight-cent mini-cameras. But one expects more of Kurosawa."

More? Kurosawa, one of the few great new masters of the medium, has had one weakness: he has often failed to find themes that were commensurate with the surge and energy of his images. At times he has seemed to be merely a virtuoso stylist, a painter turned director whose visual imagination had outstripped his content. But in at least three films, eye and mind have worked together at the highest levels. His first major international success, *Rashomon* (1950) — despite the longeurs of the opening and closing sequences — is still the classic film statement of the relativism, the unknowability of truth. *The Seven Samurai* (1954) is incomparable as a modern poem of force. It is the Western form carried to apotheosis — a vast celebration of the joys and torments of fighting, seen in new depth and scale, a brutal imaginative ballet on the nature of strength and weakness. Now, in *Yojimbo*, Kurosawa has made a farce of force. And now that he has done it, we can remember how good his comic scenes always were and that he frequently tended toward parody.

Ikiru is often called Kurosawa's masterpiece. (It *does* have one great moment — the old man's song in the swing. *Throne of Blood*, which I much prefer, has at least two great moments — Isuzu Yamada's handwashing scene, and that dazzling filmic achievement of Shakespeare's vision when Birnam Wood does come to Dunsinane.) Movies are, happily, a popular medium (which makes it difficult to understand why Dwight Macdonald with his dedication to high art sacrifices his time to them), but does that mean that people must look to them for confirmation of their soggiest humanitarian sentiments? The prissy liberals who wouldn't give a man with the D.T.'s a quarter for a shot ("He'll waste it on drink") are just the ones who love the message they take out of *Ikiru*, not that one man did manage to triumph over bureaucracy but that the meaning of life is in doing a bit of goody good good for others. I have talked to a number of these people about why they hated *The Manchurian Candidate* and I swear not one of them can remember that when the liberal senator is killed, milk pours out. *Yojimbo* seems so simple, so marvelously obvious, but those who are sentimental don't get it: they think it's a mistake, that it couldn't have been intended as a killing comedy. It's true that even Shakespeare didn't dare give his clowns hot blood to drink. But Kurosawa dares.

Devi

The Apu Trilogy has been widely acclaimed as a masterpiece, which indeed it is, though I would guess that in the years since its release fewer Americans have seen it than have seen *David and Lisa* in any *week* since its release. Fewer have seen Satyajit Ray's new film, *Devi*, than have seen *David and Lisa* in any *night* since its release. Ingmar Bergman, who was also a slow starter with American audiences, has definitely caught on; why not Ray?

Bergman is sensual and erotic; he provides "stark" beauty and exposed nerves and conventional dramatic conflicts and a theme that passes for contemporary — the coldness of intellectuals. Husbands fail their wives and drive them crazy because they don't understand them and all that. (Really, it's not people who don't understand us who drive us nuts — it's when those who shouldn't, *do*.) But I would guess that what gives his movies their immense appeal is their semi-intellectual, or, to be more rude, "metaphysical" content. His characters are like schoolboys who have just heard the startling new idea that "God is dead"; this sets them off on torments of deep thought. Bergman's greatest "dark" film, *The Seventh Seal*, reminds one of the nightmares of life and death and religion that one had as a child; the sense of mystery and the questions that no one will answer suggest the way religious symbols function in childhood and in fear. Bergman's power over audiences is that he has not developed philosophically beyond the awesome questions: audiences trained in more rational philosophy still respond emotionally to Bergman's kind of mysticism, his searching for "the meaning of life," his fatalism, and the archaic ogres of childhood and religion. Bergman is not a deep thinker, but he is an artist who moves audiences deeply by calling up their buried fears and feelings. People come out of his movies with "something to think about" or, at least, to talk about.

Those who find Bergman profound and sophisticated are very likely to find Satyajit Ray rather too simple. I think that Ray, like Kurosawa, is one of the great new film masters, and that his simplicity is a simplicity arrived at, achieved, a master's distillation from his experience; but it is — and this may be another reason why audiences prefer Bergman — the simplicity to which we must respond with *feeling*. It is not the simplicity of a film like *David and Lisa* — which is simplicity at a pre-art level, the simplicity of those who don't perceive complexities and have not yet begun to explore their medium.

People say that *David and Lisa* is a "heartfelt" experience, but they gobble it up so easily because it appeals to feelings they already had. It's a movie about mental disturbances that couldn't disturb anybody. Similarly, *Sundays and Cybèle*, also a phenomenal box-office success, is gobbled up as "artistic" (it's "artistic" the same way that *Harper's Bazaar* fiction is "beautifully literate"). Bosley Crowther says that *Sundays and Cybèle* is "what *Lolita* might conceivably have been had it been made by a poet and angled to be a rhapsodic song of innocence and not a smirking joke." Surely only a satirist like Nabokov could have invented this eminent critic whose praise gives the show away — "angled to be a rhapsodic song of innocence."

(One of the delights of life in San Francisco is observing the cultural chauvinism of New York from a safe distance. *Variety* informs us that improvement is expected in West Coast movie tastes now that the Western edition of the New York *Times* brings us Bosley Crowther. And Dwight Macdonald, who calls any place outside New York "the provinces," has a solution for the problems of American movies: they should be made closer to the intellectual life of the nation — in New York. But it's the

Eastern banks, not the Western minds, that are destroying our movies.)

The concept of humanity is so strong in Ray's films that a man who functioned as a villain could only be a limitation of vision, a defect, an intrusion of melodrama into a work of art which seeks to illuminate experience and help us feel. There is, for example, a defect of this kind in De Sica's *Umberto D*: the landlady is unsympathetically caricatured so that we do not understand and respond to her as we do to the others in the film. I don't think Ray ever makes a mistake of this kind: his films are so far from the world of melodrama that such a mistake is almost unthinkable. We see his characters not in terms of good or bad, but as we see ourselves, in terms of failures and weaknesses and strength and, above all, as part of a human continuum — fulfilling, altering, and finally accepting ourselves as part of this humanity, recognizing that no matter how much we want to burst the bounds of experience, there is only so much we can do. This larger view of human experience — the simplicity of De Sica at his best, of Renoir at his greatest, is almost miraculously present in every detail of Satyajit Ray's films. Ray's method is perhaps the most direct and least impaired by commercial stratagems in the whole history of film. He does not even invent dramatic devices, shortcuts to feelings. He made no passes at the commercial market; he didn't even reach out toward Western conceptions of drama and construction, although as one of the founders of the Calcutta film society, he must have been familiar with these conceptions. He seems to have had, from the beginning, the intuitive knowledge that this was not what he wanted.

In the background of almost every major new figure in film today we see the same great man — Jean Renoir. In France, the critic André Bazin taught a film-loving juvenile delinquent named François Truffaut "first" as Truffaut says, "to love Renoir and then to know him." The lives of Ray and Renoir intersected in 1950, when Ray, a young painter working as a layout artist for a British advertising firm, was struggling to work out a film treatment for *Pather Panchali*, and Renoir was in Calcutta filming *The River*, a movie that despite its weaknesses is perhaps a genre in itself — the only fictional film shot in a remote culture in which the director had the taste and sensitivity to present an outsider's view without condescension or a perfunctory "documentary" style. Ray has said that "the only kind of professional encouragement I got came from one single man" — Jean Renoir, who "insisted that I shouldn't give up."

There is a common misconception that Ray is a "primitive" artist and although, initially, this probably worked to his advantage in this country (*Pather Panchali* was taken to be autobiographical, and "true" and important because it dealt with rural poverty), it now works to his disadvantage, because his later films are taken to be corrupted by exposure to "art," and thus less "true." *The Apu Trilogy* expresses India in transition, showing the development of the boy Apu's consciousness from the primitive, medieval village life of *Pather Panchali* through the modern city streets and schools of Benares to the University of Calcutta in *Aparajito*, and then, in *The World of Apu*, beyond self-consciousness to the destruction of his egotism, and the rebirth of feeling, the renewal of strength. But Ray himself is not a primitive artist any more than, say, Robert Flaherty was when he chronicled the life of the Eskimos in *Nanook of the North*. Ray was a highly educated man at the beginning of his film career, and he was influenced by a wide variety of films, those of Renoir and De Sica in particular. (Sent by his employers to England for three months in 1950, he went to more than ninety films, and he has reported that the one that helped most to clarify his ideas was *The Bicycle Thief*.) Among his other influences are certainly Dovzhenko's *Earth* and Eisenstein, and probably Von Sternberg. Just as *Nanook*, although a great work, seems primitive compared with a later, more complex Flaherty film like *Man of Aran*, *Pather Panchali* has a different kind of beauty, a more primitive kind, than later Ray films. But Ray's background is not Apu's: "My grandfather was a painter, a poet, and also a scientist who, in addition to editing the first chil-

dren's magazine in Bengal, had introduced the half-tone block
to India. My father was equally well known. He . . . wrote,
among other works, Bengal's classic Book of Nonsense — an
Englishman might call him India's Edward Lear." After gradu-
ating from the University of Calcutta with honors in physics
and economics, the nineteen-year-old Ray, at the urging of Rab-
indranath Tagore, went to study at Tagore's school, Santini-
ketan. There, he "developed some skill in drawing" and "read
widely in the history of art . . . studying in particular Chinese
calligraphy." After Tagore's death, he left the school ("There
were no films there and somehow, I don't know how it happened, but films appealed to me"). In Calcutta he worked as
art director for a British advertising firm: "I stayed with them
a long while and went through every department. When I was
in a position to do so I introduced into their advertisements a
fusion of modern western and Bengal tradition, to give it a new
look."

In addition, he illustrated books, and it was after he had
illustrated an edition of the popular novel *Pather Panchali* that
he began to think about visualizing it on the screen.

What I lacked was first-hand acquaintance with the *milieu* of the
story. I could, of course, draw upon the book itself, which was a
kind of encyclopaedia of Bengali rural life, but I knew that this was
not enough. In any case, one had only to drive six miles out of the
city to get to the heart of the authentic village. While far from
being an adventure in the physical sense, these explorations . . .
nevertheless opened up a new and fascinating world. To one born
and bred in the city, it had a new flavor, a new texture; and its
values were different. It made you want to observe and probe, to
catch the revealing details, the telling gestures, the particular turns
of speech. You wanted to fathom the mysteries of "atmosphere."

Ray's statements and articles have been widely published, and
his English is perfectly clear, but the critics can't resist the
chance to play sahib. *Pather Panchali* provided Crowther with
an opportunity for a classic example of his style and perception:

"Chief among the delicate revelations that emerge from its loosely formed account of the pathetic little joys and sorrows of a poor Indian family in Bengal is the touching indication that poverty does not nullify love and that even the most afflicted people can find some modest pleasures in their worlds . . . Any picture as loose in structure or as listless in tempo as this one is would barely pass as a 'rough cut' in Hollywood." In a review of *Aparajito*, Kingsley Amis, then *Esquire*'s movie critic, thought that "Satyajit Ray, the director, seems to have set out with the idea of photographing without rearrangement the life of a poor Indian family, of reporting reality in as unshaped a form as possible." *The World of Apu*, which died at the box-office, got short shrift from Macdonald: "*Pather* was about a family in a village, *Apu* is about a young writer in a city, a more complex theme, and I'm not sure Ray is up to it." (Somehow he makes us feel that he's more sure than he ought to be; he condescends promiscuously.)

Each of the films of *The Apu Trilogy* represents a change, I think a development, of style. Unfortunately, those who responded to the slow rhythm of *Pather Panchali* felt that this pace was somehow more true to India than the faster pace of the third film, *The World of Apu*. But Ray's rhythm is derived from his subject matter, and for the college students and artists of *The World of Apu*, the leisurely flow of the seasons on which *Pather Panchali* was based would be ludicrous. Even those who prefer *Pather Panchali* to his later work should recognize that an artist cannot retain his first beautiful awkward expressiveness and innocence, and that to attempt to do so would mean redoing consciously what had been beautiful because it was not completely conscious. An artist must either give up art or develop. There are, of course, two ways of giving up: stopping altogether or taking the familiar Hollywood course — making tricks out of what was once done for love.

Ray began his film career with a masterpiece, and a trilogy at that; this makes it easy to shrug off his other films as very fine but not really up to the trilogy (even critics who disparaged each film of the trilogy as it appeared, now use the trilogy as the measure to disparage his other works). It is true that the other films are smaller in scope. But, if there had been no trilogy, I would say of *Devi*, "This is the greatest Indian film ever made." And if there had been no trilogy and no *Devi*, I would say the same of his still later *Two Daughters*, based on Tagore stories, of which the first, *The Postmaster*, is a pure and simple masterpiece of the filmed short story form. (The second has memorable scenes, beauty, and wit, but is rather wearying.) Ray's least successful film that has been imported, *The Music Room* (made early, for respite, between the second and third parts of the trilogy), has such grandeur in its best scenes that we must revise customary dramatic standards. By our usual standards it isn't a good movie: it's often crude and it's poorly constructed; but it's a great experience. It's a study of *noblesse oblige* carried to extremity, to a kind of aesthetic madness. It recalls the film of *The Magnificent Ambersons* and, of course, *The Cherry Orchard* but, more painfully, it calls up hideous memories of our own expansive gestures, our own big-role playing. We are forced to see the recklessness and egomania of our greatest moments — and at the same time we are forced to see the sordid banality of being practical. The hero is great *because* he destroys himself; he is also mad. I was exasperated by the defects of *The Music Room* when I saw it; now, a month later, I realize that I will never forget it. Worrying over its faults as a film is like worrying over whether *King Lear* is well constructed: it doesn't really matter.

Ray is sometimes (for us Westerners, and perhaps for Easterners also?) a little boring, but what major artist outside film and drama isn't? What he has to give is so rich, so contemplative in approach (and this we are completely unused to in the film medium — except perhaps in documentary) that we begin to accept our lapses of attention during the tedious moments with the same kind of relaxation and confidence and affection that we feel for the boring stretches in the great novels, the epic poems.

Although India is second only to Japan in the number of movies it produces, Ray is the *only* Indian director; he is, as yet, in a class by himself. Despite the financial conditions under which he works, despite official disapproval of his themes, despite popular indifference to his work, he is in a position that almost any film maker anywhere in the world might envy. The Indian film industry is so thoroughly corrupt that Ray could start fresh, as if it did not exist. Consider the Americans, looking under stones for some tiny piece of subject matter they can call their own, and then judge the wealth, the prodigious, fabulous heritage that an imaginative Indian can draw upon. Just because there has been almost nothing of value done in films in India, the whole country and its culture is his to explore and express to the limits of his ability; he is the first major artist to draw upon these vast and ancient reserves. The Hollywood director who re-makes biblical spectacles or Fannie Hurst stories for the third or sixth or ninth time is a poor man — no matter how big his budget — compared to the first film artist of India. American directors of talent can still try to beat the system, can still feel that maybe they can do something worth doing, and every once in a while someone almost does. In India, the poverty of the masses, and their desperate *need* for escapist films, cancels out illusions. Ray knows he can't reach a mass audience in India (he can't spend more than $40,000 on a production). Outside of West Bengal, his films are not understood (Bengali is spoken by less than fifteen percent of India's population — of those, only twenty percent can read). In other provinces his films, subtitled, appeal only to the Indian equivalent of the American art-house audience — the urban intellectuals — not only because the masses and the rural audiences want their traditional extravaganzas but because they can't read. Probably India produces so many films just because of the general illiteracy; if Indians could read subtitles, American and European films might be more popular. (India has so many languages, it's impractical to dub for the illiterates — the only justification for dubbing, by the way.)

It's doubtful if Ray could finance his films at all without the international audience that he reaches, even though it's shockingly small and he doesn't reach it easily. Indian bureaucrats, as "image" conscious as our own, and much more powerful in the control of films, prefer to send abroad the vacuous studio productions which they assure us are "technically" superior to Ray's films (everyone and everything in them is so clean and shiny and false that they suggest interminable TV commercials).

Devi, based on a theme from Tagore, is here thanks to the personal intercession of Nehru, who removed the censors' export ban. According to official Indian policy, *Devi* is misleading in its view of Indian life. We can interpret this to mean that, even though the film is set in the nineteenth century, the government is not happy about the world getting the idea that there are or ever were superstitions in India. In the film, the young heroine is believed by her rich father-in-law to be an incarnation of the goddess Kali. I don't know why the Indian government was so concerned about this — anyone who has ever tried to tell children how, for example, saints function in Catholic doctrine may recognize that we have a few things to explain, too. Those who grow up surrounded by Christian symbols and dogmas are hardly in a position to point a finger of shame at Kali worship — particularly as it seems so closely related to prayers to the Virgin Mary, Mother of God. As the film makes clear, Kali is generally called "Ma."

The film has so many Freudian undertones that I was not surprised when the film maker sitting next to me in the empty theater muttered, "Think what Buñuel would do with this." I'm grateful that it's Ray, not Buñuel, and that the undertones stay where they belong — down under. Buñuel would have made it explicit. Ray never tells us that this is the old man's way of taking his son's bride away from him; he doesn't tell us that this is the old man's way of punishing his Westernized, Christianized son; he never says that religion is the last outpost of the old man's sensuality, his return to childhood and "Ma" love. But we experience all this, just as we experience the easy drift of the lovely silly young girl into the auto-intoxication, the narcissism of believing that she *is* a goddess. She is certainly beautiful enough. In one sense the film is about what Christians might call the sin of pride: the girl who finds it not too difficult to believe that she is a goddess, fails to cure the nephew she adores; when the child dies, she goes mad. But that is a Christian oversimplification: what we see is the girl's readiness to believe, her liquid acquiescence; not so much *pride* as a desire to please — the culmination, we suspect, of what the culture expects of a high-born girl. And, surrounded by so much luxury, what is there for the girl to do but try to please? The whole indolent life is centered on pleasure.

Ray creates an atmosphere that intoxicates us as well; the household is so rich and the rich people so overripe. The handsome, soft-eyed men in their silks and brocades are unspeakably fleshly; the half-naked beggars on the steps outside are clothed in their skins, but the rich are eroticized by their garments. And perhaps because of the camera work, which seems to derive from some of the best traditions of the silent screen and the thirties, perhaps because of the Indian faces themselves, the eyes have depths — and a disturbing look of helplessness — that we are unused to. It's almost as if these people were isolated from us and from each other by their eyes. It is not just that they seem exotic to us, but that each is a stranger to the others. Their eyes link them to the painted eyes of the Hindu idols, and, in the film, it is this religion which separates them. They are lost behind their eyes.

Sharmila Tagore (Tagore's great-granddaughter), fourteen when she played Apu's bride, is the seventeen-year-old goddess; she is exquisite, perfect (a word I don't use casually) in both these roles. And the men are wonderfully selected — so that they manage to suggest both the handsomeness of almost mythological figures and the rotting weakness of their way of life. Ray has been developing his own stock company, and anyone who mistook the principal players in the trilogy for people just acting out their own lives for the camera, may be startled now to see them in a nineteenth-century mansion. In the early parts of the trilogy, Ray was able to convince many people that he had simply turned his cameras on life; he performs the same miracle of art on this decadent, vanished period. The setting of *Devi* seems to have been caught by the camera just before it decays. The past is preserved for us, disturbingly, ironically, in its jeweled frame. Are we not perhaps in the position of the "advanced," ineffective young husband who knows that his childish wife can't be Kali because he has "progressed" from Kali worship to the idols of Christianity? (Can we distinguish belief in progress from the sin of pride?)

It is a commentary on the values of *our* society that those who saw truth and greatness in *The Apu Trilogy*, particularly in the opening film with its emphasis on the mother's struggle to feed the family, are not drawn to a film in which Ray shows the landowning class and its collapse of beliefs. It is part of *our* heritage from the thirties that the poor still seem "real" and the rich "trivial." *Devi* should, however, please even Marxists if they would go to see it; it is the most convincing study of upper-class decadence I have ever seen. But it is Ray's feeling for the beauty within this disintegrating way of life that makes it convincing. Eisenstein cartooned the upper classes and made them hateful; they became puppets in the show he was staging. Ray, by giving them the respect and love that he gives the poor and struggling, helps us to understand their demoralization. The rich, deluded father-in-law of *Devi* is as human in his dreamy sensuality as Apu's own poet father. Neither can sustain his way of life or his beliefs against the new pressures; and neither can adapt.

Like Renoir and De Sica, Ray sees that life itself is good no matter how bad it is. It is difficult to discuss art which is an affirmation of life, without fear of becoming maudlin. But is there any other kind of art, on screen or elsewhere? "In cinema," Ray says, "we must select everything for the camera according to the richness of its power to reveal."

How the Long Distance Runner Throws the Race

Alan Sillitoe's short story *The Loneliness of the Long Distance Runner* is very good in a simple but disturbing and suggestive way. The long distance runner who is writing his own story expresses a rejection of official values that, to one degree or another, we all share, or at least feel. Like Kafka's heroes, or Dostoyevsky's in *Notes from Underground*, this hero's anxieties and fears and pettiness get under our skin. He is a small-minded, spiteful boy-man; nevertheless, he expresses what we often feel to be our most courageous side. He says, "I'm not having any. It's all yours." He is a close relative of those juvenile delinquents that Hollywood dropped as heroes because they became too hot to handle. It became increasingly difficult to resolve the plots, to explain them away. They went from A pictures to B and C and D pictures, where from the start they could be so ludicrous and meaningless that disposing of them wasn't any problem. Sillitoe's hero, however, is more defined than a delinquent or a rebel; his origins are in poverty and deprivation but he's not a worker; he's a proletarian, all right, but a proletarian thief, and at the end of the story he's becoming a more clever, a bigger thief.

The narrator of the story is a thief with an outsider's view of society, an outlaw's rejection of the whole shebang. He is as intransigent, as dedicated to his outlaw view — to his own brand of cunning — as Joyce's hero was to silence, exile, and cunning. But, and this is what makes the figure so peculiarly disturbing, he is almost subhuman. His contempt and resentment are the whole man: he has no responsibilities toward his family, he isn't interested in anything but living it up like a lord with some tarts for his pleasure. His only feeling of connection is with his father who lived miserably and died in horrible pain — rejecting the modern medicine offered him; Colin is as unyielding. He would kill the representatives of authority, he tells us, if he had the chance. He represents, and this is the power of his image, not only the rejection that we share, but the underlying threats of that rejection. He doesn't merely say no to the more dehumanized and brutal aspects of modern society but to education, art, humanity, sympathy, love, and all the rest of what we care about. He asks no quarter and he gives none. He is consistent in his outlaw's position — as we are not — and he is thus not a whole man. He shows us how narrow, how Pygmy-like would be our view of life if we were consistent in our rejections. He is the representative of the hatred building up in the modern urban consciousness — hatred which we know to be at least partly valid.

The movie, also written by Sillitoe, turns him into a socialist hero who, in one supremely embarrassing moment, even discovers some rudimentary form of socialism all by himself: he explains that he wouldn't mind working if the bosses didn't get the profits. As a theatrical experience this risks comparison with the unforgettably embarrassing last few minutes of Odets's *Awake and Sing* when the hero, having at last discovered the meaning of it all, rushes on stage with a copy of *The Communist Manifesto*.

Tom Courtenay's performance draws upon the original conception of Colin Smith. But Sillitoe's movie script and Tony Richardson's direction have turned the story into a study of class warfare — and a very familiar kind of class warfare at that. The race of the story with its undifferentiated competing runners, has, for example, become a competition against a posh public school. And the film is full of easy ironies — the Borstal boys singing *Jerusalem* is intercut with shots of a boy who has run away being beaten up by the authorities; the workshop scene shows the Borstal boys dismantling gas masks. The bite of the original character was that Colin wasn't merely at war with the upper classes but that he refused the proletarian role. He wasn't a worker; he was a thief. The film, supplying the usual ironies of class distinctions, ridiculing the old-school-tie once more, obscures the point, tries to make a much easier point — one more demonstration of social inequality under capitalism.

To make Colin a more conventional, "misunderstood" victim of society, his character is softened. The Colin who had the best time of his life when his mother collected the 500 pounds death benefits on his father, becomes the Colin who burns the death money his mother hands him. His fantasies about living it up with some tarts become a poignant romantic interlude with a scared, love-hungry working-class girl. In the movie he's calculating and resentful only with representatives of the authoritarian society; he's gentle and defenseless and loyal and naive and touching with his own kind — though stern as the ham in *Hamlet* when his mother misbehaves ("You brought your fancy man into the house before my father was cold"). He's a sensitive, good boy; he's even given a gamin-like charm and a sudden, crooked smile that lights up the withdrawn, aged, downtrodden face. I think we are supposed to feel — "Why, look, he never had a chance to be young. He only steals for a lark, for a bit of a good time, for fun. He's really innocent and harmless." The implication is unmistakable that in a different social system, this basically good Colin, which the movie suggests is the true Colin that society is crushing, would take over. He's defiant, not as in the story because the ugliness and mechanization of modern life make work and adaptation seem like a living death; he's defiant because of social injustice.

In making Colin more human, in making him stand for the beautiful, innocent life, and in making the usual kinds of social comments (the poor don't stand a chance), the film destroys the impact of the story. There Colin represented something in us that we have to deal with, that we can't resolve. Sillitoe and Richardson by stuffing "poetry" in, with little innocent idylls of the fun of pinching a car, and wandering hand in hand at the beach with a playmate girl, have destroyed the true poetry of the original conception — which was in the singleness of vision: a terrifying view of modern life, a madman's view that forces us to see how mad we are.

The story isn't a great story, but its power is in its narrowness. We begin by assenting to Colin's view of society; then, when we see where it's leading us, we can no longer wholly extricate ourselves. There's a kind of grandeur about Colin's dedication to his small piece of truth, his thief's honesty. He doesn't have — or even want — the happiness of the movie hero with his sweet girl; his happiness is in the power he feels when he throws the race, the power of showing what he is.

He's tough — and I mean the word as American teen-agers now use it. To be "tough" is to be casually but calculatingly defiant toward all authority, and fearless about consequences. The word has replaced the earlier term "cool"; it's obviously related to the current term in Japan, "durai" or dry. For an earlier generation, "cool" indicated an attitude toward life; for this new generation, middle class as well as working class, "tough" means something very like Colin Smith's total rejection. The term that American teen-agers now use as the opposite of "tough" is "spaz." A spaz is a person who is courteous to teachers, plans for a career, is full of soft sentiments and believes in official values. A spaz is something like what adults still call a square; I assume the word is derived from the spaz's efforts and his nervousness about doing all the right things — he isn't cool and relaxed. "Spaz" (from spastic?) is probably a somewhat more brutally graphic way of saying someone's a "jerk."

Just as the Colin Smith of the story sees himself as alive and the in-laws as dead, these American middle-class teen-agers see the adult world as a dead world of boredom, hypocrisy, a world of stupid, disappointed people. To be "tough" means largely that you're supposed to be more alive than other people because they're working to get ahead in the dead, meaningless system; you're alive because you're contemptuous of them. The joke is that, like Colin, these kids want the material benefits of the system — money, cars, good times. The middle-class Americans don't, of course, have to steal; they just sponge off their families — with methods that, from what I've observed, are as cold and spiteful as Colin's thieving.

I have been horrified hearing these kids talk about their own parents; they're accurate but they're not any more compassionate toward what they consider the enemy than Colin who wants to shoot the in-laws. They feel too superior, too sure of their aliveness and of adult deadness for compassion. What they get from books reinforces their contempt for middle-class values — as indeed it should. But they have nothing to put in the place of dead values but a style, an attitude, the "toughness" which, however, is aesthetically and intellectually preferable to spaz anxieties for good grades, security, and respectability. To be tough is a good start, it helps to clear away hypocrisy and gentility, but it's too limited, too egocentric, too contemptuous of effort. It can turn into a singleness of response, a narrowing of experience, something as subhuman as Colin Smith's idea of life.

Why, with this story that affects us in so many important ways, did the author and director change it — reducing a major conflict in morality and attitudes to the fictions and platitudes of proletarian youth battling against the prigs and bullies of the capitalist system? Perhaps because *Saturday Night and Sunday Morning*, also based on Alan Sillitoe material, had been the biggest box-office success in England in 1961, *The Loneliness of the Long Distance Runner* was reshaped for the screen to express a similar kind of social consciousness. Perhaps Sillitoe thought that the story he had written was less important than the opportunity the screen provided for class-warfare propaganda. So far as I can see the film succeeds only with the liberals of the art-house audience, those who have long since been trained to salivate when they hear the tinkle of class distinctions. Had he stuck to his story he might have jarred audiences into some new emotional responses. The anarchist thief is close enough to the emotional life and political sympathies of liberals to be an uncomfortable image; and he is, in the form of our younger generation — not necessarily of juvenile delinquents but let us say, of "prematurely-alienated" teen-agers — a basic, common symptom of our time.

I wonder if I may raise a related issue — without giving too much offense. The left wingers of the thirties and forties, partly on the basis that property was theft anyway, became contemptuous of what they chose to call bourgeois morality. Many of them casually stole books and records from shops on the basis that they really wanted them and thus had more of a right to them than the shopkeepers. And they became so casual that it was not at all unusual for them to steal from their friends and from homes where they were guests (which was safer than stealing from stores, because their liberal friends and hosts couldn't possibly call the police). Stealing as an expression of contempt for property values is not something liberals might care to discuss openly, but it is very much a part of accepted liberal attitudes.

It may be that the theme of Sillitoe's story in which the rejection of bourgeois morality becomes a way of life upset even the author, that he preferred to clean it up for the movies, to make the proletarian protagonist a victim instead of an egomaniac. The pity is that the movie audience which might have been upset, forced to think out some of its attitudes toward theft and property and work and social organization, is instead reconfirmed in its liberal complacency. The Colin of the movie is their hero: he showed the Governor. The Colin of the story might have made our liberal flesh crawl.

$8\frac{1}{2}$: Confessions of a Movie Director

Some years ago a handsome, narcissistic actor who was entertaining me with stories about his love affairs with various ladies and gentlemen, concluded by smiling seductively as he announced, "Sometimes I have so many ideas I don't know which one to choose." I recall thinking — as I edged him to the door — that he had a strange notion of what an idea was.

The director-hero of 8½ is the center of the film universe, the creator on whose word everything waits, the man sought after by everyone, the one for whom all possibilities are open. Guido can do anything, and so much possibility confuses him. He's like the movies' famous couturier who can't decide what he's going to do for the spring collection. ("I've simply got to get an idea. I'll go mad if I don't. Everybody's depending on me.") I'm afraid that Guido's notion of an "idea" isn't much more highly developed than my silly actor friend's, and it's rather shockingly like the notion of those god-awful boobs who know they could be great writers because they have a great story — they just need someone to put it into words. Indeed the director conforms to the popular notions of a *successful* genius, and our ladies-magazine fiction has always been fond of the "sophisticated" writer or director looking for a story and finding it in romance, or in his own backyard. "Accept me as I am" is Guido's final, and successful, plea to the wife-figure (although that is what she has been rejecting for over two hours).

Just as *La Dolce Vita* confirmed popular suspicions about the depravity of the rich and gifted, 8½ confirms the popular view of a "big" film director's life — the world is his once he finds that important "idea" (it's so important that the boobs will never tell theirs for fear of "giving it away," i.e., having it stolen — the fewer their "ideas," the greater their fear of plagiarism). Perhaps the irrelevance of what we see (principally his conflicts between his love for his wife, the pleasures of his mistress, his ideal of innocence, and his dreams of a harem) to the composition of a work of art may be indicated by a comparison: can one imagine that Dostoyevsky, say, or Goya or Berlioz or D. W. Griffith or whoever, resolved his personal life before producing a work, or that his personal problems of the moment were even necessarily relevant to the work at hand? This notion of an artist "facing himself" or "coming to grips with himself" as a precondition to "creation" is, however, familiar to us from the popular Freudianized lives of artists (and of everyone else).

It is perhaps easy for educated audiences to see an "advance" in film when a film maker deals with a "creative crisis" or "artist's block," a subject so often dealt with in modern writing; but is it applicable to film? What movie in the half-century history of movies has been held up by the director's having a creative block? No movie with a budget and crew, writers and sets. The irrelevance of what we see to the processes of making a movie can, of course, be explained away with, "He's having a break-down and all this is his fantasy life." Someone's fantasy life is perfectly good material for a movie *if* it is imaginative and fasci-nating in itself, or if it illuminates his non-fantasy life in some interesting way. But 8½ is neither; it's surprisingly like the con-fectionary dreams of Hollywood heroines, transported by a hack's notions of Freudian anxiety and wish fulfillment. 8½ is an incredibly externalized version of an artist's "inner" life — a gorgeous multi-ringed circus that has very little connection with what, even for a movie director, is most likely to be solitary, concentrated hard work. It's more like the fantasy life of some-one who wishes he were a movie director, someone who has soaked up those movie versions of an artist's life, in which in the midst of a carnival or ball the hero receives inspiration and dashes away to transmute life into art. "What's the film about? What's on your mind this time?" asks Guido's wife. In 8½ the two questions are one.

Creativity is the new cant — parents are advised not to hit it with a stick, schoolteachers are primed to watch for it, founda-tions encourage it, colleges and subsidized health farms nourish it in a regulated atmosphere; the government is advised to honor it. We're all supposed to be so in awe of it that when it's in crisis, the screen should be torn asunder by the conflicts. But the creativity con-game, a great subject for comedy, is rather embarrassing when it's treated only semi-satirically. When a satire on big, expensive movies is itself a big, expensive movie, how can we distinguish it from its target? When a man makes himself the butt of his own joke, we may feel too uncomfortable to laugh. Exhibitionism is its own reward.

8½ suggests some of Fellini's problems as a director, but they are not so fantastic nor so psychoanalytic as the ones he parades. A major one is the grubby, disheartening economic problem that probably affects Fellini in an intensified form precisely because of the commercial success of *La Dolce Vita* and the business hopes it raised. A movie director has two "worst" enemies: commercial failure and commercial success. After a failure, he has a difficult time raising money for his next film; after a success, his next must be bigger and "better." In recent years no major Hollywood director with a string of "big" successes has been able to finance a small, inexpensive production — and this is not for want of trying. From the point of view of studios and banks, an expenditure of half a million dollars is a much bigger risk than an investment of several million on a "name" property with big stars, a huge advertising campaign and almost guaranteed bookings. Commenting on the cost of 8½ (and Visconti's *The Leopard*), *Show* reported that "In terms of lire spent, they have nearly been Italian *Cleopatras*. But what Hollywood bought dearly in *Cleopatra* was a big empty box . . . What the Italians got in 8½ was a work of immense visual beauty and impressive philosophy, a sort of spectacle of the spirit that was more than they had paid for. A masterpiece is always a bargain." *Show*'s "philosophy" is the kind you look for, like Fellini's "ideas." 8½ does indeed make a spectacle of the spirit: what else can you do with spirit when you're expected to turn out masterpieces?

According to Fellini, we "need new criteria of judgment to appreciate this film." Yeah. "In my picture everything happens," says Guido, which is intended to mean that he is an artist-magician; but the man who trusts to alchemy is like the man who hopes to create a masterpiece in his sleep and find it miraculously *there* upon awakening. Fellini throws in his disorganized ideas, and lets the audiences sort out the meanings for themselves. 8½ is big, it's "beautiful": but what is it? Is it really a magical work of art? There is an optimum size for a house: if it becomes too big it becomes a mansion or a show-place and we no longer feel the vital connections of family life, or the way the rooms reflect personalities and habits and tastes. When a movie becomes a spectacle, we lose close involvement in the story; we may admire the action and the pageantry or, as in *8½*, the decor, the witty phantasmagoria, the superb "pro-fessionalism" ("That Fellini sure can make movies"), but it has become too big and impressive to relate to lives and feelings. Fellini's last home movie was *Nights of Cabiria*; *8½* is a mad-house for a movie director who celebrates *La Dolce Vita*, i.e., a funhouse. "What marvelous casting," his admirers exclaim, responding not to the people in his films, but to his cleverness in finding them. That is all one can respond to, because the first appearance of his "characters" tells us all that is to be known about them. They are "set" — embalmed. No acting is necessary: he uses them for a kind of instant caricature. His "magic" is that his casting couch is the world. He uses "real" aristocrats and "real" celebrities as themselves, he turns busi-nessmen into stars, and then he confesses that he's confused about life and art — the confusion which gives his films that special, "professional" chic.

Like those professors of English who boast that they're not interested in what's going on in the world, they're interested only in literature, or critics who say they're not interested in content but in structure, or young poets who tell us they're not interested in anything except their own creativity, Guido announces, "I have nothing to say but I want to say it." The less self, the more need to express it? Or, as the wife said to her drunken husband, "If you had any brains, you'd take them out and play with them."

And the "spa" is just the place to do it, as *Marienbad* dem-onstrated. Those who honed their wits interpreting what trans-pired *Last Year at Marienbad* now go to work on *8½*, separating out "memories" and fantasies from "reality." A professor who teaches film told me he had gone to see *8½* several times to test out various theories of how the shifts between the three categories were accomplished, and still hadn't discovered the answer. When I suggested that he had set himself an insoluble problem, because 8½ is all fantasy, he became very angry at what he called my perversity and cited as a clear example of "reality" the sequence of the screen tests for the mistress and wife (one of the most nightmarish episodes in the film) and as an example of "memory" the Saraghina dancing on the beach (which compares as a "memory" with, say, the monster washed up at the end of *La Dolce Vita*).

This is the first (and, predictably, not the last) movie in which the director seems to be primarily interested in glorifying his self-imprisonment. And this failure to reach out imaginatively — which traditionally has been considered artistic suicide — is acclaimed as a milestone in film art by those who accept self-absorption as "creativity."

8½ began as a "sequel" to *La Dolce Vita* — taking up the story of the "Umbrian angel." Now Fellini turns her into Claudia Cardinale, a rather full-bosomed angel with an ambiguous smile. Fluttering about diaphanously, she's not so different from Cyd Charisse or Rita Hayworth in gauze on the ramps of an MGM or Columbia production number. She becomes a showman's ideal of innocence — pulchritudinous purity, the angel-muse as "star" (of the movie and the movie within the movie) — a stalemate endlessly reflected, an infinite regression.

IV

Polemics

Is There a Cure for Film Criticism?

Or, Some Unhappy Thoughts on Siegfried Kracauer's *Theory of Film: The Redemption of Physical Reality*

Siegfried Kracauer is the sort of man who can't say "It's a lovely day" without first establishing that it *is* day, that the term "day" is meaningless without the dialectical concept of "night," that both these terms have no meaning unless there is a world in which day and night alternate, and so forth. By the time he has established an epistemological system to support his right to observe that it's a lovely day, our day has been spoiled. Kracauer doesn't mean to spoil movies for us. It's obvious that he really loves certain movies — and he does his best to justify this affection by bending and twisting his theory to include, or at least excuse, the movies he likes. This is made possible by our confusion about what the *theory* is.

It's always said of George Lukacs that his best stuff isn't in English; Kracauer's best stuff isn't in English either. Reading this book is slow going — and not because it's overwhelmingly deep. After 215 pages we get to this:

The time-honoured differentiation between form and content of artistic achievements affords a convenient starting-point for an analysis of story types. It is true that in any given case these two components of the work of art interpenetrate each other insolubly: each content includes form elements; each form is also content . . . But it is no less true that the concepts "form" and "content" have a basis in the properties of the artistic work itself. And the near-impossibility of neatly validating these concepts in the material is rather a point in their favour. With complex live entities the accuracy of definitions does not suffer from the fact that they retain a fringe of indistinct meanings. Quite the contrary, they must be elusive to achieve maximum precision — which implies that any attempt to remove their seeming vagueness for the sake of semantically irreproachable concepts is thoroughly devious.

Kracauer really cannot be accused of deviousness, and certainly his form and content are insoluble.

What do movies have to do with the "redemption" of "physical reality"? Our physical reality — what we experience about us — is what we can't redeem: if it's good, marvelous; if it isn't, we can weep or booze, or try to change it. Redemption, like sublimation, is a dear, sweet thought. And Kracauer's theory of film is a theory imposed on motion pictures: he's too much of a theoretician to develop a critical attitude or approach on the basis of what he likes (that would be too simple, too sensible). He presents a theory and then presents foundations and documentation (dogmentation, I almost said) to support it. The foundations are so laboriously laid that there is a tendency to accept certain assumptions, just to get things moving (after all, who wants to stay at the pre-film level forever?). But we may not feel too cheery about where things are heading when informed that "The following historical survey, then, is to provide the substantive conceptions on which the subsequent systematic considerations proper will depend." Doesn't exactly sound like an invitation to a party, does it? So many people who fled from Hitler, stripped of their possessions, seem to have come over carrying the worst of German pedantry in their heads.

Theory of Film: The Redemption of Physical Reality is expensively got out by Oxford University Press; it is, I suppose, Kracauer's major work since that Freudian-Marxian heavy entertainment *From Caligari to Hitler*, which is always referred to as a landmark in film scholarship — I suppose it is, in the sense that nobody else has done anything like it, *Gott sei dank!* The book carries such dust-jacket blurbs as Paul Rotha saying it is "The most important work to date in the English language on the theory and aesthetics of the Film. It will make a deep impact in all places where the Cinema is regarded as an art." And Richard Griffith, the curator of the Museum of Modern Art Film Library, says "Dr. Kracauer's work supersedes all previous aesthetic theories of the film."

There is, in any art, a tendency to turn one's own preferences into a monomaniac theory; in film criticism, the more confused and single-minded and dedicated (to untenable propositions) the theorist is, the more likely he is to be regarded as serious and important and "deep" — in contrast to relaxed men of good sense whose pluralistic approaches can be disregarded as not fundamental enough. During the years in which dialecticians were stating the thesis that "the art of the motion picture is montage" some very good movies were being made that had nothing whatever to do with "montage." (And those who were making a religion of the theory usually pointed out as examples the films Eisenstein made long after he'd abandoned — or been forced to abandon — "montage.") Related monomaniac schools developed — for example, *Sight and Sound* wants movies to be "firm" (a term one might think more applicable to a breast or a conviction).

Siegfried Kracauer is in the great, lunatic tradition: he believes that the cinema is "animated by a desire to picture transient material life, life at its most ephemeral. Street crowds, involuntary gestures, and other fleeting impressions are its very meat . . . films are true to the medium to the extent that they penetrate the world before our eyes . . . " He says that this assumption "that films are true to the medium to the extent that they penetrate the world before our eyes . . . " is "the premise and axis" of his book. But what does it mean? Either it's a general sort of remark, a harmless tautology indicating that movies have something to do with the world — like presenting images of it; or he is trying to distinguish two classes of movies, those which presumably "penetrate the world before our eyes" and those which don't. But as we don't know what he means by this penetration, we accept his "premise and axis" as meaningless and move on. At almost every step in his reasoning we must do the same: would it be some terrible evidence of superficiality if we could penetrate what he's talking about?

For Kracauer, as for Hegel, all nature and all history are marching toward one culmination:

If film is a photographic medium, it must gravitate toward the expanses of outer reality — an open-ended, limitless world which bears little resemblance to the finite and ordered cosmos set by tragedy. Unlike this cosmos, where destiny defeats chance and all the light falls on human interaction, the world of film is a flow of random shots involving both humans and inanimate objects. . . . Once you start from the assumption that the camera retains major characteristics of photography, you will find it impossible to accept the widely sanctioned belief or claim that film is an art like traditional arts. Works of art consume the raw material from which they are drawn [I'd love an example! He sounds like a materialist running amok in a neighbour's field], whereas films as an outgrowth of camera work are bound to exhibit it. [Is it the medium or Kracauer standing on its head? The camera work is an outgrowth, if we must use such vegetable terms, of the conception of the film.] However purposefully directed, the motion picture camera would cease to be a camera if it did not record visible phenomena for their own sake. It fulfils itself in rendering "the ripple of the leaves."

I am puzzled to know how this ripple of the leaves theory could possibly help us to see into the art of the film: often the worst and most embarrassing part of a film is the accidental, the uncontrolled, the amateurish failure which exhibits its unachieved intentions; and the finest moment may be a twitch of the actress's cheek achieved on the fiftieth take. There are accidents which look like art and there is art that looks accidental; but how can you build an *aesthetic* on *accident* — on the *ripple of the leaves?* How do you discriminate between the "accidental" that is banal or awkward or pointless and the "accidental" that is "cinema" — without referring to some *other* standards of excellence or even relevance? How can you say "accidents were the very soul of slapstick"? In comedy what looks accidental is generally the result of brilliant timing and deliberate anarchy and wild invention and endless practice.

What it comes down to in Kracauer is that film is Lumière's "nature caught in the act" — or neo-realism: the look of so many good movies during the period he was gestating this book becomes his definition of cinema itself.

What is this *nature* that is appealed to, a nature that *excludes* works that are staged, stylized, or even carefully wrought, if not simply another kind of *selection* from nature? Kracauer regards films dealing with the life of the poor or films using non-professionals as more "natural." Why? "Film," he tells us, "gravitates toward unstaged reality" and "the artificiality of stagy settings or compositions runs counter to the medium's declared preference for nature in the raw." How and when did the medium declare its preference, I wonder? The trouble with this kind of Hegelian prose is that the reader is at first amused by what seem to be harmless metaphors, and soon the metaphors are being used as if they were observable historical tendencies and aesthetic phenomena, and next the metaphor becomes a stick to castigate those who have other tastes, and other metaphors.

What are we to make of a statement like "Herschel not only predicted the basic features of the film camera but assigned to it a task which it has never since disowned: 'the vivid and life-like reproduction and handing down to the latest posterity of any transaction in real life . . . ' "? Well, I can't say that the film camera has ever disowned this task, any more than *it* ever claimed it. But I can certainly cite numerous people who have used it for recording life they *arranged* for the camera. Griffith and Eisenstein, for example — and just about everybody else who ever made a movie. When Kracauer says "Film . . . is uniquely equipped to record and reveal physical reality and, hence, gravitates toward it," either he is including whatever is photographed in "reality" — an empty generalization — or trying to claim that film "gravitates" toward "raw," "unstaged" reality, nature caught in the ripple of the leaves, and is once again indulging in the metaphorical sleight of mind by which he seeks to convince us that film "gravitates" — i.e., is drawn toward his idea of what movies should be. "Imagine a film which, in keeping with the basic properties, records interesting aspects of physical reality but does so in a technically imperfect manner; perhaps the lighting is awkward or the editing uninspired. Nevertheless such a film is more specifically a film than one which utilises brilliantly all the cinematic devices and tricks to produce a statement disregarding camera-reality." But what is camera-reality? What can it be but the area of reality he wants the camera to record? To put it simply and crudely, *Earth* is no more *real* than *Smiles of a Summer Night*. Kracauer is indulging in one of the oldest and most primitive types of thinking — he's like a religious zealot who thinks his life of prayer and fasting is more "real" than the worldly life of men in big cities, and that "nature" has somehow dictated his diet of nuts and berries.

"It is evident that the cinematic approach materialises in all films which follow the realistic tendency." Obviously — by his definition of cinema. Can tautology go much further? But then, once he has convinced himself that the art of the motion picture follows natural laws, he forgets that these natural "laws" are simply descriptive, and begins to talk about the "medium's recording obligations" — as if natural laws were prescriptions and commands, to be followed and obeyed. And it is but a short next step for "nature" to decide what the *content* of films should or must be.

"The hunting ground of the motion picture camera is in principle unlimited [Don't trust this man. You'd better get a license — he'd be the first to turn you in for poaching.]; it is the external world expanding in all directions. Yet there are certain subjects within that world which may be termed 'cinematic' because they seem to exert a peculiar attraction on the medium. It's as if the medium were predestined (and eager) to exhibit them." The "medium" has become such an animate creature that we might as well start looking around for ways to punish it when it misbehaves.

Starting from Kracauer's basis of looking for what cannot be done in any other medium, surely one could make an equally good case for the tricks and magic of Méliès. In what other medium would much of Cocteau's *Orphée* or Dreyer's *Vampyr* or Karel Zeman's *Invention of Destruction* be possible? Kracauer says Méliès "failed to transcend" the theater "by incorporating genuinely cinematic subjects": we can translate this to mean that once you define "genuinely cinematic" as "the ripple of the leaves" or "nature caught in the act," the staged or deliberately magical becomes "uncinematic" — by definition. But why should we go along with him in playing this game of arbitrary definitions that simply lead us back to his starting point? It's a dull game: a nursery game.

"Mary Jane, be a good girl and eat your neo-realist bread pudding."

"I had that for supper last night. Tonight I want something choice, like some Jean Cocteau *nouvelle vague* ice cream."

"But that isn't good for you. Neo-realist bread pudding is much more nourishing. If you don't eat what's good for you, you won't grow up straight and healthy."

"If you like it so much, why don't you eat it yourself?"

"You need it more than I do."

"I think I'm going to throw up."

In his effort to distinguish "cinematic subjects," Kracauer draws some curious lines of demarcation. He finds, for example, that in film "inanimate objects stand out as protagonists and all but overshadow the rest of the cast." He cites "unruly Murphy beds," "the mad automobiles in silent comedy," and so on. I would suggest that these inanimate objects are generally used on screen as props, in basically the same way they are used in vaudeville, in the theater, or in the circus — and that there is nothing the matter with such use in a film or in any other medium; no line of demarcation is either possible or necessary.

Chaplin's "Murphy bed" routine in *One A.M.* is either funny or not funny (I don't lose my mind over it); it probably could be done very similarly on stage. So what?

Other examples cited, the cruiser Potemkin and the oil derrick in *Louisiana Story*, are less feasible on stage, but how does that make them more cinematic than something which is easy to put in a theater? Both are, incidentally, much less interesting objects on the screen than they are generally asserted to be: the exciting action in *Potemkin* has little reference to the cruiser itself (extras can run around on a stage, too), and I have never discovered *any* source of great cinematic excitement in *Louisiana Story*. "The fact," says Kracauer, "that big objects are as inaccessible to the stage as small ones suffices to range them among cinematic subjects." Who cares whether the objects on the screen are accessible or inaccessible to the stage, or, for that matter, to painting, or to the novel or poetry? Who started this divide and conquer game of aesthetics in which the different media are assigned their special domains like salesmen staking out their territories — you stick to the Midwest and I'll take Florida?

Film aestheticians are forever telling us that when they have discovered what the motion picture can do that other arts can't do, they have discovered the "essence," the "true nature" of motion picture art. It is like the old nonsense that man *is* what differentiates him from the other animals — which is usually said to be his soul or his mind or his ability to transmit information from one generation to another, etc. But man is also what he shares with the other animals. And if you try to reduce him to some supposed quality that he alone has, you get an absurdly distorted view of man. And the truth is, as we learn more about animals and about man, the less we are sure about what differentiates him from other animals, or if it's so very important. And what motion picture art shares with other arts is perhaps even more important than what it may, or may *not*, have exclusively.

Those who look for the differentiating, defining "essence" generally overlook the main body of film and stage material and techniques which are very much the same. Except for the physical presence of the actors in a theater, there is almost no "difference" between stage and screen that isn't open to question; there is almost no effect possible in one that can't be simulated, and sometimes remarkably well achieved, in the other. Of course, there are effects in films that seem marvelously "filmic" — like the long tracking shots at the opening of Welles's *Touch of Evil*, or the ladies burning in Dreyer's *The Passion of Jeanne d'Arc* and *Day of Wrath*, or the good old car racing the train at the close of *Intolerance*; but it isn't beyond the range of possibility for a stage director to get very similar effects. Close-ups, long-shots, fast cutting are all possible on the stage, even though they require somewhat different techniques. And there is no more reason for a stage director to avoid fluid techniques that resemble movies (he *can't* avoid them in staging, say, Shakespeare or Büchner or *Peer Gynt* or *To Damascus*) than for a moviemaker to avoid keeping his camera inside one room — if a room is where his material belongs. We can take pleasure in the virtuoso use of visual images in Dovzhenko's *Arsenal* or Gance's *Napoleon*; we can also take pleasure in a virtuoso performer like Keaton simply changing hats in *Steamboat Bill, Jr.*

Perhaps the most lovable side of Kracauer is his desperate attempt to make musicals, which he obviously adores, fit his notion of cinema as nature in the raw. A man who likes Fred Astaire can't be all pedant. How touching he becomes when he tries to explain that it is Astaire's dancing "over tables and gravel paths into the everyday world . . . from the footlights to the heart of camera-reality" that makes him acceptable. He's like a man trying to sneak his dear — but naughty — friends into heaven.

As if our delight in the performance of a song or dance depended on the degree to which it grew out of the surrounding material — as if our pleasure had to be justified! This is a variant of the pedagogical Puritan notion that you mustn't enjoy a poem or a story unless it teaches you a lesson: you mustn't enjoy a movie unless it grows out of "nature." "In making its songs appear an outgrowth of life's contingencies, the genre shows an affinity, however mediated, for the cinematic medium." Phew! Our pleasure in song and dance, as in motion picture itself, is in the ingenuity with which man *uses* the raw material of his existence — not in the raw material itself, or in a visible link with it.

Once again he falls back on his strange use of language. "Astaire's consummate dancing is meant to belong among the real-life events with which he toys in his musicals; and it is so organised that it imperceptibly emerges from, and disappears in, the flow of these happenings." The crucial word here is "meant." *Who* means it — some cosmic force? I think it may be almost disingenuous of Kracauer to pretend that the Astaire-Rogers musicals represent the "flow of life." Isn't it enough that they represent the American film musical comedy tradition of rhythm and romance and high spirits, a tradition that has collapsed under the weight of "serious" ideas and "important" dance? He cannot accept even the early classic René Clair comedies for their wit and choreographic grace and movement, their poetic, imaginative stylization — but because " . . . it is the vicissitudes of life from which these ballets issue."

In other words, he attempts to build an aesthetic not on art (the formalized expression of experience) but on whether the raw material of art is still visible (or he can *pretend* it's visible) in the finished work — a very curious standard indeed. Why not then simply reject all art and go back to "nature"? His "aesthetics," carried out with any intellectual rigour, *rejects art.* If you can only accept dancing in films by such bizarre claims as " . . . what could be more inseparable from that flow (of life) than 'natural' dancing?" some nebulous conception of "nature" has become your standard of art. It is, of course, on this same basis that reviewers of musicals often praise works like *On the Town* or *West Side Story* — and denigrate infinitely better musicals like *Singin' in the Rain* or *The Band Wagon* — though patently nothing is more embarrassing than the transparent efforts to make it appear that the musical numbers are "growing out" of the story. The dialogue becomes as flat and functional as the recitatives of opera. In a musical production like *The King and I*, the best sequence is the theatrical presentation of the Uncle Tom's Cabin ballet; the attempted integration of song into the plot, the contrived "natural" ways in which the characters break into little songs, are puerile and depressing. It is this clumsy effort to make things look "natural" instead of accepting the stylization of song and dance which helps to make so many musicals seem simpering and infantile.

But when Astaire goes into an exuberant routine that involves leaping over luggage and chairs, we are as aware of the pretense, the *convention* that this "grows out" of the plot situation, as we are aware of the conventions of any backstage musical, with the elaborate presentation of opening night and the understudy becoming the star. Surely nobody but "serious" critics takes one set of conventions for "life" and hence cinema art, and the other set of conventions for the dreadful error of "staginess." What matters is simply how good the numbers are (and how much talent or artistry have gone into making the conventions of musical film amusing and acceptable). A poorly choreographed dance over luggage and chairs would be no better because it seemed to "grow out" of the plot.

The lengths to which many theoreticians of the film will go to avoid accepting any form of convention or stylization is extraordinary. You may begin to suspect that they regard style as decadent; as if it were nature spoiled. For example, Kracauer's lengthy consideration of photography omits color — which obviously involves types of control that would be a bit upsetting to this theory of "accidents" and "nature" and "unadulterated life." In his system the stylized use of color would be like tampering with nature. And music? "The all-important thing is . . . that musical accompaniment enlivens the pictures by evoking the more material aspects of reality." (But the more music does so, the worse it is as music. Even program music like Respighi's *Pines* or *Fountains* does not evoke pines or fountains,

but only images in the minds of people who would rather day-
dream than listen.)

And how is this for another effort to justify dancing by reference to the "candid" camera? "Records of dancing sometimes
amount to an intrusion into the dancer's intimate privacy. His
self-forgetting rapture may show in queer gestures and distorted
facial expressions which are not intended to be watched . . .
However, the supreme virtue of the camera consists precisely in
acting the voyeur." But the supreme virtue of an Astaire is
precisely that you don't see the sweat and grimaces and months
of nerve-wracking preparation: you see the *achieved* elegance.
Astaire has the wit to make the dance appear casual and, as
audience, we recognize that this nonchalant ease is the true grace
note of his control. We are never for a minute taken in by the
ruse that the dance is spontaneous; it is partly because we recognize the dance to be difficult and complex, that we enjoy the
convention that it just happened.

Here is an example of Kracauer's critical method at work on
the film *Hamlet*, with reference to Olivier's "To be or not to
be," spoken from a tower, with the ocean underneath:

No sooner does the photographed ocean appear than the spectator experiences something like a shock. He cannot help recognis-
ing that this little scene is an outright intrusion; that it abruptly
introduces an element incompatible with the rest of the imagery.
How he then reacts to it depends upon his sensibilities. Those indifferent to the peculiarities of the medium, and therefore unquestioningly accepting the staged Elsinore, are likely to resent the
unexpected emergence of crude nature as a letdown, while those
more sensitive to the properties of film will in a flash realise the
make-believe character of the castle's mythical splendour.

If you have to be *sensitive* to realize that!

Of course the ocean is an intrusion: it intrudes on the stylized sets, it disturbs our acceptance and enjoyment of the Shakespearean conventions, and it adds an extra, visual layer of
meaning to the soliloquy itself by introducing a redundancy

— another means of suicide. But those "so sensitive to the properties of film" that they want to throw out the castle and have more ocean, are throwing out Shakespeare. I don't wish to demean the visual grandeur of the ocean, but can't we have some poetry and drama, too? Those who unquestioningly accept the staged Elsinore are not "indifferent to the peculiarities of the medium"; they are testifying to the director's success in involving them in the world he has created on the screen. Yes, the ocean is a miserable mistake in *Hamlet*, but in Castellani's *Romeo and Juliet* the Friar's little outdoor scene gathering herbs is exquisite — a moment of absurd sweetness and innocence. Surely there are no hard and fast rules: it all depends on how it's done. In *Richard III*, Olivier succeeds with the soliloquies as neither he nor anyone else has done on film before; instead of treating them as outmoded or improper theatrical conventions and trying to fuse them with the dramatic action, he ignored film theories and used the soliloquy as a perfectly valid cinematic device. These moments when Richard puts the audience in his confidence are the most exciting in the film — intimate, audacious, brazen. What better demonstration could we have of the variety, the infinity of possibilities in moviemaking?

Kracauer finds that "the medium has always shown a predilection for . . . phenomena overwhelming consciousness [If consciousness is overwhelmed, what becomes of phenomena?] . . . elemental catastrophes, the atrocities of war, acts of violence and terror, sexual debauchery, and death." Is it the "medium" that shows this predilection? If so, it is not the only medium that does. Shakespeare dealt with such phenomena in poetic drama, Tolstoy in *War and Peace*, Beethoven in his symphonies, Goya in his *Disasters of War*, Picasso in *Guernica*. Was it the film "medium" that showed a predilection, or is it that artists like Griffith, Eisenstein, Pudovkin, Dovzhenko, Kurosawa wanted *at certain times* in their creative lives to deal with such phenomena, just as they might want at other times to express more personal emotions? The Shakespeare who wrote

Macbeth also wrote the sonnets; is Griffith's *Broken Blossoms* less cinematic than *The Birth of a Nation* or *Intolerance?*

In no other art do theoreticians insist that the *range* of subject matter is determined by the medium. We can love *Middlemarch* without having to reject *The Wings of the Dove.* But Odessa-steeped film critics tell us that Eisenstein's "goal, a cinematic one, was the depiction of collective action, with the masses as the true hero" — and this battle hymn has become the international anthem of film criticism. In the fall 1961 *New Politics*, Ernest Callenbach writes "a letter to a young film maker" and says "Get thee to Cuba, and after that to Latin America elsewhere, and then Africa." Would the same advice be given to a young writer or painter? Why are moviemakers obliged to make history? In the dialectics of film criticism, the violent movements of men are as "natural" as the rippling of the leaves. But, but — suppose the young film maker doesn't know Spanish, can't stand the sight of blood, was drawn to the film medium after seeing *L' Avventura*, and has prepared a fine, elliptical scenario on the uneventful life of Emily Dickinson? He'll probably make a terrible movie, but surely the first prerogative of an artist in any medium is to make a fool of himself. Callenbach, like so many film critics, regards Kracauer's position as basically sound. Writing of *Theory of Film*, he summarizes the views, and says, "True. But what of the exact ways in which the potentially good materials are handled?" In other words, after you get to Cuba, where presumably you can find Kracauer's and Callenbach's kind of filmic "collective action" which is somehow raw nature, how should you proceed? Let's leave them to work it out, but it's worth noting that Kracauer's position is still dominant in much of film criticism.

Callenbach says the "general position must be retained. *Theory of Film* is indeed a landmark." You'd think there were no movies made between post-revolutionary Russia and post-war Italy and . . . Cuba. The application of this kind of theory in the past decades has resulted in such critical evaluations as Richard Griffith's selection of *A Nous La Liberté* as René Clair's "masterpiece" (over *Le Million!*) and his decision that *La Grande Illusion* was "fatally the projection of a literary argument. Nevertheless, the film was a determined attempt to comment upon events and if possible to influence them." That tells us what *counts* in making movies, doesn't it? You can mitigate your crimes against the "medium" if you attempt to influence history — in the direction the critic approves. The standard film histories still judge movies by the values of the "Resistance." Probably de Broca's *The Five-Day Lover* can't be taken seriously unless *he* goes to Cuba; then mitigating social attitudes can be discovered in it.

American audiences and exhibitors have their own variant of the Kracauer position; they want the theater screen to do what the television screen can't do: overpower them. The wide screen is a Procrustes bed, and all movies that don't fit its proportions have their tops and bottoms cut off. In the reissue of *Gone with the Wind*, Vivien Leigh not only has lost her feet, she ends in mid-thigh; in the now standard "SuperScope" *Henry V*, Olivier has no hair, often no head. Movies are blown-up and reissued with their color drained away, the focus blurred. Just as silent movies are projected at sound speed (enabling audiences to laugh at the jerky, primitive, early flickers) every composition in a widened film may be destroyed — but movies are bigger than ever. It might be thought that the "small" movie is the domain of the foreign film theaters, but increasingly the art-houses are not only projecting everything in wide-screen but are looking forward to more "art blockbusters," on the model of *La Dolce Vita* and *Two Women*. However, if the art-house audience has its monomania for one element at the expense of others, it is for what is euphemistically described as a more "adult," "frank," or "realistic" treatment of human relations. One man's "reality" is poverty and mass movements; another man's reality is sex.

Some critics are wet behind the ears; Kracauer is dry behind the ears. "One thing is evident: whenever a film-maker turns the spotlight on a historical subject or ventures into the realm of fantasy, he runs the risk of defying the basic properties of his medium. Roughly speaking, he seems no longer concerned with physical reality but bent on incorporating worlds which to all appearances lie outside the orbit of actuality."

Why doesn't he just come out with it and admit that he thinks art is unnatural? Let's stop spinning and look at some movies: Is De Sica "defying the basic properties of his medium" when he turns the great Emma Gramatica into an angelic old rattlebrain flying through the skies of *Miracle in Milan* (never mentioned in the book)? Is he "obeying" these "basic properties of the medium" when he takes a "non-professional," a college professor, and turns him into the great *Umberto D* (cited some fifteen times)? Both films are staged and acted; how and why is the fantasy defying the medium, and how is it that *Umberto D*, which is just as staged as a movie set in medieval Japan or Gothic Ruritania, is supposed to have an "unfixable flow" — "the omnipresent streets breathe a tristesse which is palpably the outcome of unfortunate social conditions." May we not deduce that for Kracauer the "basic properties" of the film have more to do with "unfortunate social conditions" than with art? But *Miracle in Milan* also has something to do with "unfortunate social conditions" though De Sica's form is a comic fable about human brotherhood and innocence, a fantasy demonstration that the pure in heart must seek the Kingdom of Heaven because, literally and ironically, they have no kingdom on earth.

Is this too stylized a treatment of social conditions to be compatible with Kracauer's notions of cinema? But then how is it that Eisenstein's triumphs of geometry and engineering "convey to us the paroxysmal upheavals of real masses"? When he moves real masses (of extras) he's helping us to see the "blind drive of things," and some of the most imaginative stylization of all time in handling masses — in *Metropolis* — can only be justified as cinema by a real howler: "the fleeing crowds (in the flood episode) are staged veraciously and rendered through a combination of long shots and close shots which provide exactly the kind of random impressions we could receive were we to witness this spectacle in reality." But all is not really well. "Yet the cinematic impact of the crowd images suffers from the fact that the scene is laid in architectural surroundings which could not be more stylized." In other words, a movie is a movie only if you can pretend it isn't a movie. By stylized he obviously means "unreal" or "unnatural"; he should visit the new science-fiction Los Angeles airport, which is glaringly "real." There, "raw life" makes *Metropolis* seem far more prophetic than say, *October*. Perhaps a belief in progress (via the dialectic, of course) is also part of his concept of "nature."

Middle-class Marxists hate actors (who wants to be bothered by the mysteries of personality?) almost as much as they hate fantasy. Films with "non-actors" win Kracauer's special approbation: they have "a documentary touch."

Think of such story films as *The Quiet One, Los Olvidados,* or the De Sica films, *Bicycle Thieves* and *Umberto D*: in all of them the emphasis is on the world around us; their protagonists are not so much particular individuals as types representative of whole groups of people. [Jaibo a type! There isn't one great character in literature, in drama or in film who is a type. And in our daily lives, only the people we don't get to know function as types.] These narratives serve to dramatise social conditions in general. The preference for real people on the screen and the documentary approach seem to be closely related.

The inferences become inevitable: the non-actor is "real." The professor who gives such a great performance as Umberto D is acceptable because Kracauer can confuse him with nature in the raw, and he's ever so much more "real" than a highly trained actress like Emma Gramatica. (If a famous old actor had played Umberto D, Kracauer would probably have to go into prolix apologetics before reconciling the film with the "documentary approach.") But some hidden standards must also be at work: *The Roof,* which would seem to satisfy all Kracauer's notions of the "medium's" requirements, is never mentioned. Perhaps even the "medium" is depressed by dull movies.

Kracauer's description of the nature of cinema excludes, limits, rejects. *Le Sang d'un Poète* and *Un Chien Andalou* are tossed out as "a film type" — "stagy fantasy" which "cannot help producing an uncinematic effect." And with them go all the marvelous possibilities for associational editing, which for some of us makes a film like *Un Chien Andalou* seem an indication of whole new areas in art. We hadn't recognized, it seems, that such "inner life" interests ignore camera-reality. He sets us straight about Cocteau — "a *littérateur* rather than a film-maker"; that quickly disposes of some of the greatest works of our time. *Orphée* (never mentioned) is, by his system of defini-tions, not a movie at all.

Soon we learn that "a sensitive spectator or listener" at the film version of Menotti's *The Medium* is "caught in a terrifying clash between cinematic realism and operatic magic . . . he feels he is being torn asunder." (Kracauer's aesthetic sensibilities are so delicate that he suffers excruciating tortures when his film sense is violated; now how can any reasonable person get so upset by a moderately successful film version of a mediocre opera?) But not only does the audience suffer: we learn that "the cinema takes revenge upon those who desert it" — poor Powell and Pressburger, their crime was that "having thrown out the cinema as a means of capturing real life" they "reintro-duce it to evolve an imagery which is essentially stage imagery, even though it could not be staged in a theatre." (Isn't it amus-ing to discover that although what is essentially "cinema" is what can't be done in other media, there is such a thing as "essentially stage imagery, even though it could not be staged in a theatre.")

Couldn't we introduce, at this point, some sensible criteria instead of these essences and retrogressions and punishments? The trouble with *Tales of Hoffmann* is not that "it is cinema estranged from itself" or that its imagery is stagy, but that it suffers from the same monotony and failure of imagination that blight so many ballet presentations. Kracauer says, "It is natural for film — and therefore artistically promising — to prefer the enchantments of an obscure railway station to the painted splendour of enchanted woods." Couldn't we say simply that as anything a camera can record is "natural," nature is not a criterion in judging movies? An obscure railway station may be enchanting, so may painted woods. Oberon's procession in Reinhardt's A *Midsummer Night's Dream* is an exquisite, magical moment on film — indicating that what is the matter with most of the movie is not the "uncinematic" use of stylized sets, but the *way* they are conceived and used, how the actors and camera move, how the lines are spoken, the quality of the visual imagery, the rhythm of the action and editing, or any of the infinite number of elements that may come between a creative artist and the achievement of his goal. It may even be that Reinhardt's goal was not imaginative enough, or it may be the front office thought it was *too* imaginative and put restrictions on him. But there is nothing uncinematic about the attempt. What an artist wants to do can't always be set in obscure railway stations or in the streets, or in contemporary settings. Why should theorists who see the poetry of the streets want to throw out the poetry of the past and of imaginary worlds?

Reading all this exaltation of the "documentary" approach, you get the impression that cinema theorists think that Griffith shot *The Birth of a Nation* while the battles were raging, that Eisenstein was making newsreels, and that Rossellini and Buñuel were simply camera witnesses to scenes of extraordinary brutality. Ironically, the greatest director of all time to work with documentary material — the one great example Kracauer might point to — Leni Riefenstahl, whose *Triumph of the Will* and *Olympiad* are film masterpieces of a documentary nature if anything is, is not mentioned in *Theory of Film, The Redemption of Physical Reality*. Mightn't we infer that politics has something to do with Kracauer's "reality"?

I should like to see motion picture art brought back into the world of the other arts (which it has never left, except in film theory) and see movies judged by the same kind of standards that are used in other arts, not by the attempt to erect a "reality" standard. Reality, like God and History, tends to direct people to wherever they want to go. The "reality" standard leads Kracauer into this kind of criticism: ". . . Bergman's *The Seventh Seal* is essentially a miracle play, yet the medieval beliefs and superstitions it features are questioned throughout by the inquisitive mind of the knight and the outright scepticism of his squire. Both characters manifest a down-to-earth attitude. And their secular doubts result in confrontations which in a measure acclimatise the film to the medium." I would say that when a film theorist, whose book is being used as a text in many film courses, must look for "secular doubts" and "confrontations" in order to find cinematic qualities in a work, that he has sacrificed much of the art of the motion picture to his theory, and that, in his attempt to separate motion picture from other arts, he has sacrificed the most elementary responsiveness towards work in any medium — the ability to perceive a movie or a poem or an opera or a painting in something like its totality, to respond to its qualities, and to see it in relation to the artist's work as a whole. He seems overdue for secular doubts.

Obviously English is not Kracauer's native language, and it seems cruel and unfair to protest his usage of it. But how can we judge what he's saying when he sets up terms and classifications (like "mental reality") that seem to mean something for him that they could hardly mean to anyone else? Are we perhaps being more generous to his ideas than we would be if we could decipher them?

What good are Kracauer's terms if no one else can apply them? How can anyone tell what fits his scheme? It's so arbitrary, it's like a catechism to which he owns the only set of correct answers. Who could guess that Rosebud, the sled of *Citizen Kane,* is one of the "symbols true to the medium"? What about the battle on the ice in *Nevsky?* (A great game for a bookmaker — most of us would lose our shirts.) It turns out that "It is nothing but an excrescence on the body of an intrigue imposed upon the medium." This man Kracauer is really one up on us.

He's full of surprises: when he calls something "a veritable *tour de force*" this is a term of opprobrium: it means it isn't cinematic. If certain novels (*The Grapes of Wrath*) become "remarkable films" and others (*Madame Bovary* in the Jean Renoir version) "can hardly be called genuine cinema," what would be your guess as to the reason? Would you ever hit on "a difference which is in the adapted novels themselves"? "First, Steinbeck's novel deals in human groups rather than individuals . . . Through his very emphasis on collective misery, collective fears and hopes, Steinbeck meets the cinema more than halfway. Second, his novel exposes the predicament of the migratory farm workers, thus revealing and stigmatising abuses in our society. This too falls in line with the peculiar potentialities of film." Not only wouldn't I ever guess — but to go back a step, I remember Valentine Tessier at the opera and other scenes in Renoir's *Madame Bovary* ("all the traits of a theatrical film") with great pleasure, and I remember *The Grapes of Wrath* ("a classic of the screen") as a blur of embarrassing sentimental pseudo-biblical pseudo-documentary, a perfect representation of what Bertrand Russell called "the fallacy of the superior virtue of the oppressed."

How does Kracauer react to verbal comedy? To Preston Sturges, or *On Approval* or *Kind Hearts and Coronets* or, going back, to Sacha Guitry? Your guess is as good as mine, because verbal comedy doesn't really fit into his ideas of cinema and he doesn't bother with it. He refers to the Preston Sturges comedies as "borderline cases" — I assume he means on the border of his (i.e., the medium's) acceptance.

Could we ever have guessed that the avant-garde experiments would have to be justified by their beneficial results? "Nor should it be forgotten that, like Buñuel, many an avant-garde artist became realistic-minded and outward-bound; Joris Ivens and Cavalcanti, for instance, turned to social documentary."

How can we make clear to Kracauer that "the snow-covered courtyard" in *Le Sang d'un Poète* — "a stagy fantasy" and "uncinematic effect" for him — might mean more to us than all his rippling leaves? The rippling leaves are admired and then, more often than not, forgotten; Cocteau's images reverberate in our memories. And what does he single out to attack in *Un Chien Andalou* ("a hybrid") but the "small street crowd seen from far above" which is not "integrated into contexts suggestive of camera-reality." Buñuel and Dali "availed themselves of the camera in a literary rather than genuinely cinematic interest." That "small street crowd seen from far above" is one of the most startling and disturbing images in films; I, at least, have forgotten most of those street crowd scenes he thinks it should resemble.

What we actually respond to or remember from a film may be almost totally unrelated to Kracauer's definitions. (You can't exactly say he has *standards* — his standards are concealed as definitions of what a movie is. It's a timid way out: you never have to defend your choices; the medium has made them for you.) For example, although Kracauer uses René Clair to bolster his arguments against what he calls "surrealistic imagery," the only part of Clair's *Porte des Lilas* I cared for was the little set-piece of the children acting out a crime as the adults read a newspaper account of it — an almost surrealist little ballet with no connection to the rest of the film. The only sequence I recall from *Rickshaw Man* is the distant view of an Englishman's little dance of rage as he's kept waiting in his rickshaw. *Aparajito* was beautiful, but it is all hazy in memory except for that sudden ecstasy of the child reciting poetry.

In film after film, what we recall may be a gesture or a bit of dialogue, a suggestion, an imaginative moment of acting, even the use of a prop. Suddenly something — almost anything — may bring a movie to life. It is art and imagination that bring the medium to life; not as Kracauer would have it, the recording of "reality." I can't remember much of the streets and crowds and the lifelike milieu even from the neo-realist films — who does? But who can forget the cry of the boy at the end of *Shoeshine*, or the face of *Umberto D*, or Anna Magnani's death in *Open City*? I would suggest these experiences are very similar to the experiences we have in the theater. But shouldn't we take our bits and pieces of human revelation wherever we find them? There isn't so much to be had that we need to worry about whether what we get from a movie is only possible in "cinema" or whether we could have received a similar impression, or even the total conception, in a novel or in the theater.

Does every movie have to re-establish the existence of the outside world? Surely we can take something for granted when we step from the street into the movie house. Kracauer seems to think we go into the movie house to see the street we have left. The indeterminate flow of life is precisely what we are *leaving* — we go to see a distillation.

How can so many of the aspects of film — the very qualities that draw us to the medium — be *improper* to it? And the movies that suggest directions, hopes, possibilities? How is it that he has so little interest in the visual and emotional excitements of a Futurist experiment like *Menilmontant*? (What does he think of *Menilmontant* — one of the dazzling masterpieces of the screen? It narrates "fictitious incidents embedded in poetised actuality." Is that supposed to be bad or good? I rather think, bad.)

After 300 pages Kracauer triumphantly reaches "The Redemption of Physical Reality" and when he finally presents the proof of the pudding, it turns out to be — a pudding. "In order to make us experience physical reality, films must show what they picture. This requirement is so little self-evident that it raises the issue of the medium's relation to the traditional arts." And so on into the night. We've covered all that heavily trod old ground from Nietzsche to Comte to Whitehead, and Spengler to Toynbee and Durkheim. Kracauer must think we read books on the movies to get our knowledge of history and philosophy.

How is it that the "medium" stands so square for liberal, middle-class social consciousness? And how is it that in a period when even a college freshman has heard something about how our perspectives affect our notions of "reality," Kracauer goes on writing about his view of "unfortunate social conditions" as "reality"? Films are not made by cameras, though many of them look as if they were, just as a lot of dialogue sounds as if it were written by typewriters.

Art is the greatest game, the supreme entertainment, because you discover the game as you play it. There is only one rule, as we learned in *Orphée*: Astonish us! In all art we look and listen for what we have not experienced quite that way before. We want to see, to feel, to understand, to respond a new way. Why should pedants be allowed to spoil the game?

There are men whose concept of love is so boring and nagging that you decide if that's what love is, you don't want it, you want something else. That's how I feel about Kracauer's "cinema." I want something else.   [1962]

⁑⁑⁑⁑⁑⁑

Circles and Squares
Joys and Sarris

. . . the first premise of the auteur theory is the technical competence of a director as a criterion of value. . . . The second premise of the auteur theory is the distinguishable personality of the director as a criterion of value. . . . The third and ultimate premise of the auteur theory is concerned with interior meaning, the ultimate glory of the cinema as an art. Interior meaning is extrapolated from the tension between a director's personality and his material. . . .

Sometimes a great deal of corn must be husked to yield a few kernels of internal meaning. I recently saw Every Night at Eight, one of the many maddeningly routine films Raoul Walsh has directed in his long career. This 1935 effort featured George Raft, Alice Faye, Frances Langford and Patsy Kelly in one of those familiar plots about radio shows of the period. The film keeps moving along in the pleasantly unpretentious manner one would expect of Walsh until one incongruously intense scene with George Raft thrashing about in his sleep, revealing his inner fears in mumbling dream talk. The girl he loves comes into the room in the midst of his unconscious avowals of feeling, and listens sympathetically. This unusual scene was later amplified in High Sierra *with Humphrey Bogart and Ida Lupino. The point is that one of the screen's most virile directors employed an essentially feminine narrative device to dramatize the emotional vulnerability of his heroes. If I had not been aware of Walsh in* Every Night at Eight, *the crucial link to* High Sierra *would have passed unnoticed. Such are the joys of the* auteur *theory.*

— Andrew Sarris, "Notes on the Auteur Theory in 1962,"
Film Culture, Winter 1962-1963.

Perhaps a little more corn should be husked; perhaps, for example, we can husk away the word "internal" (is "internal meaning" any different from "meaning"?). We might ask why the link is "crucial"? Is it because the device was "incongruously intense" in *Every Night at Eight* and so demonstrated a try for something *deeper* on Walsh's part? But if his merit is his "pleasantly unpretentious manner" (which is to say, I suppose, that, recognizing the limitations of the script, he wasn't trying to do much) then the incongruous device was probably a misconceived attempt that disturbed the manner — like a bad playwright interrupting a comedy scene because he cannot resist the opportunity to tug at your heartstrings. We might also ask why this narrative device is "essentially feminine": is it more feminine than masculine to be asleep, or to talk in one's sleep, or to reveal feelings? Or, possibly, does Sarris regard the device as feminine because the listening woman becomes a sympathetic figure and emotional understanding is, in this "virile" context, assumed to be essentially feminine? Perhaps only if one accepts the narrow notions of virility so common in our action films can this sequence be seen as "essentially feminine," and it is amusing that a critic can both support these clichés of the male world and be so happy when they are violated.

This is how we might quibble with a different *kind* of critic but we would never get anywhere with Sarris if we tried to examine what he is saying sentence by sentence.

So let us ask, what is the meaning of the passage? Sarris has noticed that in *High Sierra* (not a very good movie) Raoul Walsh repeated an uninteresting and obvious device that he had earlier used in a worse movie. And for some inexplicable reason, Sarris concludes that he would not have had this joy of discovery without the *auteur* theory.

But in every art form, critics traditionally notice and point out the way the artists borrow from themselves (as well as from others) and how the same devices, techniques, and themes reappear in their work. This is obvious in listening to music, seeing plays, reading novels, watching actors; we take it for granted that this is how we perceive the development or the decline of an artist (and it may be necessary to point out to *auteur* critics that repetition without development is decline). When you see Hitchcock's *Saboteur* there is no doubt that he drew heavily and clumsily from *The 39 Steps*, and when you see *North by Northwest* you can see that he is once again toying with the ingredients of *The 39 Steps* — and apparently having a good time with them. Would Sarris not notice the repetition in the Walsh films without the *auteur* theory? Or shall we take the more cynical view that without some commitment to Walsh as an *auteur*, he probably wouldn't be spending his time looking at these movies?

If we may be permitted a literary analogy, we can visualize Sarris researching in the archives of the *Saturday Evening Post*, tracing the development of Clarence Budington Kelland, who, by the application of something like the *auteur* theory, would emerge as a much more important writer than Dostoyevsky; for in Kelland's case Sarris's three circles, the three premises of the *auteur* theory, have been consistently congruent. Kelland is technically competent (even "pleasantly unpretentious"), no writer has a more "distinguishable personality," and if "interior meaning" is what can be extrapolated from, say *Hatari!* or *Advise and Consent* or *What Ever Happened to Baby Jane?* then surely

Kelland's stories with their attempts to force a bit of character and humor into the familiar plot outlines are loaded with it. Poor misguided Dostoyevsky, too full of what he has to say to bother with "technical competence," tackling important themes in each work (surely the worst crime in the *auteur* book) and with his almost incredible unity of personality and material leaving you nothing to extrapolate from, he'll never make it. If the editors of *Movie* ranked authors the way they do directors, Dostoyevsky would probably be in that almost untouchable category of the "ambitious."

It should be pointed out that Sarris's defense of the *auteur* theory is based not only on aesthetics but on a rather odd pragmatic statement: "Thus to argue against the *auteur* theory in America is to assume that we have anyone of Bazin's sensibility and dedication to provide an alternative, and we simply don't." Which I take to mean that the *auteur* theory is necessary in the absence of a critic who wouldn't need it. This is a new approach to aesthetics, and I hope Sarris's humility does not camouflage his double-edged argument. If his aesthetics is based on expediency, then it may be expedient to point out that it takes extraordinary intelligence and discrimination and taste to *use* any theory in the arts, and that without those qualities, a theory becomes a rigid formula (which is indeed what is happening among *auteur* critics). The greatness of critics like Bazin in France and Agee in America may have something to do with their using their full range of intelligence and intuition, rather than relying on formulas. Criticism is an art, not a science, and a critic who follows rules will fail in one of his most important functions: perceiving what is original and important in *new* work and helping others to see.

The Outer Circle

. . . the first premise of the auteur *theory is the technical competence of a director as a criterion of value.*

This seems less the premise of a theory than a commonplace of judgment, as Sarris himself indicates when he paraphrases it as, "A great director has to be at least a good director." But this commonplace, though it *sounds* reasonable and basic, is a shaky premise: sometimes the greatest artists in a medium bypass or violate the simple technical competence that is so necessary for hacks. For example, it is doubtful if Antonioni could handle a routine directorial assignment of the type at which John Sturges is so proficient (*Escape from Fort Bravo* or *Bad Day at Black Rock*), but surely Antonioni's *L'Avventura* is the work of a great director. And the greatness of a director like Cocteau has nothing to do with mere technical competence: his greatness is in being able to achieve his own personal expression and style. And just as there were writers like Melville or Dreiser who triumphed over various kinds of technical incompetence, and who were, as artists, incomparably greater than the facile technicians of their day, a new great film director may appear whose very greatness is in his struggling toward grandeur or in massive accumulation of detail. An artist who is not a good technician can indeed create new standards, because standards of technical competence are based on comparisons with work already done.

Just as new work in other arts is often attacked because it violates the accepted standards and thus seems crude and ugly and incoherent, great new directors are very likely to be condemned precisely on the grounds that they're not even good directors, that they don't know their "business." Which, in some cases, is true, but does it matter when that "business" has little to do with what they want to express in films? It may even be a hindrance, leading them to banal slickness, instead of discovery of their own methods. For some, at least, Cocteau may be right: "The only technique worth having is the technique you invent for yourself." The director must be judged on the basis of what he produces — his films — and if he can make great films without knowing the standard methods, without the usual craftsmanship of the "good director," then that is the way he works. I would amend Sarris's premise to, "In works of a lesser rank, technical competence can help to redeem the weaknesses of the material." In fact it seems to be precisely this category that the *auteur* critics are most interested in — the routine material that a good craftsman can make into a fast and enjoyable movie. What, however, makes the *auteur* critics so incomprehensible, is not their *preference* for works of this category (in this they merely follow the lead of children who also prefer simple action films and westerns and horror films to works that make demands on their understanding) but their truly astonishing inability to exercise taste and judgment *within* their area of preference. Moviegoing kids are, I think, much more reliable guides to this kind of movie than the *auteur* critics: every kid I've talked to knows that Henry Hathaway's *North to Alaska* was a surprisingly funny, entertaining movie and *Hatari!* (classified as a "masterpiece" by half the *Cahiers* Conseil des Dix, Peter Bogdanovich, and others) was a terrible bore.

The Middle Circle

. . . the second premise of the auteur *theory is the distinguishable personality of the director as a criterion of value.*

Up to this point there has really been no theory, and now, when Sarris begins to work on his foundation, the entire edifice of civilized standards of taste collapses while he's tacking down his floorboards. Traditionally, in any art, the personalities of all those involved in a production have been a factor in judgment, but that the *distinguishability* of personality should in itself be a criterion of value completely confuses *normal* judgment. The smell of a skunk is more distinguishable than the perfume of a rose; does that make it better? Hitchcock's personality is certainly more distinguishable in *Dial M for Murder, Rear Window, Vertigo,* than Carol Reed's in *The Stars Look Down, Odd Man Out, The Fallen Idol, The Third Man, An Outcast of the Islands,* if for no other reason than because Hitchcock repeats while Reed tackles new subject matter. But how does this distinguishable personality function as a criterion for judging the works? We recognize the hands of Carné and Prévert in *Le Jour se Lève*, but that is not what makes it a beautiful film; we can just as easily recognize their hands in *Quai des Brumes* — which is not such a good film. We can recognize that *Le Plaisir* and *The Earrings of Madame de* . . . are both the work of Ophuls, but *Le Plaisir* is not a great film, and *Madame de* . . . is.

Often the works in which we are most aware of the personality of the director are his worst films — when he falls back on the devices he has already done to death. When a famous director makes a good movie, we look at the movie, we don't think about the director's personality; when he makes a stinker we notice his familiar touches because there's not much else to watch. When Preminger makes an expert, entertaining whodunit like *Laura*, we don't look for his personality (it has become part of the texture of the film); when he makes an atrocity like *Whirlpool*, there's plenty of time to look for his "personality" — if that's your idea of a good time.

It could even be argued, I think, that Hitchcock's uniformity, his mastery of tricks, and his cleverness at getting audiences to respond according to his calculations — the feedback he wants and gets from them — reveal not so much a personal style as a personal theory of audience psychology, that his methods and approach are not those of an artist but a prestidigitator. The *auteur* critics respond just as Hitchcock expects the gullible to respond. This is not so surprising — often the works *auteur* critics call masterpieces are ones that seem to reveal the contempt of the director for the audience.

It's hard to believe that Sarris seriously attempts to apply "the distinguishable personality of the director as a criterion of value" because when this premise becomes troublesome, he just tries to brazen his way out of difficulties. For example, now that John Huston's work has gone flat* Sarris casually dismisses him with:

* And, by the way, the turning point came, I think, not with *Moby Dick*, as Sarris indicates, but much earlier, with *Moulin Rouge*. This may not be so apparent to *auteur* critics concerned primarily with style and individual

"Huston is virtually a forgotten man with a few actors' classics behind him . . ." If *The Maltese Falcon*, perhaps the most high-style thriller ever made in America, a film Huston both wrote and directed, is not a director's film, what is? And if the distinguishable personality of the director is a criterion of value, then how can Sarris dismiss the Huston who comes through so unmistakably in *The Treasure of Sierra Madre*, *The African Queen*, or *Beat the Devil*, or even in a muddled Huston film like *Key Largo*? If these are actors' movies, then what on earth is a director's movie?

Isn't the *auteur* theory a hindrance to clear judgment of Huston's movies and of his career? Disregarding the theory, we see some fine film achievements and we perceive a remarkably distinctive directorial talent; we also see intervals of weak, half-hearted assignments like *Across the Pacific* and *In This Our Life*. Then, after *Moulin Rouge*, except for the blessing of *Beat the Devil*, we see a career that splutters out in ambitious failures like *Moby Dick* and confused projects like *The Roots of Heaven* and *The Misfits*, and strictly commercial projects like *Heaven Knows, Mr. Allison*. And this kind of career seems more characteristic of film history, especially in the United States, than the ripening development and final mastery envisaged by the *auteur* theory — a theory that makes it almost de rigeur to regard Hitchcock's American films as superior to his early English films. Is Huston's career so different, say, from Fritz Lang's? How is it that Huston's early good — almost great — work, must be rejected along with his mediocre recent work, but Fritz Lang, being sanctified as an *auteur*, has his bad recent work praised along with his good? Employing more usual norms, if you respect the Fritz Lang who made *M* and *You Only Live Once*, if you enjoy the excesses of style and the magnificent absurdities of a film like *Metropolis*, then it is only good sense to reject the

---

touches, because what was shocking about *Moulin Rouge* was that the content was sentimental mush. But critics who accept even the worst of Minnelli probably wouldn't have been bothered by the fact that *Moulin Rouge* was soft in the center, it had so many fancy touches at the edges.

ugly stupidity of *Journey to the Lost City*. It is an insult
to an artist to praise his bad work along with his good; it indicates that you are incapable of judging either.

A few years ago, a friend who reviewed Jean Renoir's University of California production of his play *Carola*, hailed it as "a
work of genius." When I asked my friend how he could so describe this very unfortunate play, he said, "Why, of course, it's a
work of genius. Renoir's a genius, so anything he does is a work
of genius." This could almost be a capsule version of the *auteur*
theory (just substitute *Hatari!* for *Carola*) and in this reductio
ad absurdum, viewing a work is superfluous, as the judgment is
a priori. It's like buying clothes by the label: this is Dior, so it's
good. (This is not so far from the way the *auteur* critics work,
either.)

Sarris doesn't even play his own game with any decent attention to the rules: it is as absurd to praise Lang's recent bad work
as to dismiss Huston's early good work; surely it would be more
consistent if he also tried to make a case for Huston's bad pictures? That would be more consistent than devising a category
called "actors' classics" to explain his good pictures away. If *The
Maltese Falcon* and *The Treasure of Sierra Madre* are actors'
classics, then what makes Hawks's *To Have and Have Not* and
The Big Sleep (which were obviously tailored to the personalities of Bogart and Bacall) the work of an *auteur*?

Sarris believes that what makes an *auteur* is "an élan of the
soul." (This critical language is barbarous. Where else should
élan come from? It's like saying "a digestion of the stomach."
A film critic need not be a theoretician, but it is necessary that
he know how to use words. This might, indeed, be a first premise for a theory.) Those who have this élan presumably have
it forever and their films reveal the "organic unity" of the directors' careers; and those who don't have it — well, they can
only make "actors' classics." It's ironic that a critic trying to
establish simple "objective" rules as a guide for critics who he
thinks aren't gifted enough to use taste and intelligence, ends

up — where, actually, he began — with a theory based on mystical insight. This might really make demands on the *auteur* critics if they did not simply take the easy way out by arbitrary decisions of who's got "it" and who hasn't. Their decisions are not merely not based on their theory; their decisions are *beyond* criticism. It's like a woman's telling us that she feels a certain dress *does* something for her: her feeling has about as much to do with critical judgment as the *auteur* critics' feeling that Minnelli *has* "it," but Huston never had "it."

Even if a girl had plenty of "it," she wasn't expected to keep it forever. But this "élan" is not supposed to be affected by the vicissitudes of fortune, the industrial conditions of moviemaking, the turmoil of a country, or the health of a director. Indeed, Sarris says, "If directors and other artists cannot be wrenched from their historical environments, aesthetics is reduced to a subordinate branch of ethnography." May I suggest that if, in order to judge movies, the *auteur* critics must wrench the directors from their historical environments (which is, to put it mildly, impossible) so that they can concentrate on the detection of that "élan," they are reducing aesthetics to a form of idiocy. Élan as the permanent attribute Sarris posits can only be explained in terms of a cult of personality. May I suggest that a more meaningful description of élan is what a man feels when he is working at the height of his powers — and what we respond to in works of art with the excited cry of "This time, he's really done it" or "This shows what he could do when he got the chance" or "He's found his style" or "I never realized he had it in him to do anything so good," a response to his joy in creativity.

Sarris experiences "joy" when he recognizes a pathetic little link between two Raoul Walsh pictures (he never does explain whether the discovery makes him think the pictures are any better) but he wants to see artists in a pristine state — their essences, perhaps? — separated from all the life that has formed them and to which they try to give expression.

The Inner Circle

The third and ultimate premise of the auteur *theory is concerned with interior meaning, the ultimate glory of the cinema as an art. Interior meaning is extrapolated from the tension between a director's personality and his material.*

This is a remarkable formulation: it is the opposite of what we have always taken for granted in the arts, that the artist expresses himself in the unity of form and content. What Sarris believes to be "the ultimate glory of the cinema as an art" is what has generally been considered the frustrations of a man working against the given material. Fantastic as this formulation is, it does something that the first two premises didn't do: it clarifies the interests of the *auteur* critics. If we have been puzzled because the *auteur* critics seemed so deeply involved, even dedicated, in becoming connoisseurs of trash, now we can see by this theoretical formulation that trash is indeed their chosen province of film.

Their ideal *auteur* is the man who signs a long-term contract, directs any script that's handed to him, and expresses himself by shoving bits of style up the crevasses of the plots. If his "style" is in conflict with the story line or subject matter, so much the better — more chance for tension. Now we can see why there has been so much use of the term "personality" in this aesthetics (the term which seems so inadequate when discussing the art of Griffith or Renoir or Murnau or Dreyer) — a routine, commercial movie can sure use a little "personality."

Now that we have reached the inner circle (the bull's eye turns out to be an empty socket) we can see why the shoddiest films are often praised the most. Subject matter is irrelevant (so long as it isn't treated sensitively — which is bad) and will quickly be disposed of by *auteur* critics who know that the smart director isn't responsible for that anyway; they'll get on to the important subject — his *mise-en-scène*. The director who fights to do something he cares about is a square. Now we can at least begin to understand why there was such contempt toward Huston for what was, in its way, a rather extraordinary effort — the *Moby Dick* that failed; why *Movie* considers Roger Corman a better director than Fred Zinnemann and ranks Joseph Losey next to God, why Bogdanovich, Mekas, and Sarris give their highest critical ratings to *What Ever Happened to Baby Jane?* (mighty big crevasses there). If Carol Reed had made only movies like *The Man Between* — in which he obviously worked to try to make something out of a ragbag of worn-out bits of material — he might be considered "brilliant" too. (But this is doubtful: although even the worst Reed is superior to Aldrich's *Baby Jane*, Reed would probably be detected, and rejected, as a man interested in substance rather than sensationalism.)

I am angry, but am I unjust? Here's Sarris:

A Cukor who works with all sorts of projects has a more developed abstract style than a Bergman who is free to develop his own scripts. Not that Bergman lacks personality, but his work has declined with the depletion of his ideas largely because his technique never equaled his sensibility. Joseph L. Mankiewicz and Billy Wilder are other examples of writer-directors without adequate technical mastery. By contrast, Douglas Sirk and Otto Preminger have moved up the scale because their miscellaneous projects reveal a stylistic consistency.

How neat it all is — Bergman's "work has declined with the depletion of his ideas largely because his technique never equaled his sensibility." But what on earth does that mean? How did Sarris perceive Bergman's sensibility except through his technique? Is Sarris saying what he seems to be saying, that if Bergman had developed more "technique," his work wouldn't be dependent on his ideas? I'm afraid this *is* what he means, and that when he refers to Cukor's "more developed abstract style" he means by "abstract" something unrelated to ideas, a technique not dependent on the content of the films. This is curiously reminiscent of a view common enough in the business world, that it's better not to get too involved, too personally interested in business problems, or they take over your life; and besides, you don't function as well when you've lost your objec-

tivity. But this is the *opposite* of how an artist works. His technique, his *style*, is determined by his range of involvements, and
his preference for certain themes. Cukor's style is no more
abstract(!) than Bergman's: Cukor has a range of subject matter
that he can handle and when he gets a good script within his
range (like *The Philadelphia Story* or *Pat and Mike*) he does a
good job; but he is at an immense *artistic* disadvantage, compared with Bergman, because he is dependent on the ideas of
so many (and often bad) scriptwriters and on material which
is often alien to his talents. It's amusing (and/or depressing)
to see the way *auteur* critics tend to downgrade writer-directors
— who are in the *best* position to use the film medium for personal expression.

Sarris does some pretty fast shuffling with Huston and Bergman; why doesn't he just come out and admit that writer-
directors are disqualified by his third premise? They can't arrive
at that "interior meaning, the ultimate glory of the cinema"
because a writer-director has no tension between his personality
and his material, so there's nothing for the *auteur* critic to extrapolate from.

What is all this nonsense about extrapolating "interior" meaning from the tension between a director's personality and his
material? A competent commercial director generally does the
best he can with what he's got to work with. Where is the
"tension"? And if you can locate some, what kind of meaning
could you draw out of it except that the director's having a bad
time with lousy material or material he doesn't like? Or maybe
he's trying to speed up the damned production so he can do
something else that he has some *hopes* for? Are these critics
honestly (and futilely) looking for "interior meanings" or is this
just some form of intellectual diddling that helps to sustain
their pride while they're viewing silly movies? Where is the tension in Howard Hawks's films? When he has good material, he's
capable of better than good direction, as he demonstrates in
films like *Twentieth Century, Bringing Up Baby, His Girl
Friday*; and in *To Have and Have Not* and *The Big Sleep* he

demonstrates that with help from the actors, he can jazz up ridiculous scripts. But what "interior meaning" can be extrapolated from an enjoyable, harmless, piece of kitsch like *Only Angels Have Wings;* what can the *auteur* critics see in it beyond the sex and glamor and fantasies of the high-school boys' universe — exactly what the mass audience liked it for? And when Hawks's material and/or cast is dull and when his heart isn't in the production — when by the *auteur* theory he should show his "personality," the result is something soggy like *The Big Sky.*

George Cukor's modest statement, "Give me a good script and I'll be a hundred times better as a director"* provides some notion of how a director may experience the problem of the given material. What can Cukor do with a script like *The Chapman Report* but try to kid it, to dress it up a bit, to show off the talents of Jane Fonda and Claire Bloom and Glynis Johns, and to give the total production a little flair and craftsmanship. At best, he can make an entertaining bad movie. A director with something like magical gifts *can* make a silk purse out of a sow's ear. But if he has it in him to do more in life than make silk purses, the triumph is minor — even if the purse is lined with gold. Only by the use of the *auteur* theory does this little victory become "ultimate glory." For some unexplained reason those traveling in *auteur* circles believe that making that purse out of a sow's ear is an infinitely greater accomplishment than making a solid carrying case out of a good piece of leather (as, for example, a Zinnemann does with *From Here to Eternity* or *The Nun's Story*).

I suppose we should be happy for Sirk and Preminger, ele-

* In another sense, it is perhaps immodest. I would say, give Cukor a clever script with light, witty dialogue, and he will know what to do with it. But I wouldn't expect more than glossy entertainment. (It seems almost too obvious to mention it, but can Sarris really discern the "distinguishable personality" of George Cukor and his "abstract" style in films like *Bhowani Junction, Les Girls, The Actress, A Life of Her Own, The Model and the Marriage Broker, Edward, My Son, A Woman's Face, Romeo and Juliet, A Double Life?* I wish I could put him to the test. I can only *suspect* that many *auteur* critics would have a hard time seeing those telltale traces of the beloved in their works.)

vated up the glory "scale," but I suspect that the "stylistic consistency" of, say, Preminger, could be a matter of his *limitations*, and that the only way you could tell he made some of his movies was that he used the same players so often (Linda Darnell, Jeanne Crain, Gene Tierney, Dana Andrews, et al., gave his movies the Preminger look). But the argument is ludicrous anyway, because if Preminger shows stylistic consistency with subject matter as varied as *Carmen Jones*, *Anatomy of a Murder*, and *Advise and Consent*, then by any rational standards he should be attacked rather than elevated. I don't think these films are stylistically consistent, nor do I think Preminger is a great director — for the very simple reason that his films are consistently superficial and facile. (*Advise and Consent*, an *auteur* "masterpiece" — Ian Cameron, Paul Mayersberg, and Mark Shivas of *Movie* and Jean Douchet of *Cahiers du Cinéma* rate it first on their ten best lists of 1962 and Sarris gives it his top rating — seems not so much Preminger-directed as other-directed. That is to say, it seems calculated to provide what as many different groups as possible want to see: there's something for the liberals, something for the conservatives, something for the homosexuals, something for the family.) An editorial in *Movie* states: "In order to enjoy Preminger's films the spectator must apply an unprejudiced intelligence; he is constantly required to examine the quality not only of the characters' decisions but also of his own reactions," and "He presupposes an intelligence active enough to allow the spectator to make connections, comparisons and judgments." May I suggest that this spectator would have better things to do than the editors of *Movie* who put out Preminger issues? They may have, of course, the joys of discovering links between *Centennial Summer*, *Forever Amber*, *That Lady in Ermine*, and *The Thirteenth Letter*, but I refuse to believe in these ever-so-intellectual protestations. The *auteur* critics aren't a very *convincing* group.

I assume that Sarris's theory is not based on his premises (the necessary causal relationships are absent), but rather that the premises were devised in a clumsy attempt to prop up the "theory." (It's a good thing he stopped at three: a few more circles and we'd really be in hell, which might turn out to be the last refinement of film tastes — Abbott and Costello comedies, perhaps?) These critics work embarrassingly hard trying to give some semblance of intellectual respectability to a preoccupation with mindless, repetitive commercial products — the kind of action movies that the restless, rootless men who wander on Forty-second Street and in the Tenderloin of all our big cities have always preferred just because they could respond to them without thought. These movies soak up your time. I would suggest that they don't serve a very different function for Sarris or Bogdanovich or the young men of *Movie* — even though they devise elaborate theories to justify soaking up their time. An educated man must have to work pretty hard to set his intellectual horizons at the level of *I Was a Male War Bride* (which, incidentally, wasn't even a good *commercial* movie).

"Interior meaning" seems to be what those in the know know. It's a mystique — and a mistake. The *auteur* critics never tell us by what divining rods they have discovered the élan of a Minnelli or a Nicholas Ray or a Leo McCarey. They're not critics; they're inside dopesters. There must be another circle that Sarris forgot to get to — the one where the secrets are kept.

Outside the Circles, or What Is a Film Critic?

I suspect that there's some primitive form of Platonism in the underbrush of Sarris's aesthetics.* He says, for example, that "Bazin's greatness as a critic . . . rested in his disinterested conception of the cinema as a universal entity." I don't know what a "universal entity" is, but I rather imagine Bazin's stature as a critic has less to do with "universals" than with intelligence, knowledge, experience, sensitivity, perceptions, fervor, imagina-

---

* This might help to explain such quaint statements as: Bazin "was, if anything, generous to a fault, seeking in every film some vestige of the cinematic art" — as if cinema were not simply the movies that have been made and are being made, but some preëxistent entity. If Bazin thought in these terms, does Sarris go along with him?

tion, dedication, lucidity — the traditional qualities associated with great critics. The role of the critic is to help people see what is in the work, what is in it that shouldn't be, what is not in it that could be. He is a good critic if he helps people understand more about the work than they could see for themselves; he is a great critic, if by his understanding and feeling for the work, by his passion, he can excite people so that they want to experience more of the art that is there, waiting to be seized. He is not necessarily a bad critic if he makes errors in judgment. (Infallible taste is inconceivable; what could it be measured against?) He is a bad critic if he does not awaken the curiosity, enlarge the interests and understanding of his audience. The art of the critic is to transmit his knowledge of and enthusiasm for art to others.

I do not understand what goes on in the mind of a critic who thinks a *theory* is what his confrères need because they are not "great" critics. Any honest man can perform the critical function to the limits of his tastes and powers. I daresay that Bogdanovich and V. F. Perkins and Rudi Franchi and Mark Shivas and all the rest of the new breed of specialists know more about movies than some people and could serve at least a modest critical function if they could remember that art is an expression of human experience. If they are men of feeling and intelligence, isn't it time for them to be a little ashamed of their "detailed criticism" of movies like *River of No Return?*

I believe that we respond most and best to work in any art form (and to other experience as well) if we are pluralistic, flexible, relative in our judgments, if we are eclectic. But this does not mean a scrambling and confusion of systems. Eclecticism is not the same as lack of scruple; eclecticism is the selection of the best standards and principles from various systems of ideas. It requires more care, more orderliness to be a pluralist than to apply a single theory. Sarris, who thinks he is applying a single theory, is too undisciplined to recognize the conflicting implications of his arguments. If he means to take a Platonic position, then is it not necessary for him to tell us what his ideals of movies are and how various examples of film live up to or fail to meet his ideals? And if there is an ideal to be achieved, an objective standard, then what does élan have to do with it? (The ideal could be achieved by plodding hard work or by inspiration or any other way; the method of achieving the ideal would be as irrelevant as the "personality" of the creator.) As Sarris uses them, vitalism and Platonism and pragmatism do not support his *auteur* theory; they undermine it.

Those, like Sarris, who ask for objective standards seem to want a theory of criticism which makes the critic unnecessary. And he *is* expendable if categories replace experience; a critic with a single theory is like a gardener who uses a lawn mower on everything that grows. Their desire for a theory that will solve all the riddles of creativity is in itself perhaps an indication of their narrowness and confusion; they're like those puzzled, lost people who inevitably approach one after a lecture and ask, "But what is your basis for judging a movie?" When one answers that new films are judged in terms of how they extend our experience and give us pleasure, and that our ways of judging how they do this are drawn not only from older films but from other works of art, and theories of art, that new films are generally related to what is going on in the other arts, that as wide a background as possible in literature, painting, music, philosophy, political thought, etc., helps, that it is the wealth and variety of what he has to bring to new works that makes the critic's reaction to them valuable, the questioners are always unsatisfied. They wanted a simple answer, a formula; if they approached a chef they would probably ask for the one magic recipe that could be followed in all cooking.

And it is very difficult to explain to such people that criticism is exciting just because there is no formula to apply, just because you must use everything you are and everything you know that is relevant, and that film criticism is particularly exciting just because of the multiplicity of elements in film art.

This range of experience, and dependence on experience, is pitifully absent from the work of the *auteur* critics; they seem to view movies, not merely in isolation from the other arts, but in isolation even from their own experience. Those who become film specialists early in life are often fixated on the period of film during which they first began going to movies, so it's not too surprising that the *Movie* group — just out of college and some still in — are so devoted to the films of the forties and fifties. But if they don't widen their interests to include earlier work, how can they evaluate films in anything like their historical continuity, how can they perceive what is distinctive in films of the forties? And if they don't have interests outside films, how can they evaluate what goes on in films? Film aesthetics as a distinct, specialized field is a bad joke: the *Movie* group is like an intellectual club for the intellectually handicapped. And when is Sarris going to discover that aesthetics is indeed a branch of ethnography; what does he think it is — a sphere of its own, separate from the study of man in his environment?

Some Speculations on the Appeal of the *Auteur* Theory

If relatively sound, reasonably reliable judgments were all that we wanted from film criticism, then *Sight and Sound* might be considered a great magazine. It isn't, it's something far less — a good, dull, informative, well-written, safe magazine, the best film magazine in English, but it doesn't satisfy desires for an excitement of the senses. Its critics don't often outrage us, neither do they open much up for us; its intellectual range is too narrow, its approach too professional. (If we recall an article or review, it's almost impossible to remember which Peter or which Derek wrote it.) Standards of quality are not enough, and *Sight and Sound* tends to dampen enthusiasm. *Movie*, by contrast, seems spirited: one feels that these writers do, at least, love movies, that they're not condescending. But they too, perhaps even more so, are indistinguishable read-alikes, united by fanaticism in a ludicrous cause; and for a group that discounts content and story, that believes the director is the *auteur* of what gives the film value, they show an inexplicable fondness — almost an obsession — for detailing plot and quoting dialogue. With all the zeal of youth serving an ideal, they carefully reduce movies to trivia.

It is not merely that the *auteur* theory distorts experience (all theory does that, and helps us to see more sharply for having done so) but that it is an aesthetics which is fundamentally anti-art. And this, I think, is the most serious charge that can possibly be brought against an aesthetics. The *auteur* theory, which probably helped to liberate the energies of the French critics, plays a very different role in England and with the *Film Culture* and New York *Film Bulletin auteur* critics in the United States — an anti-intellectual, anti-art role.

The French *auteur* critics, rejecting the socially conscious, problem pictures so dear to the older generation of American critics, became connoisseurs of values in American pictures that Americans took for granted, and if they were educated Americans, often held in contempt. The French adored the American gangsters, and the vitality, the strength, of our action pictures — all those films in which a couple of tough men slug it out for a girl, after going through hell together in oil fields, or building a railroad, or blazing a trail. In one sense, the French were perfectly right — these were often much more skillfully made and far more interesting visually than the movies with a message which Americans were so proud of, considered so *adult*. Vulgar melodrama with a fast pace can be much more exciting — and more honest, too — than feeble, pretentious attempts at drama — which usually meant just putting "ideas" into melodrama, anyway. Where the French went off was in finding elaborate intellectual and psychological meanings in these simple action films. (No doubt we make some comparable mistakes in interpreting French films.)

Like most swings of the critical pendulum, the theory was a *corrective*, and it helped to remind us of the energies and crude strength and good humor that Europeans enjoyed in our movies.

The French saw something in our movies that their own movies lacked; they admired it, and to some degree, they have taken it over and used it in their own way (triumphantly in *Breathless* and *Shoot the Piano Player*, not very successfully in their semi-American thrillers). Our movies were a product of American industry, and in a sense, it was America itself that they loved in our movies — our last frontiers, our robber-barons, our naiveté, our violence, our efficiency and speed and technology, our bizarre combination of sentimentality and inhuman mechanization.

But for us, the situation is different. It is good for us to be reminded that our mass culture is not altogether poisonous in its effect on other countries, but what is appealingly exotic — "American" — for them is often intolerable for us. The freeways of cities like Los Angeles may seem mad and marvelous to a foreign visitor; to us they are the nightmares we spend our days in. The industrial products of Hollywood that we grew up on are not enough to satisfy our interests as adults. We want a great deal more from our movies than we get from the gangster carnage and the John Ford westerns that Europeans adore. I enjoy some movies by George Cukor and Howard Hawks but I wouldn't be much interested in the medium if that were all that movies could be. We see many elements in foreign films that *our* movies lack. We also see that our films have lost the beauty and innocence and individuality of the silent period, and the sparkle and wit of the thirties. There was no special reason for the French critics, preoccupied with *their* needs, to become sensitive to *ours*. And it was not surprising that, in France, where film directors work in circumstances more comparable to those of a dramatist or a composer, critics would become fixated on American directors, not understanding how confused and inextricable are the roles of the front office, the producers, writers, editors, and all the rest of them — even the marketing research consultants who may pretest the drawing powers of the story and stars — in Hollywood. For the French, the name of a director *was* a guide on what American films to see; if a director was associated with a certain type of film that they liked, or if a director's work showed the speed and efficiency that they enjoyed. I assume that anyone interested in movies uses the director's name as some sort of guide, both positive and negative, even though we recognize that at times he is little more than a stage manager. For example, in the forties, my friends and I would keep an eye out for the Robert Siodmak films and avoid Irving Rapper films (except when they starred Bette Davis whom we wanted to see even in bad movies); I avoid Mervyn LeRoy films (though I went to see *Home Before Dark* for Jean Simmons's performance); I wish I could avoid Peter Glenville's pictures but he uses actors I want to see. It's obvious that a director like Don Siegel or Phil Karlson does a better job with what he's got to work with than Peter Glenville, but that doesn't mean there's any pressing need to go see every tawdry little gangster picture Siegel or Karlson directs; and perhaps if they tackled more difficult subjects they wouldn't do a better job than Glenville. There is no rule or theory involved in any of this, just simple discrimination; we judge the man from his films and learn to predict a little about his next films, we don't judge the films from the man.

But what has happened to the judgment of the English and New York critics who have taken over the *auteur* theory and used it to erect a film aesthetics based on those commercial movies that answered a need for the French, but which are not merely ludicrously inadequate to our needs, but are the results of a system of production that places a hammerlock on American directors? And how can they, with straight faces, probe for deep meanings in these products? Even the kids they're made for know enough not to take them seriously. How can these critics, sensible enough to deflate our overblown message movies, reject the total content of a work as unimportant and concentrate on signs of a director's "personality" and "interior meaning"? It's understandable that they're trying to find movie art in the loopholes of commercial production — it's a harmless hobby and we all play it now and then. What's incomprehensible is that they *prefer* their loopholes to unified film expression. If they weren't so determined to exalt products over works that attempt to express human experience, wouldn't they have figured out that the *mise-en-scène* which they seek out in these products, the director's personal style which comes through despite the material, is only a mere suggestion, a hint of what an artist can do when he's in control of the material, when the whole film becomes expressive? Isn't it obvious that *mise-en-scène* and subject material — form and content — can be judged separately only in bad movies or trivial ones? It must be black comedy for directors to read this new criticism and discover that films in which they felt trapped and disgusted are now said to be their masterpieces. It's an aesthetics for 1984: failure is success.

I am too far from the English scene to guess at motives, and far away also from New York, but perhaps close enough to guess that the Americans (consciously or unconsciously) are making a kind of social comment: like the pop artists, the New Realists with their comic strips and Campbell's soup can paintings, they are saying, "See what America is, this junk is the fact of our lives. Art and avant-gardism are phony; what isn't any good, is good. Only squares believe in art. The artifacts of industrial civilization are the supreme truth, the supreme joke." This is a period when men who consider themselves creative scoff at art and tradition. It is perhaps no accident that in the same issue of *Film Culture* with Sarris's *auteur* theory there is a lavishly illustrated spread on "The Perfect Filmic Appositeness of Maria Montez" — a fairly close movie equivalent for that outsized can of Campbell's soup. The editor, Jonas Mekas, has his kind of social comment. This is his approach to editing a film magazine: "As long as the 'lucidly minded' critics will stay out, with all their 'form,' 'content,' 'art,' 'structure,' 'clarity,' 'importance' — everything will be all right, just keep them out. For the new soul is still a bud, still going through its most dangerous, most sensitive stage." Doesn't exactly make one feel welcome, does it? I'm sure I don't know what the problem is: are there so many "lucidly minded" critics in this country (like Andrew

Sarris?) that they must be fought off? And aren't these little "buds" that have to be protected from critical judgments the same little film makers who are so convinced of their importance that they can scarcely conceive of a five-minute film which doesn't end with what they, no doubt, regard as the ultimate social comment: the mushroom cloud rising. Those "buds" often behave more like tough nuts.

Sarris with his love of commercial trash and Mekas who writes of the "cul-de-sac of Western culture" which is "stifling the spiritual life of man" seem to have irreconcilable points of view. Sarris with his joys in Raoul Walsh seems a long way from Mekas, the spokesman for the "independent film makers" (who couldn't worm their way into Sarris's outer circle). Mekas makes statements like "The new artist, by directing his ear inward, is beginning to catch bits of man's true vision." (Dear Lon Chaney Mekas, please get your ear out of your eye. Mekas has at least one thing in common with good directors: he likes to drama- tize.) But to love trash and to feel that you are stifled by it are perhaps very close positions. Does the man who paints the can of Campbell's soup love it or hate it? I think the answer is both: that he is obsessed by it as a fact of our lives and a symbol of America. When Mekas announces, "I don't want any part of the Big Art Game" he comes even closer to Sarris. And doesn't the *auteur* theory fit nicely into the pages of an "independent film makers" journal when you consider that the work of those film makers might compare very unfavorably with good films, but can look fairly interesting when compared with commercial products. It can even look original to those who don't know much film history. The "independent film makers," Lord knows, are already convinced about their importance as the creative figures — the *auteurs*; a theory which suggested the importance of writing to film art might seriously damage their egos. They go even farther than the *auteur* critics' notion that the script is merely something to transcend: they often act as if anyone who's concerned with scripts is a square who doesn't dig film. (It's obvious, of course, that this aesthetic based on images and

a contempt for words is a function of economics and technology, and that as soon as a cheap, lightweight 16mm camera
with good synchronous sound gets on the market, the independent film makers will develop a different aesthetic.)

The *auteur* theory, silly as it is, can nevertheless be a dangerous theory — not only because it constricts the experience of
the critics who employ it, but because it offers nothing but commercial goals to the young artists who may be trying to do something in film. *Movie* with its celebration of Samuel Fuller's
"brutality" and the Mackie Mekas who "knows that everything
he has learned from his society about life and death is false" give
readers more of a charge than they get from the limp pages of
Sight and Sound and this journal. This is not intended to be a
snide remark about *Sight and Sound* and *Film Quarterly*: if
they are not more sensational, it is because they are attempting
to be responsible, to hoard the treasures of our usable past. But
they will be wiped off the cinema landscape, if they can't meet
the blasts of anti-art with some fire of their own.

The union of Mekas and Sarris may be merely a marriage of
convenience; but if it is strong enough to withstand Sarris's
"Hello and Goodbye to the New American Cinema" (in the
Village Voice, September 20, 1962), perhaps the explanation
lies in the many shared attitudes of the Mekas group and the
auteur critics. Neither group, for example, is interested in a bal-
anced view of a film; Mekas says he doesn't believe in "negative
criticism" and the *auteur* critics (just like our grammar-school
teachers) conceive of a review as "an appreciation." The directors they reject are so far beyond the pale that their films are
not even considered worth discussion. (Sarris who distributes
zero ratings impartially to films as varied as *Yojimbo*, *The Manchurian Candidate*, and *Billy Budd* could hardly be expected to
take time off from his devotional exercises with Raoul Walsh
to explain why these films are worthless.) Sarris, too, can resort
to the language of the hipster — "What is it the old jazz man
says of his art? If you gotta ask what it is, it ain't? Well, the
cinema is like that." This is right at home in *Film Culture*, al-

though Sarris (to his everlasting credit) doesn't employ the accusatory, paranoid style of Mekas: "You criticize our work from a purist, formalistic and classicist point of view. But we say to you: What's the use of cinema if man's soul goes rotten?" The "you" is, I suppose, the same you who figures in so much (bad) contemporary prophetic, righteous poetry and prose, the "you" who is responsible for the Bomb and who, by some fantastically self-indulgent thought processes, is turned into the enemy, the *critic*. Mekas, the childlike, innocent, pure Mekas, is not about to be caught by "the tightening web of lies"; he refuses "to continue the Big Lie of Culture." I'm sure that, in this scheme, any attempt at clear thinking immediately places us in the enemy camp, turns us into the bomb-guilty "you," and I am forced to conclude that Mekas is not altogether wrong — that if we believe in the necessity (not to mention the beauty) of clear thinking, we are indeed his enemy. I don't know how it's possible for anyone to criticize his work from a "purist, formalistic and classicist point of view" — the method would be too far from the object; but can't we ask Mekas: is man's soul going to be in better shape because your work is protected from criticism? How much nonsense dare these men permit themselves? When Sarris tells us, "If the *auteur* critics of the Fifties had not scored so many coups of clairvoyance, the *auteur* theory would not be worth discussing in the Sixties," does he mean any more than that he has taken over the fiats of the *auteur* critics in the fifties and goes on applying them in the sixties? Does he seriously regard his own Minnelli-worship as some sort of objective verification of the critics who praised Minnelli in the fifties? If that's his concept of critical method, he might just as well join forces with other writers in *Film Culture*. In addition to Mekas ("Poets are surrounding America, flanking it from all sides,") there is, for example, Ron Rice: "And the beautiful part about it all is that you can, my dear critics, scream protest to the skies, you're too late. The Musicians, Painters, Writers, Poets and Film-Makers all fly in the same sky, and know Exactly where It's 'AT.' " Rice knows where he's at about as much as Stan Brakhage who says, "So the money vendors have begun it again. To the catacombs then . . ." In the pages of *Film Culture* they escape from the money changers in Jerusalem by going to the catacombs in Rome. "Forget ideology," Brakhage tells us, "for film unborn as it is has no language and speaks like an aborigine." We're all familiar with Brakhage's passion for obstetrics, but does being a primitive man mean being a foetus? I don't understand that unborn aborigine talk, but I'm prepared to believe that grunt by grunt, or squeal by squeal, it will be as meaningful as most of *Film Culture*. I am also prepared to believe that for Jonas Mekas, culture is a "Big Lie." And Sarris, looking for another culture under those seats coated with chewing gum, coming up now and then to announce a "discovery" like Joanne Dru, has he found his spiritual home down there?

Isn't the anti-art attitude of the *auteur* critics, both in England and here, implicit also in their peculiar emphasis on virility? (Walsh is, for Sarris, "one of the screen's most virile directors." In *Movie* we discover: "When one talks about the heroes of *Red River*, or *Rio Bravo*, or *Hatari!* one is talking about Hawks himself. . . . Finally everything that can be said in presenting Hawks boils down to one simple statement: here is a man.") I don't think critics would use terms like "virile" or "masculine" to describe artists like Dreyer or Renoir; there is something too *limited* about describing them this way (just as when we describe a woman as sensitive and feminine, we are indicating her *special* nature). We might describe Kipling as a virile writer but who would think of calling Shakespeare a virile writer? But for the *auteur* critics calling a director virile is the highest praise because, I suggest, it is some kind of assurance that he is not trying to express himself in an art form, but treats moviemaking as a professional job. (*Movie*: Hawks "makes the very best adventure films because he is at one with his heroes. . . . Only Raoul Walsh is as deeply an adventurer as Hawks. . . . Hawks' heroes are all professionals doing jobs — scientists, sheriffs, cattlemen, big game hunters: real professionals who know their capabilities.

. . . They know exactly what they can do with the available resources, expecting of others only what they know can be given.") The *auteur* critics are so enthralled with their narcissistic male fantasies (*Movie:* "Because Hawks' films and their heroes are so genuinely mature, they don't need to announce the fact for all to hear") that they seem unable to relinquish their schoolboy notions of human experience. (If there are any female practitioners of *auteur* criticism, I have not yet discovered them.) Can we conclude that, in England and the United States, the *auteur* theory is an attempt by adult males to justify staying inside the small range of experience of their boyhood and adolescence — that period when masculinity looked so great and important but art was something talked about by poseurs and phonies and sensitive-feminine types? And is it perhaps also their way of making a comment on our civilization by the suggestion that trash is the true film art? I ask; I do not know.

[1963]

Morality Plays Right and Left

Advertising: *Night People*

Ads for men's suits show the model standing against a suspended mobile. But the man who buys knows that the mobile doesn't come with the suit: it's there to make him feel that the old business suit is different now. The anti-Sovietism of *Night People* serves a similar function. But the filmgoer who saw the anti-Nazi films of ten years ago will have no trouble recognizing the characters in *Night People*, just as ten years ago he could have detected (under the Nazi black shirts) psychopathic killers, trigger-happy cattle rustlers, and the screen villain of earliest vintage — the man who will foreclose the mortgage if he doesn't get the girl. The Soviet creatures of the night are direct descendants of the early film archetype, the bad man. Those who make films like *Night People* may or may not be privately concerned with the film's political message (the suit manufacturer may or may not be concerned with the future of wire sculpture); in the film politics is period décor — used to give melodrama the up-to-date look that will sell.

Night People is set in Berlin: a U.S. soldier is kidnaped; he is rescued by a U.S. Intelligence Officer (Gregory Peck) who knows how to deal with the Russians. They are "head-hunting cannibals" and must be treated as such. The film is given a superficial credibility by documentary-style shots of American soldiers, by glimpses of Berlin, and by the audience's knowledge that Americans in Europe have in fact been kidnaped. One might even conceive that someone who understood the nature of Communism might view certain Communists as "cannibals." But it would be a mistake to confuse the political attitudes presented in *Night People* with anything derived from historical understanding. Nunnally Johnson, who wrote, directed, and produced the film, has referred to it as "Dick Tracy in Berlin." His earlier anti-Nazi production *The Moon is Down* could be described as "Dick Tracy in Norway," and many of his films could be adequately designated as just plain "Dick Tracy."

Actual kidnapings have posed intricate political and moral problems. Should the victim be ransomed by economic concessions, should a nation submit to extortion? Were some of the victims observers for the U.S. and where does observation stop and espionage begin? We know that our government must have espionage agents in Europe — can we believe in the innocence of every victim? If they were guilty of some charges but not guilty of all the charges, what kind of protest is morally possible? The drama in the case of a Robert Vogeler or a William Oatis is in the fathoming of moral and political ambiguities. While purportedly about an East-West kidnaping, *Night People* presents a crime and a rescue. The hero has righted the wrong before we have even had a chance to explore our recollections of what may be involved in political kidnapings. Soviet ambitions and intrigue become a simple convenience to the film maker: the label "Communism" is the guarantee that the hero is up against a solid evil threat. For the sake of the melodrama, the Communism cannot be more than a label.

Night People is not much worse or much better than a lot of other movies — they're made cynically enough and they may, for all we know, be accepted cynically. David Riesman has pointed out that nobody believes advertising, neither those who write it nor those who absorb it. And the same can be said for most of our movies. Somebody turns the stuff out to make a living; it would seem naive to hold him responsible for it. In a state of suspended belief a writer can put the conflict of East and West into the capable hands of Dick Tracy: the film wasn't really written, it was *turned out*. And the audiences that buy standardized commodities may be too sophisticated about mass production to believe films and advertising, but they are willing to absorb products and claims — with suspended belief. Audiences don't believe, but they don't *not* believe either. And when you accept something without believing it, you accept it on *faith*. You buy the product by name. Who would *believe* in *Rose-Marie?* Yet the audience, after taking it in, emerges singing the Indian Love Call and it becomes a substantial part of American sentimental tone. Who would believe that *Night People* presents a political analysis? Yet the political attitudes that don't originate in political analysis become part of national political tone. Acceptance is not *belief*, but acceptance may imply the willingness to let it go at that and to prefer the accessible politics (to which one can feel as cynical and "knowing" as toward an ad) to political thought that requires effort, attention, and involvement.

The bit players who once had steady employment as S.S. guards are right at home in their new Soviet milieu; the familiar psychopathic faces provide a kind of reassurance that the new world situation is not so different from the old one (we beat these bullies once already). Perhaps *Night People* can even seem realistic because it *is* so familiar. The make-believe that is acted out often enough attains a special status: it becomes a real part of our experience. (Films like *Quo Vadis, The Prisoner of Zenda, Showboat, The Merry Widow* have been made so many times that to the mass audience they have the status of classics; are they not immortal if three generations have seen them?) Advertising, using the same appeals — the familiar with the "new" look — also depends upon repetition to make its point. If we *believed* an advertising claim, hearing it once would be enough. It is because we do not believe that advertising uses repetition and variation into infinity to get its claims accepted.

The suggestion that politics as used in melodrama is advertising décor is not intended metaphorically. I wish to suggest that films (and other forms of commercial entertainment) are becoming inseparable from advertising, and that advertising sets the stage for our national morality play.

Advertising has been borrowing from literature, art, and the theater; films meanwhile are taking over not merely the look of advertising art — clear, blatant poster design — but the very content of advertising. Put together an advertising photograph and a movie still from *How to Marry a Millionaire* (another Nunnally Johnson production) and they merge into each other: they belong to the same genre. The new young Hollywood heroine is not too readily distinguishable from the model in the Van Raalte ad; if the ad is a few years old, chances are this *is* the same girl. In a few months she will be on the front of movie magazines and on the back of news magazines endorsing her favorite cigarette. She is both a commodity for sale and a salesman for other commodities (and her value as one depends upon her value as the other). In any traditional sense, Gregory Peck is not an actor at all; he is a model, and the model has become the American ideal. Advertising dramatizes a way of life with certain consumption patterns, social attitudes and goals, the same way of life dramatized in films; films are becoming advertising in motion.

Is *Executive Suite** in substance any different from an institutional ad — "This Company Believes in the Future of America"? Break it down into shots — the hero's home, the manufacturing process scene, the mother playing catch with her son, and you are looking at pages in *Sunset, Life,* and *Today's Woman.* Then open *Time,* and there are the actors from the film speaking into dictaphones to illustrate the message: "Cameron Hawley, author of *Executive Suite,* says 'I use my Dictaphone TIME-MASTER constantly and with great success.'" If we are no longer sure what medium we are in, the reason is that there are no longer any organic differences.

The common aim of attracting and pleasing the public has synthesized their methods and their content. The film and the ad tell their story so that the customer can take it all in at a glance. They show him to himself as he wants to be, and if flattery is not enough, science and progress may clinch the sale. The new toothpaste has an activating agent; new shirts and shorts have polyester fibers running through them; *Night People* is filmed in CinemaScope with Stereophonic Sound. Can we balk at technical advances that "2000 years of experiment and research have brought to us"? New "technical advances" increase not only the physical accessibility of cultural goods, the content of the goods becomes increasingly accessible. The film's material has been assembled, the plot adapted; sound engineers have amplified the hero's voice, and the heroine's figure has been surgically reconstructed (actresses who scorn falsies can now have plastic breasts built-in). The new wide screen surrounds us and sounds converge upon us. Just one thing is lost: the essence

---

* In contrast with the situation in the film, some of the actual problems of furniture manufacturers might provide material for farce: how to make furniture that will collapse after a carefully calculated interval (refrigerator manufacturers are studying the problem of "replacement" — i.e., designing refrigerators that will necessitate replacement in ten years rather than fifteen or twenty years) or that will be outmoded by a new style (automobile manufacturers are wrestling with consumers' lag — people just don't yet understand that the 1950 car is to be discarded with the 1950 hat). The designer-hero of *Executive Suite* can be a real menace to American business: good designs last too long.

of film "magic" which lay in our imaginative absorption, our entering into the film (as we might enter into the world of a Dostoyevsky novel or *Middlemarch*). Now the film can come to us — one more consummation of the efforts to diminish the labor (and the joy) of imaginative participation.

All this has been done for us; all that's left for us is to buy. Suppose an audience does buy a film — what do they do with it? The audience is not exactly passive, it has its likes and its dislikes and it expresses them — in terms drawn more from advertising, however, than from art. The audience talks freely about the actor's personality, the actress's appeal, the likableness of their actions. Film critics become experts in "craftsmanship" and mechanics; Dreyer's *Day of Wrath* is considered impossibly slow and dim, while *Night People* is found to be "racy," "well-made," and "fast-paced" — praise more suitable to the art of a Studebaker than to the art of the film. A patron who wanted to mull a Hollywood film over for a while would be judged archaic — and rightly so. There is nothing to mull over: a trained crew did all that in advance.

Melodrama, perhaps the most highly developed type of American film, is the chief vehicle for political thought in our films (*Casablanca, Edge of Darkness, To Have and Have Not, North Star*). Melodrama, like the morality play, is a popular form; structurally melodrama is the morality play with the sermons omitted and the pattern of oppositions issuing in sensational action. Its intention is primarily to entertain (by excitation) rather than to instruct (entertainingly). Labels stand for the sermons that are dispensed with, and the action is central.

In some of the war and postwar films the writers and directors seemed to feel they were triumphing over Hollywood and over melodrama itself by putting the form to worthwhile social ends: they put sermons back in. The democratic messages delayed and impeded the action, of course, but they helped to save the faces of those engaged in the work. (Perhaps without the pseudo-justification provided by speeches about democracy, the artists would have been shattered by the recognition that films like *Cornered* aroused and appealed to an appetite for violence.) While the hypocrisy of the method made the films insulting and the democratic moralizing became offensive dogma, the effort did indicate the moral and political disturbances, and the sense of responsibility, of the film makers. *Night People* reduces the political thought to what it was anyway — labeling — and nothing impedes the action. The film is almost "pure" melodrama. The author doesn't try to convince himself or the public that he's performing an educational service or that the film should be taken seriously. The cynicism is easier to take than hypocrisy, but it also shows just how far we are going.

Heroism is the substance of melodrama, as of standard westerns and adventure films, but there is little effort in Hollywood to make it convincing or even to relate it to the hero's character (in *Night People* a few additional labels — the hero went to a Catholic college, he was a professional football player — suffice). We have come a long way since the days when Douglas Fairbanks, Sr., winked at the audience as he performed his feats; now the audience winks at the screen.*

The political facts of life may shatter the stereotypes of Hollywood melodrama but economic facts support them. The formula hero-defeats-villain has been tested at the box office since the beginning of film history and it may last until the end. Melodrama is simple and rigid and yet flexible enough to accommodate itself to historical changes. The hero is always the defender of the right and he is *our* representative. He rarely changes labels; on the few occasions when he is not an American he demonstrates that those on our side are just like us. (Gregory Peck's first screen role was in *Days of Glory*: as a heroic Soviet soldier he fought the evil Nazis.)

* The *New Yorker* carries sophisticated consumption to extremes: it is "knowing" about everything. The reader is supposed to "see through" what he buys — whether it's a production of *Macbeth*, a lace peignoir, a biography of Freud, or a $10 haircut (executed by Vergnes himself). One must admit that the consumer who doesn't take anything too seriously is aesthetically preferable to the unsportsmanlike consumer who takes buying so seriously that he pores over *Consumer Reports*.

The villains are marked by one constant: they are subhuman. If the hero of *Night People* did not know that the enemy are cannibals, he might feel some qualms about the free dispensation of strychnine (he must feel as sure as Hitler that those opposing him are beyond reconciliation). Film melodrama, like political ideology with which it has much in common, has a convenient way of disposing of the humanity of enemies: *we* stand for humanity; *they* stand for something else. The robbers who are shot, the Nazis who are knifed — they are cowards or fanatics and they don't deserve to live. Fear, on the one hand, and, on the other, devotion to a "misguided" cause to the disregard of personal safety are evidence of subhumanity. The villains are usually more expressive than the heroes because their inhumanity is demonstrated precisely by the display of extreme human emotions. (Gregory Peck, who is always a hero, is rarely called upon to register any emotion whatever. The devil can be expressive, but the hero is a stick of wood.) The villains are not human; if they were, they'd be on our side. When historical circumstances change and our former enemies become allies, we let bygones be bygones and they are restored to human estate. Thus the little yellow bastards are now cultured Japanese; the blood-guilty Germans are now hardworking people, so akin to Americans in their moral standards and ability to organize an efficient economy; now it is the Russians, the courageous pioneers and fighting men of the war years, who are treacherous and subhuman. (In *Night People* the enemy are variously described as "the creeps over there," "burglars," "a methodical bunch of lice.") Political melodrama looks ahead.

This is the level of the anti-Communism of *Night People*. And it is at this level that the advertising-entertainment medium has political effect. In a culture which has been movie-centered for thirty years, films are a reflection of popular American thought as well as an influence upon it. At the Army-McCarthy hearings, the participants, conscious of the radio and television audience, find it necessary to proclaim, each in his turn, that he *hates* Communists. McCarthy imputes weakness and political unreliability to the Secretary of the Army by suggesting that Stevens merely *dislikes* Communists. In other words, if he knew what they were, he would *hate* them: he lacks the hero's sureness. McCarthy draws political support by the crude, yet surprisingly controlled, intensity of his hatred of Communists; the intensity suggests that he, like Intelligence Officer Peck, knows how to take care of rats, and his lack of scruples becomes a political asset. Further knowledge is irrelevant; the hero does not need to look too closely into the heart of evil.

Knowledge may even be dangerous. The hero should know that Communists are rats without needing to examine the nature of Communism. Is our thinking so primitive that we fear that a close look will not only expose us to destruction but will turn us into rats, that Communism is contagious? Is that why there is so much fear that people may read Communist literature, and why those who have had no contact with Communism are deemed the only safe anti-Communists? The man of conscience who examines the enemy sees human beings — the primitive explanation is that he got too close and was infected. If you know enough to hate Communists, you know enough; if you know more, perhaps you can no longer hate. The ritualistic nature of this popular anti-Communism was made apparent in the public reaction to Acheson's remark that he wouldn't turn his back on Alger Hiss. Acheson spoke as one human being talking about another; he was attacked for his failure to recognize that Soviet agents are not supposed to be regarded as human beings.

The morality play had meaning as an instructive dramatization, an externalization of the conflict within man. Our popular culture and popular politics and even our popular religion take this conflict and project it onto the outside world. The resulting simplification has immediate advantages: we are exonerated, they are guilty. In contrast with drama which sensitizes man to human complexity, melodrama desensitizes men. No wonder the public has no patience with real political issues, nor with the moral complexities of Shakespeare or Greek tragedy. The movies know how to do it better: in a film, Stevens or McCarthy would prove his case; in a film, Oppenheimer would be innocent or guilty. A reporter who made a telephone survey asking, "Are you listening to the Army-McCarthy hearings?" got the housewife's response: "No, that's not my idea of entertainment." It is the stereotyped heroes and villains of her brand of entertainment who react upon our public figures — so that if Stevens admitted that he had functioned in the real world of conciliation and compromise, he would be publicly dishonored (yet he cannot prove his basic honesty without making that admission).

Senator McCarthy has not the look of a man in the grip of a fixed idea; rather he has the look of a man who has the fixed idea well in hand. When national issues can be discussed in terms of "ferreting out rats" (and even McCarthy's political opponents accept the term) the man with the fixed idea is the man who appears to stand for something. He has found the role to play. When Senator McCarthy identifies himself with *right* and identifies anyone who opposes him with the Communist conspiracy, he carries the political morality play to its paranoid conclusion — a reductio ad absurdum in which right and wrong, and political good and evil, dissolve into: are you for me or against me? But the question may be asked, are not this morality and this politics fundamentally just as absurd and just as dangerous when practiced on a national scale in our commercial culture? The world is *not* divided into good and evil, enemies are *not* all alike, Communists are *not* just Nazis with a different accent; and it is precisely the task of political analysis (and the incidental function of literature and drama) to help us understand the nature of our enemies and the nature of our opposition to them. A country which accepts wars as contests between good and evil is suffering from the delusion that the morality play symbolizes real political conflicts.

Some political theorists would like to manipulate this delusion: they hold that the only way to combat Communism is to employ the "useful myth" that the current world struggle is a battle between Christianity and atheism, that the free world represents God on earth and the Communist countries, the anti-Christ. Such a "useful myth" may very likely, however, be purchased (for the most part) just as cynically as it is sold. Is a myth a myth for the public that accepts it without conviction? Or does "Fight for God" become more like the advertising slogan "Always Buy Chesterfields" — a slogan which does not prevent the Chesterfield smoker from having nagging fears of lung cancer and heart disease? The modern man who fights in a mythical holy crusade knows he's compelled to fight — whether it's for God or not.

Cecil B. DeMille, who might lay claim to having falsified history as much as any man alive, is now at work on *The Ten Commandments* (in Vista Vision). He states: "It's amazing how much our story parallels the world situation today" — the parallel may be a bit elusive, but no doubt DeMille will make his point. Other film makers, suddenly confronted with Cinema-Scope, have been raiding his domain; they appear to be so dazzled by the width of the screen they feel it can only be filled by God. Their primitive awe is similar to that of the public which is attracted to "big" pictures. Though it is easy to scoff at the advertising which emphasizes the *size* of a picture — the cast of thousands, the number of millions spent — magnitude in itself represents an achievement to the public. The whole family goes to *The Robe* or *The Greatest Show on Earth* — it's an event like *Gone with the Wind* or *Duel in the Sun*, as big as a natural catastrophe. Primitivism takes many forms. We no longer hear' arguments on all sides about what causes wars: global atomic warfare is so big it seems to be something only God can explain. (*Night People* is not a small picture: the closing shot leaves the hero confronting the heavens.)

The danger in manipulation and cynicism is not that those who extol the greatness of the democratic idea and the greatness of the common man while treating the public as common fools are Machiavellians scheming to impose an ideology upon the public. The democratic ideology has been imposed on *them*:

they are driven by economic necessity (and political necessity) to give the public what it wants. The real danger is that we may lose the capacity for those extensions in height, in depth, in space which are the experience of art and thought. If the public becomes accustomed to being pleased and pandered to, the content is drained out of democratic political life. (The pimp who peddles good clean stuff is nevertheless engaged in prostitution.)

After dozens of anti-Nazi films and countless slick stories and articles, the public had had enough of Hitler. What they wearied of had only the slenderest connection with the subject of Nazism; they got tired of the old formula with the Nazi label. But they didn't reject the formula, they settled for a change of labels. In the same way Hollywood may well exhaust anti-Communism before it has gotten near it. *Night People* is just the beginning of a new cycle — a cycle which begins by exploiting public curiosity and ends by satiating it.

All our advertising is propaganda, of course, but it has become so much a part of our life, is so pervasive, that we just don't know what it is propaganda *for*. Somehow it keeps the wheels rolling and that seems to be what it's for. Why don't other peoples see that we are the heroes and the Russians cannibals? One reason is that America's public relations romance with itself is a spectacle to the rest of the world. In Hollywood productions, the American soldiers and civilians abroad are soft touches, chivalrous under the wisecracks, patronizing and generous towards unfortunate little people the world over; aroused by injustice, the American is Robin Hood freed by birth from the threat of the Sheriff of Nottingham. Though this propaganda fails us abroad (too many Americans having been there) it functions at home as an entertaining form of self-congratulation and self-glorification: it makes the audience feel good. While we consume our own propaganda, other people are not so gullible about us. They have a different way of being gullible: they are influenced by Communist propaganda about us.

Propaganda — *Salt of the Earth*

One wonders if the hero of *Night People,* so sharp at detecting the cannibal under the Communist tunic, would recognize the Communist *position* when he saw it. *Salt of the Earth* is as clear a piece of Communist propaganda as we have had in many years, but the critic of the New York *Times* saw, ". . . in substance, simply a strong pro-labour film with a particularly sympathetic interest in the Mexican-Americans with whom it deals," and the critic of the Los Angeles *Daily News* had this to say: "If there is propaganda in this picture it is not an alien one, but an assertion of principles no thoughtful American can reject." There are Americans, then, who have not learned that Communist propaganda concentrates on local grievances. They fail to recognize that Communism makes use of principles that no thoughtful American (or Frenchman or Englishman) can reject. Communism in each region appears to be divested of its Soviet accoutrements; its aspect is not alien in Central America, South America, Europe, Asia, or Africa. It is effective because it organizes, or captures the direction of, groups struggling for status.

Despite the reactions of some critics, it is not likely that the American film audience would react favorably to the publicity campaign, "At last! An honest movie about American working people." If American working people seek an image of their attitudes and beliefs they will find it in Hollywood films — they have helped to put it there. Though a Hollywood version glamorizes their lives, it does justice to their dreams. If they did go to see *Salt* it is not likely that more than a small proportion would see anything that struck home, and that perhaps would be only as a reminder of depression days.

At special showings or at art film houses, it's a different story. *Salt* can seem true and real for those liberals and progressives whose political thinking has never gone beyond the thirties. Depression social consciousness is their exposed nerve: touch it and it becomes the only reality, more vivid than the actual conditions they live in. Many Americans felt the first stirrings of political awareness in the thirties, and nothing that has happened since has affected them comparably. They look back to the social theater and WPA art as to a Golden Age. The prosperity that followed is viewed almost as a trick, a device to conceal the truth and to prevent the oppressed workers from joining together to defeat ruthless big business. Prosperity is integrated with so much advertising and cynicism that it seems a sham — it doesn't look *real*. In search of something to believe in, they see the hollowness of the films played out in modern apartments and neat little cottages and tend to situate truth in the worst possible setting — in what has been left out of Hollywood films. What looks ugly and depressing must be true, since what looks prosperous is as empty as an ad. (The film that uses a Santa Barbara mansion for the home of its heroine doesn't advertise its documentary background, but a film using a shack, even if it is a facade, stresses truth and realism.) The depths to which they may fall have a greater emotional claim on them than the prosperity they (fearfully) enjoy. The worst makes the greatest claim to truth.

Salt of the Earth is not likely to be effective propaganda for overthrowing the capitalist bosses at home, a task which the Communists are not likely to envision in the United States anyway. But it is extremely shrewd propaganda for the urgent business of the U.S.S.R.: making colonial peoples believe that they can expect no good from the United States; convincing Europe and Asia and the rest of the world that there are no civil liberties in the U.S.A. and that our capitalism is really fascism. The American Communists are not so much interested these days in glorifying the Soviet Union as in destroying European and Asiatic faith in the United States. Fifteen years ago it would have been easy to toss off a film like *Salt* with "it's worse than propaganda, it's a dull movie." Flippancy makes us rather uneasy today: Communist propaganda, seizing upon our failures and our imperfections, and, when these are not strong enough, inventing others, has very nearly succeeded in discrediting us to the whole world. The discreditable aspects of American life are realities to be dealt with. Communist propaganda, however, treats them as opportunities.

The raw material of *Salt of the Earth* is a 1951–1952 strike of Mexican-American zinc miners in New Mexico. The film, made in 1953, was sponsored by the International Union of Mine, Mill and Smelter Workers (expelled from the CIO in 1950 as Communist-dominated), and financed by Independent Productions Corporation (the money was "borrowed from liberal Americans"). The writer, director, and producer are blacklisted in Hollywood as fellow travelers.

What brought these people together to make a film — zinc miners, liberal Americans, blacklisted film makers? This was no mere commercial enterprise, and in our brief history as a nation of film addicts, there has never been anything like a group of several hundred people working together in devotion to film art. If art was their aim, how misguided their effort — for what work of art, in any field, has ever resulted from "group discussion and collective constructive criticism" ("no less than 400 people had read, or heard a reading of, the screenplay by the time we commenced production"). Collective constructive criticism — where have we heard that term before? It is not irony but justice that the artists who chose this method came out with a film as dreary and programmatic as the films made by those who have collective criticism forced upon them.

Here is the opening of the film and our introduction to the heroine, Esperanza: "A woman at work chopping wood. Though her back is to the camera, we sense her weariness in toil by the set of her shoulders . . . we begin to gather that she is large with child. The woman carries the load of wood to an outdoor fire, staggering under its weight. . . ." It doesn't take us long to find out that this is eternal downtrodden woman, but if we're slow, her first words set us straight: "How shall I begin my story that has no beginning? How shall I start the telling of all that is yet becoming?"

The miners of *Salt of the Earth* are striking for equality (principally equality of safety conditions) with the "Anglos," but the strike is not a bargaining weapon for definite limited objectives. It is inflated with lessons, suggestions and implications until it acquires symbolic status. This is the dialogue as the hero Ramon watches Esperanza, his wife, nursing the baby:

Ramon: A fighter, huh?

Esperanza: He was born fighting. And born hungry.

Ramon: Drink, drink, Juanito. You'll never have it so good.

Esperanza: He'll have it good. Some day.

Ramon (half-whispering): Not just Juanito. You'll have it good too, Esperanza. We're going to win this strike.

Esperanza: What makes you so sure?

Ramon (brooding): Because if we lose, we lose more than a strike. We lose the union. And the men know this. And if we win, we win more than a few demands. We win . . . (groping for words) something bigger. Hope. Hope for our kids. Juanito can't grow strong on milk alone.

This is a strike in which the workers *grow.* "Have you learned nothing from this strike?" Esperanza asks her husband, and speaks of her own development: "I want to rise. And push everything up with me as I go. . . ." "Strike" in *Salt of the Earth* is used in its revolutionary meaning, as a training ground in solidarity, a preparation for the big strike to come — a microcosm of the coming revolution.

If the author had cut up a pamphlet and passed out the parts, he wouldn't have given out anything very different from this:

Esperanza: They tried to turn people against us. They printed lies about us in their newspapers. . . . They said . . . that all the Mexicans ought to be sent back where they came from. But the men said . . .

Antonio (slapping newspaper): How can I go back where I came from. The shack I was born in is buried under company property.

Kalinsky: Why don't nobody ever tell the bosses to go back where they came from?

'Cente: Wouldn't be no bosses in the state of New Mexico if they did.

Alfredo (dreamily): Brother! Live to see the day!

Antonio: Talk about wide open spaces! Far as the eye can see —no Anglos.

Ramon holds up a finger, correcting him.

Ramon: No Anglo *bosses*.

This pedagogical tone, so reminiscent of the thirties, is maintained throughout much of the film. Social realism has never been able to pass up an opportunity for instruction: these strikers are always teaching each other little constructive lessons. Here is Ramon reprimanding Frank, the "Anglo" union organizer, for his failure to recognize a picture of Juarez:

Ramon: . . . If I didn't know a picture of George Washington, you'd say I was an awful dumb Mexican.

Frank (deeply chagrined): I'm an awful dumb Anglo . . . I've got a lot to learn.

Then, of course, there are the big lessons: when Esperanza is in labor and the Sheriff is asked to get the doctor he responds with, "You kiddin'? Company doctor won't come to no picket line." A miner's widow then speaks to the men picketing: "They, up there, your bosses — they don't care whether your children live or die. Let them be born like animals! (A pause.) Remember this while you're marching, you men. Remember well." (She spits in the road.)

Another facet of social realism is the inflation of dialogue to the rank of folk wisdom (*Ramon:* " 'No money down. Easy term payments.' I tell you something: this instalment plan, it's the curse of the working class.") and folk wit (*Esperanza:* "Finding scabs in Zinc town, Ramon said, was like looking for a rich man in heaven . . ."). These "oppressed" are not confused by book-learning and bosses' lies. They are the custodians of the real social truth.

The story is not just slanted: the slant *is* the story. Even the baby's christening party — in the nighttime — is interrupted by deputy sheriffs with a repossession order for the radio. When the company gets an eviction order, we see the deputies "dumping the precious accumulations of a lifetime on to the road: the shrine, a kewpie doll, a faded photograph." And, of course, the photograph of Juarez is "smashed in the dust." If you have half an eye for this sort of thing, you'll know when you first see Esperanza's shiny radio that it will be taken away from her, just as you'll know when you see the photograph of Juarez that it wouldn't be framed except to be smashed.

Detail upon detail adds up to a picture of fascism. How can responsible critics fail to see what they're getting? Well, something has been added to this old popular front morality play, something that seems to give it new credibility.

The superintendent of the mine (from his Cadillac) suggests to the sheriff that it would be nice to cut Ramon "down to size." The sheriff "touches his Stetson courteously" and, a few moments later, gives the signal to four deputies — Vance, Kimbrough and two others. They arrest Ramon (who offers no resistance), handcuff him and thrust him into their car. Vance, "a pale, cavernous, slackjawed man," is "slowly drawing on a pigskin glove." After an exchange of a few words, the "gloved hand comes up, swipes Ramon across his mouth," as Vance says softly, "Now you know that ain't no way to talk to a white man."

Ramon sits tense now, awaiting the next blow. A trickle of blood runs down his chin. The two deputies in front sit like wax dummies, paying no attention to what is going on in back.

Kimbrough: Hey, Vance. You said this Mex was full of pepper. He don't look so peppery now.

Vance: Oh, but he is. This bullfighter's full of chile.

He drives a gloved fist into Ramon's belly. Ramon gasps, his eyes bulge. . . . Vance strikes him in the abdomen again. Kimbrough snickers. . . . Ramon is doubled up, his head between his legs. Vance pulls him erect.

Vance: Hold your head up, Pancho. That ain't no way to sit.

Ramon (a mutter in Spanish): I'll outlive you all, you lice.

Vance (softly): How's that? What's that Spic talk?

He strikes Ramon in the belly. Ramon gives a choked cry. . . . Kimbrough holds up Ramon's head while Vance punches him methodically. Ramon gasps in Spanish:

Ramon: Mother of God . . . have mercy. . . .

As if this were not enough, the next shots of Ramon being struck in the belly are intercut with Esperanza's contractions as she gives birth. Finally, "the two images merge, and undulate, and blur . . . we hear the feeble wail of a newborn infant."

This full dress racial treatment is the politically significant ingredient in *Salt of the Earth*. Although socially, economically and legally the United States has been expiating its sins against minorities in record time, it is still vulnerable. The Communists exploit this vulnerability: the message for export is that America is a fascist country which brutally oppresses the darker peoples.

Frank, *Salt's* union organizer, tells us that "equality's the one thing the bosses can't afford." The explanation offered is pitifully inadequate: "The biggest club they have over the Anglo locals is, 'well — at least you get more than the Mexicans.' " Ramon replies, "Okay, so discrimination hurts the Anglo too, but it hurts me more. And I've had enough of it." This catechism of Communist economics has a creaky sound. A rational Ramon in a film set in 1951 might very well ask: Why can't this company afford equality when so many others can?

To ask that would expose the mystification central to *Salt of the Earth* by indicating that this community is no microcosm of our society, and that the situation depicted is grotesquely far from typical. The film's strike has not been placed against the background of American life which would provide prespective and contrast. It stays within a carefully composed system of references. (Esperanza describes the help the striking miners got — "messages of solidarity and the crumpled dollar bills of working men." After fifteen years of wanting to know who the company president is, the miners come across a picture of him in a "Man of Distinction" ad. One of the men in the union truck that delivers food to the starving miners is a Negro; when a miner comes over, "the Negro leans down and shakes his hand warmly.")

Let's take a look at the film's claims to truth and "honesty." The union president (who played Ramon) has written that a Production Committee had "the responsibility of seeing that our picture ran true to life from start to finish. Occasionally there were meetings in which the union people pointed out to our Hollywood friends that a scene we had just shot was not true in certain details. When that happened, we all pitched in to correct the mistake." I think we may accept the evidence that those several hundred people who made the film believed that it was *true*; from this it does not follow, however, that we can assume that all the film's incidents belong to the period of the 1951-1952 strike.

Let's take a further look at what the union president writes: "We don't have separate pay rates any more. . . . Thank God for our union and for the men who organized it. Back in the 'thirties, they were blacklisted, thrown off company property and told to take their houses with them . . . *Salt of the Earth* was not intended to be a documentary record of that particular strike (1951-1952). But I will say this. It is a true account of our people's lives and struggles." So perhaps the eviction in the film does not derive from the 1951-1952 strike; perhaps the miners in 1951-1952 were not striking for equal safety conditions at all. And it would still be a "true," honest movie to those who made it. If they accept this film as "fundamentally" true of their lives, a "symbolic" truth that is higher, *more* true than the plain details of that strike, then, probably, they can also take the next step, and believe that their struggle is typical and symbolic of American society (the sheriff who takes orders and bribes from the bosses symbolizes government as capitalism's hired man; the company officers represent the decadent quality of American business; the love story of Ramon and Esperanza symbolizes the vitality of the masses, etc.).

Can the people who had a "constructive" hand in the script

believe in the abstract, symbolic characters as representations of their lives? Don't the miners' wives see that something is wrong somewhere when the famous Mexican actress who plays Esperanza, the symbol of *their* lives, is so unlike them? The miners' wives — big women in slacks and jackets, with short permanented hair, and a pleasant, rather coarse plainness — suggest the active, liberated manner of free American women. Esperanza, fine-boned, gentle and passive, her long hair pulled back, dressed in drab, long skirts, is the Madonna on the picket line. Can the women accept nobility incarnate as the image of themselves? Or is it that they have gotten so far into symbolic thinking that they believe in this heroine not merely as their representative but as the symbol of all suffering humanity ("Esperanza" means "hope") — so that she doesn't really have to be at all like them, since she represents a higher truth about them? I think we must allow for the possibility that those who see themselves as symbols are capable also of holding rather symbolic notions of truth.

Just for fun, let's try out *Salt*'s realistic method. We decide that a true account of Negro life in a Northern city begs to be done. We take the simple story of a Negro girl led into a life of vice and crime by a white business man who seduces her and then casts her off on his corrupt cronies. We follow her to the brothel where she is forced to work (our brothel scenes are the first authentic record of a brothel to be included in a work of art). We take incidents from actual newspaper stories (the police own the brothel; city big-shots cover-up for the police). Real prostitutes not only play themselves, they supply us with information that makes it possible for us to give accurate representations of the impotent and perverted white businessmen who are their clients. The girls are rather a buxom crew, but our heroine (we were fortunate indeed to secure the services of Miss Greer Garson, who had dreamed all her life of playing a noble Negro prostitute)* suggests endurance and infinite pa-

---

* Miss Rosaura Revueltas (*Esperanza*): "In a way it seemed I had waited all my life to be in this picture. My own mother was a miner's daughter."

tience. The heroine's only friends are among the other prostitutes — and, as there is a white girl among them, she learns that not all white people are customers: there are white workers, too. The brutal mechanization of the heroine's existence is forcefully presented in a sequence intercutting from her room to the rooms of the other girls. When, finally, the girls realize that in solidarity there is strength, they force the white madam (a cold, shrewd, hard-eyed aristocrat) to grant them better percentages.

Have we told any lies? There is nothing in it that hasn't happened at some time. All we had to do was select the data carefully and build up the story so that no "extraneous" material showing other forms of Negro life entered in. And it would be simple enough to inflate the dialogue so that the brothel becomes a microcosm of America, a symbol of race relations under fascism. Perhaps the best way to expose the falsification is to point out the brothel down the street — with white workers and a Negro clientele, and hence to suggest that perhaps America is too vast and pluralistic an enterprise to be symbolized in any one brothel.

If we want to know something about the treatment of minority peoples in the United States we don't look at one community, we examine and compare data in various communities, cities, industries and institutions. We examine the extraordinary social phenomenon of pecking (in one town the Irish peck the Italians, in the next the Italians peck the Mexicans, in other towns the Mexicans peck the Negroes, and some cities are a regular chicken yard, with Armenians or Portuguese last in the line) and other forms of internecine warfare among minorities. We look at the life of the integrated as well as the unintegrated minorities; we don't assume that the life of the Mexican-American zinc miner is more symbolic of the treatment of minorities than the life of the corner grocer whose name is Ramirez.

Compare *Salt of the Earth* with the films — *social* films, too — of artists whose work is informed with individual imagination. Buñuel, whose shocking *Los Olvidados* gives the lie to the concept that the oppressed are the salt of the earth. De Sica, whose joyful little masterpiece *Miracle in Milan* flouted the expectations of Americans who looked to Italian neo-realism for sombre, serious "truth." Eisenstein, who selected and stacked his images for ideological purposes, but who did it, at least, on a grand scale. The enemy was flamboyantly gross and evil, the violence obsessively brutal. Barbaric splendor, excesses overflowed the bounds of the ideology — just as Griffith's fairy tale riches could not be contained in the moralistic framework of *Intolerance*. These artists use the film as a feast for eye and mind.

The proletarian morality play is a strict form: the heroes and villains illustrate a lesson. The hero is humanity, the struggling worker trying to reach consciousness of his historical role. He is vital, full of untapped strength; the brutal oppression to which he has been subjected has made him all the more human.* He is a man who can learn. The villains are the hero's class enemies — they are representatives of a decadent ruling class and they must be taught a lesson. Though they control economic power, they are personally weak: they have lost the life-force. They are subhuman. The play is not so much a sermon as a guide to action. It serves as a demonstration of the potential strength of the working class — or, in this case, minority peoples. *Salt of the Earth* is full of violence; it avails itself of the excitations of melodrama, but the violence is symbolic.

Communists have their own fear of infection: the member or sympathizer who explores other ideas may be deflected from orthodoxy; he may succumb to the attractions of "bourgeois" thought. Unless he stays within the bounds of the approved

---

* The glorification of the common man denies him his humanity in the very process of setting him up as more human than others. If you believe in the greatness of the oppressed, you are very likely not looking at the oppressed at all, but at an image of what they should be. Marx predicted that a degenerate society would degrade the working class; the latter day "Marxists" accept the notion of a degenerate society but hold as a concomitant the curious notion of an uncontaminated "oppressed." The concept is not analytic, of course, but propagandistic.

ideas, he jeopardizes his own dedication to the cause and he may infect the circle of his acquaintances.

"Social realism" is supposed to derive its art from reality. The art is negligible and nothing could be further from reality than these abstractions performing symbolic actions in a depressing setting. The setting does refer to the real world, however, and *Salt of the Earth* can seem "true" to people who have been in the Imperial Valley or New Mexico or the southern states. They have seen shocking living conditions and they may feel the moral necessity to do something about them. Communist propaganda takes this desire and converts it into a sense of anxiety and distress by "demonstrating" that all of American power supports this shocking situation and thus uses this situation for a total condemnation of American life. The moral sensibility that has given vitality to American principles is manipulated by these propagandists into a denial that America stands for those principles, and into an insistence that the *real* principles of American life are revealed in the sore spot. The moral person feels helpless and alienated unless he accepts the path that is offered to him — identifying his moral interests with the revolutionary aims of the working class.

It is symptomatic of the dangers in a commercialized culture that these people — the ones who made the film and the ones who believe it — can find nothing else in American life to which they can give allegiance. They are articulate, literate. They are, no doubt, sincere in their dedication to the cause of the downtrodden. A film like *Salt of the Earth* seems so ridiculously and patently false that it requires something like determination to consider that those who make it believe in it. They serve a higher truth — and, of course, they have a guiding thread for their beliefs, a lifeline which directs them through the maze of realities and symbols. Those who hold the other end of the line are very shrewd in jerking it — now this way, now that. But what artist with vision or imagination could keep his fist closed so tight?

Salt of the Earth

The Editor, Sight and Sound

Sir, — Had I praised *Salt of the Earth* no doubt your correspondents would have considered me properly "objective" and my line of thought would not have been turned into an obstacle course. As I expressed something less than delight, Walter Lassally found that, "*Her description . . . clearly derives from the viewpoint of one who has never been in close contact with working class people,*" J. D. Corbluth thought it "*a pity that some critics are rather far away from real life and those sections of the populace who work with their hands.*"

Surely Mr. Corbluth has let the cat out of the social realist bag: manual workers are more real than other people. The callus is mightier than the pen.

The crude view of reality held by some of the correspondents is, not too surprisingly, shared by the producer and director — "*we were agreed that our films must be based in actuality. . . . A true account of the miners of the South-West and their families, predominantly Mexican-Americans, begged to be told. . . . We asked the miners and their families to play themselves . . .*" etc. For social realists, artistic truth means not the artist's fidelity to his individual vision, but an approximation, a recreation of "actual" existence. (Cocteau seeks to "rehabilitate the commonplace," the social realist seeks to deify it.) The miners are not to play roles but to "play themselves." This aesthetic would take art back to before the beginnings of art: it aims, ostensibly, to reproduce the raw material from which art derives. A ludicrous aesthetic but not without a purpose: by means of it, material which is not really raw at all can be offered as more true (based in "actuality"!) than art which is a clear and open transformation of experience. *Salt* is real to them because, they claim, it happened once; *Les Parents Terribles* is not real — though it happens forever.

Ralph Bond suggests that the method of "*collective construc-*

tive criticism" means simply that you consult strikers when you are making a film about a strike — as if it were no more than using good sense. We are all aware, or I thought we were, that artists who begin by sacrificing independent judgment in order to serve and express the masses, end up merely dramatizing political directives. What a parody of democracy the makers of *Salt* hold up for our admiration: four hundred people sit in on the script! Visualize Dreyer confronted with a committee asking for a little more earthly humor in a scene, or Cocteau trying to explain to a few hundred people why he needed the glazier in the "zone."

To the degree that Christopher Brunel can so confuse the film with a slice of life that he can reprove me for not being *"moved by the struggles of the Mexican Americans for a better life,"* the social realist method has succeeded, with him at least. *Salt* wasn't a strike, it was a movie; but the confusion goes to the heart of the propagandistic aesthetic — you're considered a strike breaker if you didn't like it.

Communist propagandists do not attack the values of American prosperity because that prosperity would be too attractive to poverty-ridden countries. They claim it's an illusion, "a big lie," and that the "real" America is a picture of class war: poor workers are dispossessed, capitalists set race against race, only the plutocrats enjoy the benefits of productivity, etc. (Russian propaganda identifies Cadillacs with capitalists, Americans identify Cadillacs with Negroes.)

G. M. Hoellering is mistaken in thinking that had I not known who made the film, I would not have objected to it. Esperanza tells us that the house belongs to the company *"but the flowers, the flowers are ours"* — does one have to be briefed? (Did Mr. Hoellering accept the saccharine nobility of Greer Garson or the wartime Claudette Colbert? Why should he be more willing to accept Miss Revueltas's saccharine deprivation?) If we're familiar with propaganda methods we know that "oppressed" women don't have babies like the rest of us, that they go through epic labor pains, with the life force finally triumphant in the birth of the little worker. How else is mediocre propaganda to achieve symbolic stature? When "the oppressed" see themselves as a chosen people, and they certainly do in *Salt*, they become as morally and aesthetically offensive as any other righteous band. If those who made the film experienced "fearful pressures," so did the Seventh Day Adventists in Hitler's concentration camps — did it ennoble them or make their dogma any more acceptable? A man may be ennobled when he fights for a good cause; a cause is not ennobled by fighting men.

At no point did I suggest that Communists, fellow travelers, or anyone else should be prevented from making movies, publishing books, or otherwise addressing the public. But, believing in the free dissemination of ideas, I must defend my right to criticize any of those ideas. Is it in good faith that some of the correspondents set up a double standard — defending freedom of expression for those who would set up an image of a fascist United States, and attacking freedom of expression for anti-Communists as witch hunting? I cannot accept the implication that because Communists and fellow travelers have been subjected to some abuse in the United States, they are therefore exempt from analysis of their methods, purposes, and results. Is one not to call a spade a spade, because Senator McCarthy lumps together spades, shovels, and plain garden hoes?

Are we to pretend that there are no spades? Are we to look at *Salt* and say with Mr. Brunel, "*All right, so it's propaganda — for a better understanding between races.*" But why, then, does the film caricature the Anglo-Saxons and why are the representatives of business and government all Anglo-Saxons? If *Salt* is supposed to be an accurate "realistic" picture of the United States, what explains this split — which is at complete variance with the statistical facts of American life?

The social realist aesthetic develops out of a political dogma, and the whole meaning of the aesthetic is that art must, so to speak, pay its way — by serving immediate socio-political ends. When a film is as loaded as *Salt*, surely the critic is obliged

to examine what it's aiming at. Or is the film critic supposed
to limit himself to sight and sound as if they had no relation to
meaning?

Yours faithfully,

PAULINE KAEL

San Francisco.

[1954]

Index

5/14/81   The Apprenticeship of
Duddy Kravitz - (1974)
    Richard Dreyfuss
based on book by Mordecai
Richler) -

(Cochran) ~~Eastern~~ ~~young~~

" queer as a clockwork orange "

Burgess

pub' 62

garden of Eden produced Christ —
original sin necessary for
Christ

St Augustine —

write in cinematic way